The Hidden Places of

DORSET, HAMPSHIRE

and

THE ISLE OF WIGHT

By
Peter Long

© Travel Publishing Ltd.

ii

Published by:
Travel Publishing Ltd
7a Apollo House, Calleva Park
Aldermaston, Berks, RG7 8TN

ISBN 1-902-00760-3
© Travel Publishing Ltd

First Published:	*1990*	*Fourth Edition:*	*1999*
Second Edition:	*1994*	*Fifth Edition:*	*2001*
Third Edition:	*1997*		

HIDDEN PLACES REGIONAL TITLES

Cambs & Lincolnshire
Cornwall
Devon
East Anglia
Heart of England
Highlands & Islands
Lake District & Cumbria
Lincolnshire
Somerset
Thames Valley

Chilterns
Derbyshire
Dorset, Hants & Isle of Wight
Gloucestershire & Wiltshire
Hereford, Worcs & Shropshire
Kent
Lancashire & Cheshire
Northumberland & Durham
Sussex
Yorkshire

HIDDEN PLACES NATIONAL TITLES

England
Scotland

Ireland
Wales

Printing by: Scotprint, Haddington
Maps by: © Maps in Minutes ™ (2000)
Editor: Peter Long
Cover Design: Lines & Words, Aldermaston
Cover Photographs: Lulworth Cove, Dorset; Rockbourne, Hampshire; Brighstone, Isle
of Wight © www.britainonview.com

Foreword

The Hidden Places is a collection of easy to use travel guides taking you, in this instance, on a relaxed but informative tour of Dorset, Hampshire and the Isle of Wight. *Dorset is a county* that encompasses rolling chalk downs, dark heathland (so beloved of Thomas Hardy), the long ridge of the Purbeck Hills and an incomparable coastline with its wealth of magnificent rock formations sculptured by the sea. *Hampshire and the Isle of Wight* offer the visitor a combination of seafaring tradition in the many coastal towns and villages as well as wonderful countryside epitomized by the New Forest and the rolling hills of northeast Hampshire. Both counties are a haven for "hidden places" and the book provides the reader with plenty of interesting historical facts and stories.

This edition of *The Hidden Places of Dorset, Hampshire and the Isle of Wight* is published *in full colour*. All *Hidden Places* titles will now be published in colour which will ensure that readers can properly appreciate the attractive scenery and impressive places of interest in this county and, of course, in the rest of the British Isles. We do hope that you like the new format.

Our books contain a wealth of interesting information on the history, the countryside, the towns and villages and the more established places of interest in the county. But they also promote the more secluded and little known visitor attractions and places to stay, eat and drink many of which are easy to miss unless you know exactly where you are going.

We include hotels, inns, restaurants, public houses, teashops, various types of accommodation, historic houses, museums, gardens, garden centres, craft centres and many other attractions throughout the area, all of which are comprehensively indexed. Most places are accompanied by an attractive photograph and are easily located by using the map at the beginning of each chapter. We do not award merit marks or rankings but concentrate on describing the more interesting, unusual or unique features of each place with the aim of making the reader's stay in the local area an enjoyable and stimulating experience.

Whether you are visiting the area for business or pleasure or in fact are living in the counties we do hope that you enjoy reading and using this book. We are always interested in what readers think of places covered (or not covered) in our guides so please do not hesitate to use the reader reaction forms provided to give us your considered comments. We also welcome any general comments which will help us improve the guides themselves. Finally if you are planning to visit any other corner of the British Isles we would like to refer you to the list of other *Hidden Places* titles to be found at the rear of the book and to the Travel Publishing website at www.travelpublishing.co.uk.

Travel Publishing

iv

Regional Map

Contents

1 Northeast Hampshire

An area of the North Downs, which are actually uplands, gently rolling, wooded hills whose folds shelter many picturesque little villages. But other parts are quite heavily populated, with prosperous towns such as Basingstoke, Aldershot and Farnborough sprawling across the map. Basingstoke, which now presents a resolutely modern face to the world, has a history that predates Domesday, but only really began to boom in the 1960s. Aldershot, too, was a little village before the British Army moved in, since when it has been *the* army town above all others. Its neighbour Farnborough is closely linked with the history of aviation, from the time in 1908 when the first powered flight in Britain took place to the air show that brings thousands of visitors from all over the world.

There are few really grand houses in the area, although The Vyne near Basingstoke and Stratfield Saye House are both grand and imposing. Two smaller and much more humble dwellings attract crowds to the area in droves: Jane Austen's house at Chawton, near Alton, and The

Fishing on the River Test

Wakes, the Selborne home of the celebrated naturalist Gilbert White. This is, like much of the county and indeed much of Dorset and the Isle of Wight, great country for walking and cycling, with numerous paths and trails criss-crossing the region and some spectacular views. Some of the valleys and their villages are among the most beautiful in the land. Boat trips have been introduced on a restored section of the old Basingstoke Canal, and lovers of steam railways can take a nostalgic ride on the Watercress Line, which runs between Alresford and Alton. On the edge of the county, near the border with Berkshire, is one of the most important archaeological sites in the country. This is the Roman Calleva Atrebatum, now called Silchester, where the occupying forces built a considerable town with temples, an amphitheatre and even an early Christian church. The pick of the finds are in Reading Museum, but the site remains a fascinating place to visit.

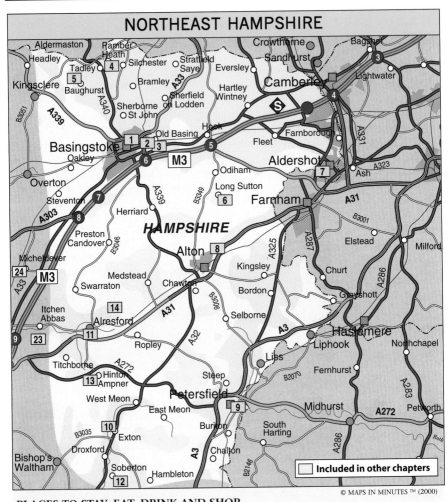

NORTHEAST HAMPSHIRE

© MAPS IN MINUTES ™ (2000)

PLACES TO STAY, EAT, DRINK AND SHOP

BASINGSTOKE

A thriving industrial and commercial town with a long history that is not always apparent from its predominantly modern look. The expansion began after the Second World War and really took off in the 1960s, when the old town was virtually submerged under the new developments. But something of old Basingstoke can still be seen, including the peaceful and evocative ruins of the 13th century Chapel of the Holy Ghost and the 14th century Church of St Michael the Archangel. The old Town Hall, dating from 1832, is now home to the **Willis Museum** with its exhibits of Basingstoke over the last 200 years and a collection of maps and clocks. The museum is named after George Willis, a clockmaker and sometime Mayor of Basingstoke, who established the museum in 1931. A more recent attraction - The

Milestones Museum - was opened in November 2000 (see panel below)

AROUND BASINGSTOKE

OLD BASING
2 miles NE of Basingstoke off the A30

The modern town offers its residents a wide choice of up-to-date amenities, but two miles to the east, Old Basing, with its narrow streets, old cottages and the much-visited ruins of **Basing House**, could be on another planet. Built on a massive scale inside the walls of a medieval castle, the house was sacked by Cromwell's men (and Cromwell himself was at the scene) after a siege that lasted the best part of three years (see panel below). A bridge on the site of Basing House crosses the old **Basingstoke Canal**, which was opened in 1794 linking the

MILESTONES

Leisure Park, Churchill Way West, Basingstoke, Hampshire RG21 6YR
Tel: 01256 477766 Fax: 01256 477784
website: milestones-museum.com

Opened in November 2000, this is Hampshire's living history museum, where the county's heritage comes to life in cobbled streets with shops, factories, interactive areas, staff in period costume and superb exhibits relating to industrial and everyday life.

Among the many highlights are the Tasker and Thorneycroft collections of agricultural and commercial vehicles, and the renowned AA collection.

BASING HOUSE

Redbridge Lane, Basing, Basingstoke, Hampshire RG24 7HB
Tel: 01256 467294

Built on a massive scale inside the walls of a medieval castle, the house was once the largest private residence in the country. The ruins of the old and new houses, the riverside walk, the dovecotes and the spectacular 16th century grange barn add up to an attraction of great appeal, and the beauty of the place is enhanced by the recently re-created 17th century garden inside the Tudor walls. The house was sacked by Cromwell's men, with Cromwell himself present, after a long and arduous siege. The ruins include the historic Garrison gateway and the foundations and cellars of the old house, and the remains of the north wing of the new. Open Wed-Sun and Bank Holiday afternoons in summer.

THE BOLTON ARMS

The Street, Old Basing, Hampshire RG24 7DA
Tel: 01256 322085

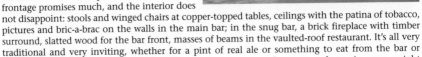

Two miles from Basingstoke but a world away from its bustle, Old Basing is quiet, pleasant and picturesque, and the **Bolton Arms** is a most agreeable spot to pause on a visit. Built in the 16th century, it was originally called the Yew Tree Inn after the grand old yew that watches over the village; its name was changed in the early 18th century to honour the Lord of the Manor of the time. The pristine black and white frontage promises much, and the interior does not disappoint: stools and winged chairs at copper-topped tables, ceilings with the patina of tobacco, pictures and bric-a-brac on the walls in the main bar; in the snug bar, a brick fireplace with timber surround, slatted wood for the bar front, masses of beams in the vaulted-roof restaurant. It's all very traditional and very inviting, whether for a pint of real ale or something to eat from the bar or restaurant menu. Starters on the main menu might include home-made paté served with a crusty baguette or oriental prawn balls, while main courses run from cod with chips and peas to salmon with lobster sauce, mozzarella-filled chicken breast and the ever-popular Bolton's steak & Theakston ale pie. Food is available lunchtime and evening except for Sunday, Monday and Tuesday evenings, and booking is recommended for a table on Friday or Saturday. Nick and Joanna Bell took over the lease of this grand old pub at the beginning of 2001 and their plans include, among others, themed food evenings.

town with London. The canal was never as widely used as had been hoped and gradually fell into disuse, but large sections have now been restored and boat trips can be taken in summer from the smart Canal Visitor Centre at Mytchett, near Camberley in Surrey. On the theme of the transport of yesteryear, a passenger railway once operated between Basingstoke and Alton, and one of its stations, Cliddesden, was used for the filming of the 1937 Will Hay classic *Oh! Mr Porter*.

PRESTON CANDOVER
7 miles S of Basingstoke on the B3046

This is the largest of the local Candovers (the others, to the south, are Candover Brown and Candover Chilton), with a Victorian church and the ruins of a much older church.

STEVENTON
8 miles W of Basingstoke off the A303/B3400

This is the village where Jane Austen was born in 1775 and where she spent the first 25 years of her life. During this time she wrote *Pride and Prejudice*, *Sense and Sensibility* and *Northanger Abbey*, though they were not published while she was here (her father offered *Pride and Prejudice* to a publisher in 1797, but he turned it down without even reading it!). The village church, where her father was rector, contains some memorials to the Austen family and also some fragments of medieval wall painting. Some of the Austens are buried in the churchyard, where a 900-year-old yew stands proudly.

The Beginnings of the River Test, nr Ashe

OVERTON
8 miles W of Basingstoke on the B3400

A sizeable village near the source of the River Test, its broad main street is lined with handsome Georgian houses. It was once an important staging post on the London-Winchester coach route, and the annual sheep fair was one of the largest in the county; it lasted for centuries until coming to an end in the 1930s. The area north of Overton towards Kingsclere includes **Watership Down**, high up on a ridge, with wonderful views. This is the setting of the eponymous book by Richard Adams; it is now a nature reserve and, yes, there are lots of rabbits. The Down is on the long-distance footpath the **Wayfarer's Walk**, which runs from Inkpen Beacon just over the border in Berkshire with Emsworth on the Hampshire coast.

SHERBORNE ST JOHN
3 miles N of Basingstoke off the A340

One of the best known buildings in the county, **The Vyne** was built in the 16th century for Lord Sandys, Lord Chamberlain at the Court of Henry Vlll. Of particular note are the classical portico (the first in Britain when added in the 17th century), some marvellous linenfold panelling in the Oak Gallery and a Tudor chapel with Renaissance stained glass, Flemish Majolica tiles and Gothic painted vaultings.

BRAMLEY
5 miles N of Basingstoke off the A340

The **Church of St James** has immense appeal with its combination of the homely and the grand. Its main treasure is its wall painting, notably of St Christopher and of Thomas à Becket. The south transept is the work of the renowned architect Sir John Soane - for him a rare sortie into ecclesiastical fields.

STRATFIELD SAYE
7 miles NE of Basingstoke off the A33

The estate and **Stratfield Saye House** were presented to the Duke of Wellington

The Drawing Room, Stratfield Saye House

as a reward for his defeat of Napoleon at Waterloo. The long two-storey house is full of Wellington relics, including books, flags and his splendidly ornate funeral carriage, made from cannon captured at Waterloo. A whole room is devoted to Wellington's beloved charger Copenhagen, who is buried in the grounds. Wellington Country Park, with fine walks and numerous attractions, is three miles away.

PAMBER HEATH
8 miles N of Basingstoke off the A340

Between the villages of Pamber Green and Pamber Heath lies **Pamber Forest**, a

THE PELICAN

Silchester Road, Pamber Heath,
Hampshire RG26 3EA
Tel: 0118 970 0286

There are three Pambers located in the countryside along the A340, and the one to head for by anyone in search of a good country pub is Pamber Heath. Lots of country pubs have a few pots scattered around the bars, but the collection at **The Pelican** puts nearly all others to shame. There are literally hundreds of them hanging from the ceiling beams, in every shape and colour you can imagine, some made of pewter and some ceramic. They've been amassed over the years by Liz Saunders, who together with her husband Danny, runs this lively and sociable pub. Both have been in the licensed trade for many years, so they definitely know how to make visitors welcome. From time to time regulars return from holiday with a pot to add to the collection, and somehow room is always found for it.

Good food is very much part of the Pelican's appeal, and the recently added, fully air-conditioned 30-cover restaurant is a popular choice for a meal. Liz looks after the cooking and her menu offers an

excellent choice of appetising fare. Garlic mushrooms or potato skins with dips (cheese, cheese & bacon, or plain & blue cheese or garlic) could get the meal under way, followed perhaps by chilli with rice, scampi with chips and peas, chicken Kiev or steak & stout pie with a puff pastry top. Baguettes served with spicy spiral fries, burgers, omelettes and jacket potatoes are just right for lighter snacks. The blackboard lists daily specials and vegetarian options. Liz's Sunday roasts are particularly popular, and her skills are much in demand for functions, special occasions and outside catering.

A visit to the Pelican is always thoroughly recommended, and if you arrive on a sunny day the pleasant beer garden is the perfect place to enjoy your refreshment.

nature reserve where a variety of habitats, from dry open heathland to wood pasture and stream valleys, each supports its own distinctive range of wildlife. The third Pamber is Pamber End, where the ruins of a 12th century priory church can be seen.

SILCHESTER
9 miles N of Basingstoke off the A340

Excavation continues to unearth treasures at the famous Roman site of Silchester, where earlier work gave us the most complete plan of any Roman town in Britain. The Romans called it **Calleva Atrebatum** - the Atrabates were a local British tribe who founded the settlement just before the Romans arrived. The perimeter wall can still be traced, and one of the many impressive remains is that of the 1st century amphitheatre beyond the walls. Most of the treasures discovered at the site are now in Reading Museum. Also of note in Silchester is the whitewashed

12th century **Church of St Mary**, which boasts some superb woodwork, 13th century wall paintings and a 14th century stone effigy of an early restorer. It lies within the walls of the Roman town.

SHERFIELD ON LODDON
4 miles NE of Basingstoke off the A33

Follow the brown signs at Sherfield on Loddon roundabout to find **Longbridge Mill**, a restored water mill housed in a timber-framed 16th century building. Flour-milling demonstrations are given each month.

ODIHAM
7 miles E of Basingstoke on the A287

Several buildings of note in this fascinating old market town. The 15th century church is the largest in the county and has a rarity in the shape of a hudd, a portable cloth-covered wooden

THE BADGERS WOOD

Wolverton Road, Baughurst, Tadley, Hampshire RG26 5JH
Tel: 0118 981 4395

A 200-year-old village pub with a cream-painted facade that's invitingly lit up at night. Chris Thompson and Sally Aylward have a warm welcome for regulars and first-timers alike, and there's a very pleasant atmosphere in the lounge and bar. Fans of real ales will be pleased to find a choice of no fewer than five brews on tap at any one time, and lunchtime brings a particularly extensive selection of food to cope with the smallest and the largest appetites - and anything in between: sandwiches and baguettes with a variety of generous fillings, 'mini-snacks', burgers and pasties, basket meals, jacket potatoes, fish & chips, spaghetti bolognese, cottage pie, chicken pie, chicken tikka - and, of course, the popular Sunday roast.

Badgers Wood is a hub of the local community and the most sociable of pubs, with men's and ladies' darts and pool teams, quiz nights, themed evenings and regular treasure hunts setting out from the pub. Car parking spaces are available at the side, and at the back is a garden with a barbecue area. The village of Baughurst lies close to the county border with Berkshire; in the southern, more rural part of the village stands the Church of St Stephen, built in 1845.

frame which would provide some shelter for the rector while conducting burial services in the rain. In a corner of the churchyard stands the **Pest House**, built around 1625 as an isolation ward for patients with infectious diseases, including the plague. Later an almshouse, it is now a little museum. All that remains of once grand **Odiham Castle** is an octagonal keep; the castle was only a few years old when it played host to King John on the eve of his journey to Runnymede to put his signature on Magna Carta.

LONG SUTTON
8 miles SE of Basingstoke off the A32

Set admidst very attractive walking, cycling and horse-riding country Long Sutton is a classic Hampshire village complete with duckpond. The village is also home to **Lord Wandsworth School**

with a sporting pedigree which has produced many well-known sportsmen including Jonny Wilkinson, Englands top-scoring flyhalf.

HARTLEY WINTNEY
9 miles NE of Basingstoke on the A30

Riding through Hartley Wintney in 1821, William Cobbett, the author of *Rural Rides*, was delighted to see young oaks planted on the village green. These oaks, known as the Mildmay Oaks, were a gift from the Lady of the Manor, Lady Mildmay, and were planted after Trafalgar as a source of timber for ships. They were never needed for that purpose and have continued to provide the village centre with a lovely sylvan setting. South of the village, the old **Church of St Mary**, largely untouched since a renovation in 1834, features high-sided box pews along the main aisle, elegant galleries spanning

THE FOUR HORSESHOES

Long Sutton, Nr Hook,
Hampshire RG29 1TA
Tel/Fax: 01256 862488
e-mail: tony.brooks@bun.com

Experienced publicans Tony and Sheila Brooks, welcome visitors of all ages, to their charming country freehouse. Customers come on foot, by bicycle and in cars to this homely 200-year-old pub, not far from junction 5 of the M3 motorwayand indicated by a Heritage signpost on the main road.

Inside,the pub's main area is open-plan, with a hardwood block floor, low beamed ceilings, cane-backed chairs, open fires and an eyecatching array of brass and copper ornaments, prints and photographs. The kitchen dishes up plenty of variety for the hungry visitor, from bar snacks to full meals, spanning sandwiches for lighter bites to filled jacket potatoes, savoury pies and a popular Sunday carvery.

The pubs regular quiz and music nights are always well attended, while for something more active there is a choice of darts in the bar or petanque in the beer garden. For visitors wishing to stay overnight, the **Four Horseshoes** has three comfortable bedrooms, all en suite, with tv and tea-making facilities. Long Sutton, a village of brick and timber cottages, lies south of Odiham in open countryside off the B3349; the parish church of All Saints dates from the 13th century and a set of 16th century bells.

the nave and transepts, and colourful funeral hatchments. A mile west of Hartley, **West Green House Garden**, in the care of the National Trust, is a series of charming gardens set around an equally appealing 18th century house. Among the highlights are stunning herbaceous beds, an ornamental kitchen garden and a grand water garden or nymphaeum.

EVERSLEY
12 miles NE of Basingstoke on the A327

The best-known resident of this village in the far north of the county was Charles Kingsley, author of *The Water Babies* and *Westward Ho!*. Sometime chaplain to Queen Victoria, he is buried in his own churchyard, and his life is commemorated in a hall in the village. And the school gates, put up in 1951 for the Festival of Britain, include the figure of a boy chimney sweep.

ALDERSHOT
15 miles E of Basingstoke on the A331

Aldershot was a little-known village of some 800 souls until the Army decided to settle here in considerable numbers, since when the population has grown to around 55,000 and the town has become the most famous military centre in the country. The story of how Aldershot became the home of the British Army is told in the **Aldershot Military Museum**, which occupies the last two surviving Victorian barracks blocks in the middle of the camp. The fascinating exhibits include a Victorian barrack room recreated in its original setting and an Edwardian kitchen. Special events are held throughout the year, and there's always a special thrill when a Chieftain battle tank is part of the show. The Rushmoor Local History Gallery in the same premises tells the history of the civilian side of

ALDERSHOT MILITARY MUSEUM

Queens Avenue, Aldershot, Hampshire GU11 2LG
Tel: 01252 314598

The Museum covers the histories of Aldershot military town and the adjoining civil towns of Aldershot and Farnborough. The complex contains a rich mixture of buildings, objects, displays, vehicles and archives, and each of the several galleries has a different theme and character.

The John Reed Gallery covers the history of the Army in Aldershot from its arrival in 1854, and includes a rare example of a Victorian barrack room displayed in its original setting. Rushmoor Local History Gallery, which with the John Reed Gallery occupies a pair of unique barrack bungalows built in 1894, deals with the history of the civil towns of Aldershot and Farnborough. The Cody Gallery is named after an American, Samuel Franklin Cody, who made Britain's first powered flight at Farnborough in 1908. The Gallery includes a reconstruction of part of his workshop and many original objects, among them his flying helmet.

The Montgomery Gallery, which stood originally in the grounds of Monty's home at Isington near Alton, houses a collection of larger exhibits, including field guns and other vehicles. The museum's collection of vehicles,

some here, some kept outside, ranges from the mass-produced Willys jeep of 1943 to the formidable 60-ton Chieftain tank; most are in full working order.

Aldershot and its neighbour Farnborough (see panel on page 9).

The airborne side of the towns is covered in the **Airborne Forces Museum** in Browning Barracks, about half a mile from the Military Museum. The Heroes Shrine in Manor Park, Aldershot commemorates the dead of the First World War, while a nearby sunken garden remembers those who fell in the Second World War. The Duke of Wellington is singled out for honour by an imposing bronze statue on Round Hill. The statue originally stood on top of the Triumphal Arch at Hyde Park Corner in London but was moved to Aldershot in 1885. The men of Aldershot became the first aviators in the country, using Farnborough Common for their flying and building their aircraft sheds where the Royal Aircraft Establishment stands today. The first occupant of the site was the Ballooning Factory, which became the Royal Aircraft Factory and then the RAE.

FARNBOROUGH
15 miles E of Basingstoke on the A331

Visitors arrive in Farnborough in their thousands for the Farnborough Air Show, held every two years, but a less well-known site just outside Farnborough is **St Michael's Abbey**, built in flamboyant French style by the Empress Eugenie in honour of her husband the Emperor Napoleon lll. She came to live in England with her son and was joined later in exile by her husband, who died at Chislehurst after an operation to remove bladder stones. The Emperor, the Empress and their son are buried in three five-ton tombs in an ornate mausoleum next to the abbey. Also buried here is the family's devoted Corsican secretary Franchescini Pietri.

ALTON

Surrounded by hop fields and some of Hampshire's loveliest countryside, Alton has a history that can be traced to pre-Roman times. Long known for its brewing industry, it was also an important centre for cloth-making, and its position on the route from London to Winchester accounts for the large number of coaching inns in the town. One of the most important landmarks is the impressive double-naved, partly-Norman **St Lawrence's Church**, which was the scene of a dramatic episode during the Civil War. A large force of Roundheads drove some 80 Royalists into the church, killing 60 of them.

Harrier Hawk Jump Jet, Farnborough Air Show

Flood Meadows, Alton

including a wolf gnawing a bone and two donkeys kicking their heels in the air. Nearby, in the old cemetery, is the grave of Fanny Adams, who, aged 8, was killed and hacked to pieces by one Frederick Baker. The story of the horrid murder was widely reported, and sailors with a macabre sense of humour began to use the phrase 'Sweet Fanny Adams' for the somewhat dubious tinned mutton which had recently been issued among their rations. In time, the saying became used for anything contemptuously considered worthless (and eventually for nothing at all!). The **Allen Gallery** in Church Street contains a fine collection of porcelain, pottery and tiles, including the famous Elizabethan Tichborne spoons. There is a delightful walled garden behind

The Royalist commander, Colonel Boles, made a heroic last stand from the splendid Jacobean pulpit but was eventually shot and killed. The church door and several of the Norman pillars are still scarred with the bullet marks left in that conflict. A more peaceful legacy of the past is the series of comical 11th century carvings of animals and birds,

THE QUEENS HEAD

20 London Road, Holybourne, Alton,
Hampshire GU34 4EG
Tel: 01420 86331

Donna Clarke is the tenant at the **Queens Head**, where locals young and old share the convivial surroundings with the many tourists and motorists who pass this way. The pub was built in the 17th century as a coaching house and it presents a handsome sight with its white-painted facade, steeply-raked tiled roof and dormer windows. Inside are two newly refurbished bar areas, one with traditional pub games (the pub fields darts and pool teams in the local leagues), the other a comfortable conservatory bar and lounge

with 30 covers for taking meals. The menu, available from midday onwards, caters for varied tastes and appetites, running from sandwiches and filled jacket potatoes to chicken and steak dishes and the popular Sunday roasts. There's plenty of parking space at the front of the pub and more at the back, where the garden has a safe children's play area. Local bands make for lively weekends at this very appealing pub, and once a year a music festival draws the crowds.

Holybourne has almost been swallowed up by Alton, but there's still something of a village atmosphere in the centre, and the village church, its Norman tower topped by a 19th century spire, is well worth a visit. It stands by a large pond fed by the springs - bourns - that gave the village its name.

the gallery and a smart new lounge where coffee and cakes are served. In the High Street, the **Curtis Museum**, named after its founder Dr William Curtis, features exhibits of natural history, geology and archaeology, as well as the story of the local hop-picking and brewing industry. Among the highlights are the Roman Selborne Cup and the imposing Anglo-Saxon Alton Buckle, while children will make straight for the Gallery of Childhood, a colourful little gallery packed with toys, dolls and books. Alton, whose High Street was once part of the old Pilgrims Way, is the point at which the Watercress Line (see under Alresford) joins the national railway system.

Jane Austen Museum, Chawton

On the northern edge of Alton, **Holybourne** is an ancient village constructed on the Roman town of Vindomis. The church is built on the source of the River Bourne. Mrs Gaskell, author and friend of the Brontës, lived here.

A little way east of Alton on the B3004, **St Mary's Church** in **East Worldham** contains an effigy thought to be that of Phillipa, wife of Geoffrey Chaucer. It could very well be that good lady, as their son Thomas was Lord of the Manor here from 1418 to 1434.

AROUND ALTON

CHAWTON
2 miles S of Alton off the A31

The **Jane Austen Museum** is located in Chawton House, a redbrick property where the author lived from 1809 until shortly before her death in 1817. Here she revised the manuscripts of earlier novels and wrote *Emma, Persuasion* and *Mansfield Park*. The rooms where she lived and worked can be visited, and in other rooms are a period costume display and memorabilia of Jane's brothers Frank and Charles, who both served in the Royal Navy. Jane's donkey carriage stands in the old bakehouse. Her mother and sister Cassandra, who lived at the house with her, are buried in the graveyard of the nearby Church of St Nicholas (Jane spent the last few weeks of her life in Winchester and is buried in Winchester Cathedral).

SELBORNE
3 miles S of Alton on the B3066

Selborne is an attractive village in a little valley in beautiful countryside, famous for its association with the 18th century naturalist Gilbert White. Born in 1720, White studied at Oriel College, Oxford, took holy orders and was a curate in several parishes before returning to Selborne, the place of his birth. Selborne was the property of another Oxford College, Magdalen, so it was not until the last few years of his life (1784-1793) that he was curate of the village that he made famous in his *Natural History and Antiquities of Selborne*, published in 1788 and never out of print since. He was buried in the graveyard of the village church, where he is commemorated by two fine stained glass windows. Also to be seen in the churchyard is the stump of a yew tree, believed to have been up to 1,400 years old when it succumbed to a storm in 1990. Parts of the top were used to make a font cover and an altar. White's home, The Wakes, is now the **Gilbert White Museum**, where visitors can see the original manuscript of his book along with some of his furniture and some lovely bed-hangings made by his doting aunts. The garden is being restored to White's own design and contains many 18th century plants, topiary and a herb

garden. The same house also contains the **Oates Museum**, devoted to Francis Oates, Victorian explorer, and his nephew Captain Lawrence Oates, who was with Captain Scott on his ill-fated South Pole expedition. The words of Oates - 'I am just going outside. I may be some time.' - are known far and wide, so too the note in Scott's diary on the decision of Oates to leave the tent to help the others: 'the act of a very gallant gentleman'.

PETERSFIELD

A pleasant market town in a wide valley in the shadow of Butser Hill, the highest point of the South Downs. Its fine old square is looked over by an equestrian statue of King William lll in Roman dress, erected in 1753 with a bequest of £500 from the local MP Sir William Jolliffe. Some of the town's oldest houses are set

NUMBER 15

High Street, Petersfield, Hampshire GU32 3JT
Tel/Fax: 01730 263925
website: www.hampshireguide.co.uk/number_15

Number 15 is a splendid town house on the main street of Petersfield, bought by Rosemary and Tony Lewis in January 1999 and opened for Bed & Breakfast in November of that year. Refurbishment has enhanced the original charm of the property, which dates from 1591 and has seen service as a grocer's shop, bakery, soap-maker's and even a bank - the old bank vaults can still be seen from the hallway. The guest accommodation is on the second floor and comprises one single and two double bedrooms, each with en suite shower room, all well-furnished, warm, quiet and comfortable, with tv and tea/coffee-making kit. A choice of full English or Continental breakfast is served in a dining room that adjoins the bedrooms. Tony and Rosemary previously owned a small family hotel in Petersfield, and friendly hospitality remains a watchword at Number 15. The entrance to the house is at the rear and is reached by a small alley to the side of the building. There's ample parking nearby and plenty of excellent pubs and restaurants for lunch and dinner. Number 15 - no pets and no smoking - is an ideal base for either business visits or for exploring the town and the surrounding area.

around The Spain, an attractive green whose name commemorates the markets held here by dealers in Spanish wool. Plenty of time should be allowed for a stroll round the town and its major places of interest. The oldest building is the **Church of St Peter** with its 12th century chancel arch and splendid north nave. in the churchyard a headstone remembers the cricketer and maker of cricket balls John Small (1737-1826). **Petersfield Museum** in the old courthouse uses a good deal of local archive material in telling the history of the town from the 12th century to the present day. The **Bear Museum** was the first of its kind in Britain and is home to a varied collection of Teddy Bears, some close to celebrating their 100th birthdays. Visitors are invited to bring along their own bears so that the resident experts can shed some light on their family trees. The **Physic Garden**, set in an ancient walled burgage plot behind 16 High Street, is a charming little garden laid out in the style of the 17th century, a style that would have been familiar to the distinguished botanist John Goodyer, who lived in Petersfield. The **Flora Twort Gallery** contains the delightful drawings and paintings of local scenes produced over a period of 40 years by the accomplished eponymous artist, who bequeathed her cottage studio to Hampshire County Council on her death at the age of 91 in 1985. The restaurant on the premises has a fine reputation.

AROUND PETERSFIELD

STEEP
2 miles NW of Petersfield off the A325

In **All Saints Church** are two engraved lancet windows installed in 1978 to mark the centenary of the birth of the writer and poet Edward Thomas, who moved with his family from London to Steep in 1907. He was killed in action in the First World War. On Shoulder of Mutton Hill, above the village, is a memorial stone to the poet, erected in 1937 when the hillside was dedicated to his memory.

BURITON
3 miles S of Petersfield off the A3

Buriton is a very pleasant village with a wonderful tree-lined duckpond sited in ideal walking country. The **Church of St Mary** has a notable treasure in its Norman font made of Purbeck marble. The church has for a neighbour an early 18th century manor house (in private hands) where the historian Edward Gibbon wrote much of his magnum opus, *The Decline and Fall of the Roman Empire*.

SOUTH HARTING
3 miles SE of Petersfield on the B2146

The most notable building hereabouts is the National Trust's **Uppark**, a fine Wren-style country mansion built in 1690 high on the South Downs. It was extensively damaged by fire in 1989 and the restoration plans are the subject of an award-winning exhibition. The interior houses rescued paintings, fine furnishings and famous dolls houses, and the garden has been restored to the original Repton design. The servants' rooms are as they were in 1874, when the mother of HG Wells was housekeeper (he mentions Uppark fondly in his autobiography).

CHALTON
5 miles S of Petersfield off the A3

Chalton is the site of **Butser Ancient Farm**, a reconstruction of an Iron Age Farm at the foot of Butser Hill. The site is in effect an open-air archaeological laboratory, where experts are undertaking studies into the lives, homes and farming methods of the ancient people who once lived here.

Thatched Cottage, East Meon

EAST MEON

5 miles W of Petersfield off the A3 or A272

The Meon Valley is an area of great beauty and East Meon can claim to be the loveliest village in the whole valley. It also boasts one of the finest churches in the county. The central tower, with walls four feet thick, dates from the 12th century, while inside, the greatest treasure is the remarkable 12th century **Tournai font** in black marble, exquisitely carved with scenes that include the Creation and the Expulsion of Adam and Eve from the Garden of Eden. Only seven such fonts are known to exist in England, the work of Flemish master carvers, and East Meon's is certainly among the most magnificent of them all. Thomas Lord, founder of the cricket ground in London, and the spy Guy Burgess are buried in the churchyard.

Opposite the church is another building of distinction, a 15th century courthouse where the Bishops of Winchester, the Lords of the Manor, held their courts.

EXTON

8 miles W of Petersfield on the A32

A beautiful Meon Valley village with a wide expanse of grass bordering the river

THE SHOE INN

Shoe Lane, Exton,
Hampshire SO32 3NT
Tel: 01489 877526

Heather Seymour, with many years experience in the trade, is the licensee at the **Shoe Inn**, a Wadworth pub in a prime location down by the River Meon. A terrace runs across the front of the pub, with the garden and the river just across the road.

Inside, open fires blaze a winter welcome, and the chimney breast separates the two bars - the Fremantle Bar named in honour of a local worthy, and the non-smoking bar and restaurant area. The rooms are oak-panelled throughout and the floors carpeted, and the bars are adorned with numerous pieces of porcelain and brassware, regimental plaques and a collection of boots and shoes donated by local patrons.

Heather is a keen walker and also an enthusiastic cook, which shows in the length and variety of the main menu. Home-made chicken liver and brandy paté is a very tasty starter, which could be followed by lasagne (also home-made), lamb shank, pan-fried trout or a tempting butterfly chicken breast topped with ham and brie. There's a good choice for vegetarians, a special children's menu and a super selection of desserts. Daily specials widen the choice still further, and for a quicker snack or smaller appetite, the Bar & Garden menu offers sandwiches, salads, burgers, jacket potatoes and basket meals.

THE HORSE & GROOM INN

Broad Street, Alresford,
Nr Winchester,
Hampshire SO24 9AQ
Tel: 01962 734809

Among the most notable of the many shops and hostelries on historic Broad Street is the **Horse & Groom**, whose history goes back to the 1600s. Behind the charming half-timbered facade is an interior of ancient beams, open fires, old pictures and prints and lots of cosy nooks and crannies. The pub is run in fine style by Gerry and Phil Budge, who took over in 1997 when Phil retired from the Army after 26 years' service with REME. He is a great rugby fan and officiates as a referee at many matches in the county.

Food has long been an attraction at the Horse & Groom and the tenants continue to put great emphasis on the quality and range of the fare served in the 34-cover non-smoking restaurant, anywhere in the bar (70 more covers) or out in the spacious courtyard and beer garden. Some of the dishes are traditional favourites - ham, egg and chips; rump steak with tomato, mushrooms, onion rings and chips; the super Sunday roasts - but the majority are dishes you will probably find on no other pub

menus: Cajun spiced crabcakes with a corn and bacon chowder, wild boar and apple paté with autumn fruit chutney, braised lamb steak on colcannon with a redcurrant and rosemary sauce, woodland mushrooms and goat's cheese with an almond crumble and a tomato and tarragon sauce. Quiche of the day, catch of the day and the daily sausage special are always great favourites, and it is appropriate that watercress, most of which is grown in this area, features in many dishes, typified by kipper paté with watercress salad and beetroot chutney, or medallions of peppered beef on roasted celeriac and watercress with a red wine and peppercorn cream. Such fine food deserves fine wine, and at the Horse & Groom the well-chosen list runs to some 30 items, with no fewer than ten (five red and five white) available by the 1.75cl or 2.50cl glass.

Broad Street is one of the county's most beautiful streets and it is entirely fitting that one of its occupants should be a pub of such distinction. The dignified Georgian town has much to offer the visitor, including the Bishop's Reservoir with its varied wildlife and the steam-hauled Watercress Line that runs to Alton, but when food is the topic, it's the Horse & Groom that takes centre stage.

THE WHITE LION

School Hill, Soberton, Nr Droxford, Hampshire SO32 3PF
Tel: 01489 877346 e-mail: bookings@thewhitelion.idps.co.uk

Next to the church at the heart of one of the longest villages in the county, the **White Lion** is a front-runner in the Meon Valley hospitality stakes. The building dates back as far as the 17th century, and bars and restaurant are rich in traditional charm, with low beamed ceilings, local period prints and lots of nooks and crannies. The Village Bar is warmed by a log fire, and in the Quiet Bar visitors can, for a small fee, use the latest computer equipment. This bar has a cosy eating area, and there's also a separate restaurant with a menu that could include anything from moules marinière to pasta with prawns, Barnsley chop or beef, stout and Stilton pie. Baguettes and potato skins fit the bill for a quick

snack. Things get hot on a Tuesday night, when curries are accompanied by a jam session!

At the back of the pub there is an attractive garden with lawns and flower beds. Mine host at this most agreeable of pubs is Graham Acres and his dog "Spike". He has a cheerful greeting for both regulars and first-timers, who include visitors to the common and walkers on the Wayfarers' Walk, which passes by the front door. In summer the Morris Men are an occasional attraction.

and close to the Old Winchester Hill archaeology trail.

DROXFORD
10 miles W of Petersfield on the A32

In Droxford church there is a plaque to Izaak Walton, a great lover of the area, whose son-in-law was rector. In a siding outside Droxford station Churchill and Eisenhower set in train the D-Day invasion.

SOBERTON
12 miles W of Petersfield off the A32

A wide-flung village at the point where the Meon Valley broadens and the chalk gives way to clay.

HAMBLEDON
8 miles W of Petersfield off the A3

A village of redbrick Georgian houses, known for its wine and even better

known for its cricketing connections. It was in the Hambledon Club that the rules of the game were laid down in 1774. A granite monument stands on **Broadhalfpenny Down**, where the early games were played, and a number of cricketers are buried in the churchyard at the village church of St Peter and St Paul.

NEW ALRESFORD

In the valley of the River Alre, New Alresford (pronounced Allsford) was new in about 1200, created by Geoffrey de Lucy, Bishop of Winchester, as part of a grand plan to build a waterway from Winchester to Southampton. The huge reservoir he built is smaller now, and home to otters and varied birdlife. Once among the country's leading wool markets, Alresford has long been at the centre of the watercress industry, and one

HINTON AMPNER GARDENS (NATIONAL TRUST)

Bramdean, Alresford, Hampshire SO24 0LA
Tel: 01962 771305

The **Hinton Ampner** of today is largely the creation of Ralph Dutton, the 8th and last Lord Sherborne. Born here in 1898, he inherited the house in 1936 and set about remodelling the house and garden in a carefully considered marriage of modern gardening, neo-Georgian building and neo-Classical furnishings. His plan for the garden was to lead visitors gently from mood to mood; the design is formal but the planting informal, and he created delightful walks with unexpected vistas by the thoughtful siting of trees and statues. What he wanted above all from a garden was tranquillity, and any visitor to Hinton Ampner would agree that he achieved it triumphantly. There are, just as Ralph Dutton planned, delights and surprises at every turn.

The lily pond, which he laid out on his father's croquet lawn, is home to nine different varieties of water lily and a good number of golden orfe and goldfish. The Sunken Garden, the first area planned by Dutton, boasts some of the wonderful topiary that is such an identifying feature of Hinton Ampner.

The Long Walk is a perfectly straight path linking the east and west extremities of the garden and featuring an avenue of 30 clipped Irish yews. The Dell, the Philadelphus Walk, the Yew Garden and the Temple - built as a folly, gazebo and resting place - are other highlights of this quite superb garden.

Ralph Dutton also greatly altered the house, more or less demolishing his grandfather's gloomy Victorian mansion and restoring the Georgian style that he much preferred. In 1960 a fire badly damaged the house and its contents, and in its subsequent rebuilding Dutton made further changes and set about collecting Regency furniture and Italian paintings to replace those lost in the fire.

On his death in 1985, there being no heir, Ralph Dutton bequeathed the house, the gardens and the hamlet of Hinton Ampner to the National Trust. The house is privately tenanted but the ground-floor rooms can be visited at certain times.

The Watercress Line

of its many attractions is the **Watercress Line**. This is the nickname of the Mid-Hants Railway, which once carried wagonloads of watercress to join the lines to London and beyond. Ten miles of the line are now run by enthusiasts as a steam railway. The line runs from Alresford to Alton by way of Ropley, the engineering centre of the railway and a station with a notable display of topiary. The next stop is Medstead & Four Marks, which at 630' above sea level is the highest in the south of England. The gradients of up to 1 in 60 caused crews using this route to say that they were going 'over the Alps'. The steepness of the line calls for powerful locomotives, and ferrequinologists (railway buffs) will thrill at the sight of an ex-Southern region S15 4-6-0, a Standard Class 5 4-6-0 number 73096 and most of all at the mighty 34016 *Bodmin*, a Bulleid Pacific of the West Country class. The final station is Alton, where the line joins the main railway network.

Though 800 years old, Alresford has a mainly Georgian look, the result of the major fires which ravaged the town down the years. The fulling mill and the ancient parish church are both worth a visit, and the town has many interesting specialist shops. Alresford's most famous son was

Admiral Lord Rodney, a contemporary of Lord Nelson who built the grand manor house near the church. Mary Sumner, wife of a rector of the church, founded the Mothers Union here in 1876. Alresford was also the home of the author and poet Mary Russell Mitford, best known for her portraits of country life, and in particular *Our Village*. Alresford has very strong links with the early years of cricket, and Mitford wrote: '*Hampshire is the Greece of cricketers, and Alresford the Athens.*'

A short way north of Alresford on the B3046 stands the imposing shell of **Northington Grange**, a grand neo-classical country mansion built around 1815 by William Wilkins and inspired by a tour of Greece. The most notable feature of the Grecian facade is the row of vast Doric columns, said to be based on the Temple of Theseus in Athens.

AROUND NEW ALRESFORD

HINTON AMPNER
4 miles S of New Alresford on the A272

The River Itchen, renowned for trout and watercress beds, rises a little way west of Hinton Ampner to begin its 25-mile journey to the sea at Southampton; the Itchen Way follows the river throughout its course. **Hinton Ampner House and Gardens**, now in the care of the National Trust, was the creation of Ralph Dutton between 1936 when he inherited the house and 1985 on his death (see panel opposite).

THE THREE HORSESHOES

Bighton, Alresford, Hampshire SO24 9RE
Tel: 01962 732859

The picturesque hamlet of Bighton is located a couple of miles northeast of Alresford and can be reached by minor roads off the A31, the B3046 or the B3047. Motorists, cyclists and walkers in the know all make a beeline for the **Three Horseshoes**, a fine old village pub which was taken over by Margaret and Mick Alexander and their daughter Nicola as recently as February 2001. The building dates from the late 18th or early 19th century and was at one time an alehouse and smithy.

The purposeful black and white frontage, set well back from the road, hides an interior that simply oozes old-world charm, with country furniture and studded leather-backed chairs, a massive brick

fireplace with timber surrounds, another with a jaunty thatched canopy, exposed brick walls, beams and everywhere a pleasing jumble of old blacksmith's implements, pictures, prints and bric-a-brac. Margaret does the cooking, making excellent use of fresh local produce for across-the-board menus that include a traditional Sunday lunch (book for this). Food is not served Wednesday evening, Sunday evening or Monday lunch (the pub is closed Monday lunchtime except for Bank Holidays).

TICHBORNE

3 miles E of Winchester off the A31

Two famous stories will be forever associated with this lovely village of thatched and half-timbered cottages. The legend of the **Tichborne Dole** dates from the time of Henry l, when the owner of Tichborne Park, the dastardly Sir Roger Tichborne, told his crippled wife Mabella that she could have her dying wish to provide food for the poor, but only from an area she could crawl round. The brave woman managed to encircle an area of more than 20 acres of arable land, while holding a flaming torch. Ever since then the Park's owners have provided bags of flour every year to the villagers of Tichborne and Cheriton, and the field is still known as "The Crawls". Equally notorious is the episode of the **Tichborne Claimant**, a sensational trial of 1871 involving a certain Arthur Orton, son of a

Wapping butcher, who appeared from his home in Wagga Wagga, Australia, claiming to be the heir to the estate. Although he bore no resemblance to the rightful heir, Roger Charles Doughty Tichborne, who had disappeared while sailing round the world, he was 'recognised' and supported in his claim by Roger's mother, who disliked her husband's family and was determined to believe the impostor. Orton's claim was rejected in a trial that lasted 100 days, and he was put on trial for perjury; after a further 188 days he was found guilty and sentenced to 14 years in prison.

A mile or so south of Tichborne, on the B3046, is the village of **Cheriton**, whose church is thought to stand over a prehistoric burial ground. In 1644, the Battle of Cheriton, fought near Cheriton Wood, resulted in the deaths of 2,000 men as the Roundheads defeated the Royalists.

2 Northwest Hampshire

Northeast Hampshire has one major city, Winchester, one major town, Andover, and scores of scattered villages in a part of the county with some really grand scenery, particularly as the North Downs roll westwards to meet Salisbury Plain.

River Itchen

In the northern part are the peaceful open chalklands, while towards the south the rivers and streams and water meadows are the focus, bringing anglers from near and far for the finest trout fishing in the land. Winchester, which was already an important community in the Roman period, became the capital of the Kingdom of Wessex under the Anglo-Saxons and the capital of the whole country in the reign of Alfred the Great. Winchester is best known for its wonderful Cathedral and its renowned public school, but its other attractions could easily fill a whole book, and this area of Hampshire has a great deal to offer outside its major city, from historic and pre-historic sites to Victorian extravaganza at Highclere, the largest house in the county, and 20th century nostalgia on the

Thatched Cottage, Wherwell

Watercress Line steam railway. This line once served as the main means of distributing watercress, which grew, and still grows, in the specially contructed beds by the shallow streams around Alresford. Andover, which grew in size with the influx of Londoners in the 1960s, was once an important centre of the wool trade, and many old buildings survive from the early days of prosperity. Evidence of Iron Age occupation is particularly strong around Andover, most importantly at the hill fort of Danebury, which was a stronghold of the Atrebates tribe. The whole region is criss-crossed by marked trails and paths and cycle routes and some of the scenery and views are spectacular. The highest point in the region is Farley Mount, a country park with an abundant variety of flora and fauna.

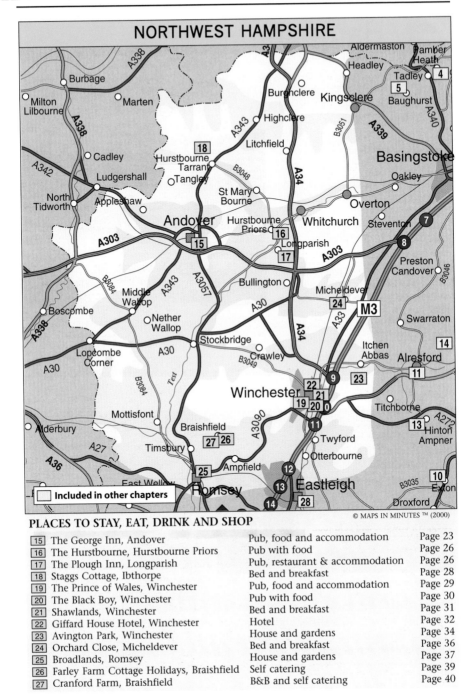

NORTHWEST HAMPSHIRE

© MAPS IN MINUTES ™ (2000)

PLACES TO STAY, EAT, DRINK AND SHOP

ANDOVER

A picturesque market town with a history going back to Saxon times. One outstanding landmark is the hilltop **Church of St Mary**, which was completely rebuilt in the 1840s with a generous gift from Dr William Goddard, a retired headmaster of Winchester College. The interior is said to have been modelled on Salisbury Cathedral; it falls a little short of that marvellous building but is nonetheless worth a visit. Dominating the market place in the town centre is the handsome Guildhall, built in 1825, and many of the old coaching inns that once filled the town still stand. Andover was an important stopping place on the major routes to and from London, Oxford and Southampton, and as many as 50 coaches a day would stop at the inns to change horses and to allow the passengers to stretch their legs and take refreshment.

The story of the town from pre-Roman times is told in the **Andover Museum & the Museum of the Iron Age** in Church Close.

Another way of getting to know the town is to join a guided walk on the heritage trail starting at the Tourist Information Centre; also starting from the TIC are two trails which lead to collections of poems in praise of the lovely Test Valley. The poems, set in granite or bronze, are scattered through the town and lead the walker past public works of art by the River Anton. **The Test Vale Tapestry** is a fascinating piece of community embroidery which is kept in the Council Offices and can be seen by appointment - ask at the TIC. Four miles west of Andover at **Weyhill**, signposted from the main A303, a great day out for the family can be enjoyed at the **Hawk Conservancy and Country Park**, home to more than 200 birds from all over the

THE GEORGE INN

George Yard, High Street,
Andover, Hampshire SP10 1PD
Tel: 01264 336562

A large white-painted building with a redbrick extension, the **George Inn** is centrally located but also tucked away. It stands in the centre of Andover, its entrance down a pedestrian way off the High Street. Open for breakfast and morning coffee, the George offers a welcome respite for shoppers, and hot and cold food is served between 10 o'clock and 3. Children are welcome when eating. One of the inn's great assets is its location, and its accommodation makes it an ideal base for both business visitors and motorists touring the region. The eight letting bedrooms, available all the year round, reflect this mix of business, comprising a family room, three doubles and four singles. A live band performs from 9 till 10.30 on Thursday evenings, and a DJ does his stuff from 8 o'clock to midnight on Friday and Saturday. The most convenient place for parking is the George Yard car park, from which it's the shortest of walks to the inn. Walking is the best way to get to know the historic parts of the town, and the Andover Heritage Trail, lasting about 90 minutes, is a guided walk that takes place on Tuesday and Saturday afternoons. The George Inn is the first venture into the licensed trade for Doreen Ashley and her son Duncan, who took over as tenants here in the autumn of 2000.

Thatched Cottage, Wherwell

tributary of the Test, Middle Wallop became famous during the Battle of Britain, when the nearby airfield was the base for squadrons of Spitfires and Hurricanes. Many of the old buildings have been incorporated into the **Museum of Army Flying**, which is home to an important collection of military kites, balloons, aircraft and helicopters. Dioramas trace the development of Army flying from the days before the First World War with a display of 35 aircraft and the finest collection of military gliders in Europe. Explorers' World is the Museum's interactive science and

world. Thrilling flying displays take place three times a day and include owls, eagles, falcons, kites and hawks. Seven of the 22 acres have been developed into a wild flower meadow and conservation area dedicated to the Conservancy's founder Reg Smith. The October Weyhill Fair was an event of great importance in its day and appears as the Weydon Priors Market in Thomas Hardy's *Mayor of Casterbridge*, where the future mayor sells his wife and child.

A little further along the A303 thrills of a different kind are guaranteed at **Thruxton Motor Racing Circuit**, whose annual calendar of events takes in many aspects of the sport, including Formula Three, Touring Cars, Superbikes, Trucks and Karts.

Middle Wallop

education centre, with a number hands-on activities and a fine camera obscura giving an amazing view of the surrounding countryside.

AROUND ANDOVER

MIDDLE WALLOP
7 miles SW of Andover off the A343

The middle of three villages strung out along the valley of the Wallop Brook, a

NETHER WALLOP
7 miles SW of Andover off the A30

Nether Wallop is the prettiest of the Wallops, its stream lined with willows, many of its houses thatched or timbered. The most notable building in the village is **the Church of St Andrew** with its

Nether Wallop

striking medieval wall paintings. Almost 1,000 years old, they lay hidden beneath plaster for centuries until being rediscovered in the 1950s. The most impressive and unusual of the paintings depicts St George fighting the Dragon. Outside the church is a curiosity in the shape of a dark grey stone pyramid, 15ft high, with red stone flames rising from its tip. This imposing piece was erected at his own expense and in his own memory by Francis Couce, a local doctor who died in 1760.

STOCKBRIDGE
7 miles S of Andover on the A30

The trout-rich River Test flows through, under and alongside the broad main street of Stockbridge, which attracts visitors from near and far with its antique shops, art

galleries and charming tea rooms. Fishing on the Test is strictly controlled at this point by two exclusive clubs, both with long waiting lists.

South of the A30, on a minor road from Stockbridge to Houghton lie **Houghton Lodge Gardens & Hydroponicum.** An 18th century 'Cottage Ornée' surrounded by lawns and trees stands by the Test, with lovely views over the valley - understandably this is a favourite location for films and television. Chalkcob walls shelter a kitchen garden with ancient espaliered fruit trees, glasshouses and herb garden. The hydroponic greenhouse tour includes a lecture on 'How to grow plants easily at home with soil and toil and without pesticides'.

Two miles northwest of Stockbridge off the A30 is the impressive **Danebury Iron Age Hill Fort,** whose earthworks, ditches and banks were excavated over a period of years to give us a detailed view of life more than 2,000 years ago. Many of the finds from the site are now in Andover Museum.

LONGPARISH
5 miles E of Andover on the B3048

A straggling village on a stretch of the River Test famed for its excellent trout

River Test, Stockbridge

THE HURSTBOURNE

Hurstbourne Priors, Nr Whitchurch,
Hampshire RG28 7SE
Tel: 01256 892000 Fax: 01256 895351

Bill and Karen Essen's 200-year-old hostelry is one of the most versatile public houses in the area, a friendly, cheerful place to relax over a drink or a meal, a popular venue for parties and functions, and a good base for visitors to the area, whether on business or enjoying a break from the usual routine. Food is served lunchtime and evening seven days a week, with a daily changing specials list supplementing a wide selection of table d'hote meals. Many of

the much-loved pub classics are to be found on the menu, including prawn cocktail, garlic mushrooms, lasagne and steak & kidney pie.

It's a very sociable sort of place, with regular live music sessions, karaoke nights, quiz nights, pool and darts, and private parties and get-togethers can be arranged at Stripes function room. **The Hurstbourne**, which has car parking spaces front and rear, is easy to find near the junction of the B3400 and B3048. Andover and Whitchurch are both a short drive away, and south of Andover stretches Harewood Forest, a large expanse of ancient woodland through which the walkers' favourite, the 46-mile Test Way walk passes. The village of Hurstbourne Priors itself lies along the valley of the Bourne, a well-known fishing river.

THE PLOUGH INN

Longparish, Andover, Hampshire SP11 6PB
Tel: 01264 720358 Fax: 01264 720377

The Plough Inn is a splendid old-world country pub of immense appeal, with a creeper-clad facade and award-winning gardens. Inside is no less fetching, with exposed brick walls, old beams, rustic furniture and an assortment of prints, pictures and bric-a-brac contributing to a cosy, traditional ambience. Pauline and Chris Dale have built up an enviable reputation for hospitality and good cheer in the seven years since they took over as leaseholders. food is served lunchtime and evenings (except Sunday evenings from January to the end of March) and covers both bar and restaurant menus. Booking is advisable for Friday and Saturday evenings and Sunday lunch. The main menu of classic dishes is always supplemented by blackboard specials, which could include such mouthwatering possibilities as lamb chops with a hot mint sauce, halibut in a seafood sauce or sea bass steamed with ginger and spring onions. To accompany the excellent food, or to enjoy on their own, are no fewer than five real ales (including the locally brewed King Alfred), plus a good selection of other beers and wines from around the world. Children are welcome, and part of the eating area is reserved for non-smokers. The Plough Inn also caters for guests staying overnight in two Bed & Breakfast rooms, one big enough for a family.

fishing. A Longparish resident, Colonel Peter Hawker, notes in his diary for 1818 that he landed a ton of the fish in that year! **Longparish Upper Mill**, in a lovely location on the river, is a large flour mill with a working waterwheel. Visitors can see the restoration work in progress.

WHITCHURCH
6 miles E of Andover on the B3400

A little town on the River Test that was once the first important coach stop on the London-Exeter run. Its coaching inns have gone but it has a unique attraction in the **Whitchurch Silk Mill**, the last working silk mill in the South of England. The waterwheel has been fully restored but the power is now provided by electricity, and the mill functions as a museum making silks for interiors and costume dramas, with a costume exhibition and a shop. The mill, which stands on Frog Island on the Test, provided some of the silk for the costumes in the BBC's acclaimed production of *Pride and Prejudice*. Bere Mill, on the eastern edge of Whitchurch, is a weatherboarded mill on the Test where a Frenchman, Henri Portal, set up a paper-making business in the 18th century.

APPLESHAW
4 miles NW of Andover off the A342

Many of the houses that stand on either side of the village's broad single street are thatched, and the old-world atmosphere is enhanced by the clock installed in the middle of the street to celebrate Queen Victoria's Diamond Jubilee. The village's most notable buildings are the neo-Gothic parish church and the Georgian former vicarage.

TANGLEY
6 miles NW of Andover off the A342/A343

Tangley sits among woods on a hilltop high above Tangley Bottom, the low-lying ground which forms the county boundary with Wiltshire. Its mostly Victorian church is notable for its rare lead font, the only one of its kind in Hampshire and one of only a handful in the country. Dating back to the 1600s, it is decorated with Tudor roses, crowned thistles and fleurs-de-lys. The old Roman road from Winchester to Cirencester, the Icknield Way, runs through the parish of Tangley, which includes the parishes of Vernham Dean and Hatherden. Most of this part of the county is designated an Area of Outstanding Natural Beauty, and the views are stupendous.

HIGHCLERE
14 miles N of Andover on the A343

Sir Charles Barry, architect of the Houses of Parliament, was in similarly exuberant mood when engaged on the rebuilding of **Highclere Castle**. The largest mansion in the whole county is a really splendid, grandiose affair, with turrets at the angles and a huge pinnacled tower in the centre. It occupies the site of a

Freefolk, nr Whitchurch

Highclere Gardens

Moorish and rococo styles and a wealth of old masters and other treasures. The castle is the home of the 7th Earl and Countess of Carnarvon; he is the Queen's racing manager, and visitors can see a display that reflects the racing interest of the family. In the basement is an exhibition of ancient artefacts collected by the 5th Earl, who was with Howard Carter on the 1922 expedition that discovered the tomb of Tutankhamun. This fascinating hoard had lain undiscovered in the basement for almost 70 years before being found in a hidden chamber by a butler. Highclere Castle has been used as a location for many films and television productions, including *Inspector Morse.*

former Palace of the Bishops of Winchester, and the lovely park in which it stands is one of the finest of all the works of Lancelot 'Capability' Brown. The interior of the castle is no less ornate than the outside, with a mixture of Gothic,

STAGGS COTTAGE

Windmill Hill, Ibthorpe, Nr. Andover, Hampshire SP11 OBP
Tel: 01264 736235 Fax: 01264 736597
e-mail: staggscottage@aol.com

On a hill overlooking the village of Ibthorpe, **Staggs Cottage** offers all the home comforts in peaceful, picturesque surroundings with magnificent views over the Bourne Valley. Neat, modern and practical, with a happy atmosphere generated by owners Colin and Jane Norton, the house has three guest bedrooms - a single, a double and a twin - with a shared bathroom. The rooms are equipped with television, radio alarm clock and tea/coffee-making facilities. A traditional English breakfast with all the options starts the day, and evening meals can be provided with notice.

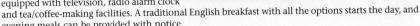

The countryside around Ibthorpe is great walking territory, and the Nortons can organise a special package and rates for walkers. Each morning they will drive guests to where they want to start the day's walk (fuelled of course by that excellent breakfast!). At the end of the day the guests phone the cottage (the owners will even provide a mobile phone) to be picked up at the point they have reached and taken back to the cottage to be fed and watered. The next day the guests are taken back to the point they reached the previous day...... and so on! This is a great service for really keen walkers: they don't have to book several places to stay; they can bring as much luggage as they like but only have to carry the minimum for the walk; and they don't even have to come by car - the ever-helpful Colin and Jane will meet guests at the nearest station, which is Andover. They offer the service for the Test Way, Clarendon Way, Avon Valley Path, the Wayfarers and part of the Kennet & Avon Canal - get those boots out and start planning!

BURGHCLERE
15 miles N of Andover off the A34

A couple of miles from Highclere, the **Sandham Memorial Chapel** hides a unique and very moving treasure behind a fairly unprepossessing redbrick facade. The interior walls are entirely covered with murals by Stanley Spencer and reflect his own experiences as an orderly in the First World War. Most of the scenes depict soldiers in the day-to-day business of war, but one wall shows the resurrection of soldiers killed in combat. In the foreground is a pile of white crosses cast aside by the soldiers. This marvellous expressionist work, which took five years to complete and is considered to be among Spencer's finest, was commissioned in the 1920s by Mr and Mrs Behrend in memory of a relation, Lieutenant Sandham, who died in 1919 of an illness contracted during the Macedonian campaign. There is no lighting in the chapel, so the murals are best viewed on a bright day.

WINCHESTER

Winchester is one of the country's most historic cities, with settlements dating back to the Iron Age. It was an important military base from Roman times (they called it Venta Belgarum), and King Alfred chose it as the capital of his kingdom of Wessex, which at the time included most of southern England. The decline that set in after the Imperial Legions returned to Rome was halted by Alfred in the late 800s, and two centuries later, on the site of a 7th century Saxon cathedral, work began on the magnificent **Winchester Cathedral**, which has ever since brought worshippers and sightseers from all over the world. The work was started by Bishop Wakelin on a swampy site that

THE PRINCE OF WALES

26 Hyde Street, Winchester, Hampshire SO23 7DX
Tel: 01962 854257

Near the centre of Winchester, but away from the real bustle, the **Prince of Wales** was built as a row cottages and became a pub in 1865. New tenants Simon and Maire Daniels arrived in January 2001 and are already enhancing the pub's reputation as a place to seek out to enjoy friendly hospitality and something good to eat and drink.

Maire's cooking can be sampled in the invitingly traditional bars from 12 to 2.30 and from 5 until closing time Monday to Friday and all day at the weekends. Her steak and kidney pudding, traditional stews and mixed grills are certain to satisfy the heartiest appetite,

and even the speciality sandwiches (cream cheese and grapes, triple-layer pork with stuffing and apple sauce) served with coleslaw and crisps are meals in themselves. Sunday brings a choice of three roasts, each served with roast potatoes, roasted vegetables and of course the appropriate accompaniments - bread sauce, sausage and bacon with the chicken, Yorkshire pudding with the beef.

This is definitely a place to linger - for the night if you like, as the pub has three letting B&B rooms sharing two shower rooms. A good breakfast starts the day, and special deals are available for longer stays.

THE BLACK BOY

1 Wharf Hill, Winchester, Hampshire SO23 9NQ
Tel: 01962 861754

The name is certainly unique in the county, but the **Black Boy** is highly unusual in other respects, too. David Nicholson arrived at this 16th century hostelry in 1995 after worldwide experience in the catering business, and together with his wife Sarah has assembled an absolutely fascinating display of

out-of-the-ordinary objects of all kinds imaginable. Every nook and cranny, every wall and every beam is home to part of this incredible array: crown green bowls hanging over a scrubbed table in a cradle made of cord; a library of old, often rare books; a collection of watch faces; a bar counter made from bottle tops; thousands of hanging keys; pump handles which can squirt water at customers.

Also on hand is a range of pub games both traditional and modern, including one where the player has to swing a chain so that the ring on the end of the chain catches on a hook on the wall - trickier than it looks, and it needs a steady hand and eye! An open log fire warms the two bar areas, where caricatures of local worthies look down from the walls.

Outside is a beer garden with a patio where space heaters banish the evening chill. The Black Boy specialises in real ales produced by local breweries, with as many as five usually on tap at any one time, and also satisfies the inner man with a range of simple, tasty, home-made fare. The food is not

always available, but when it is it could include stuffed potatoes, garlic mushrooms and chilli.

The Nicholson household is completed by recently arrived baby son Wilfred and the resident dogs Megan and Rats. For centuries, Winchester has attracted visitors from all over the world, in fact ever since King Alfred the Great adopted it as the capital of his Kingdom of Wessex in 871.

Thorneycroft's handsome statue of the King looks down the High Street, which has few rivals anywhere in the land in terms of historical associations. The tourists flock to see the magnificent Cathedral, the College and all the many other historic buildings, and increasingly they make tracks for Wharf Hill and this remarkable pub, which deserves to be a must on the sightseer's itinerary.

necessitated foundations of vast logs. Bishop William of Wykeham added ribs and mouldings and fan vaulting in the 14th century, essentially creating the building we see today. The Cathedral, which has the longest nave of any in Europe, is filled with priceless treasures, including sumptuous medieval monuments and copies of the Winchester Bible and Bede's *Ecclesiastical History*. The tombs of William ll (Rufus), Jane Austen and Izaak Walton are among the many in the Cathedral, along with that of St Swithin, to whom the Cathedral is dedicated. St Swithin was a 9th century bishop who, at his own humble request, was buried in the Cathedral grounds, not inside the building itself. When, on July 15th 971, his remains were brought inside on the orders of Bishop Aethelwold and honoured with a fine shrine, it rained heavily for 40 days, a phenomenon that was said to show the Saint's displeasure.

Ever since that day it has been said that if it rains on July 15th it will rain for 40 days. One of the statues in the Cathedral is that of a less well known figure, a diver named William Walker. This man spent seven years from 1906 in laboriously removing the logs that had supported the Cathedral for 800 years and replacing those rotting foundations with cement.

The area around the Cathedral provides a wealth of interest for the visitor: the Deanery, occupied continuously since the 13th century; the **Pilgrims' Hall** with its marvellous hammerbeam roof; **Cheyney Court**, once the Bishops' courthouse; Dean Garnier's recently recreated Victorian garden; Kingsgate, one of two surviving ancient city gates, and beyond it the simple, evocative Church of St Swithin; Jane Austen's House, where the novelist spent the last six weeks of her life until her death in 1817; the renowned College with its beautiful chapel, founded

SHAWLANDS

46 Kilham Lane, Winchester,
Hampshire SO22 5QD
Tel/Fax: 01962 861166
e-mail: kathy@pollshaw.u-net.com

Bill and Kathy Pollock offer exceptionally comfortable Bed & Breakfast accommodation in their well-appointed detached suburban home. **Shawlands**, which was built in 1960, is located in a quiet lane overlooking fields, but is only a mile and a half from the centre of historic Winchester, with quick and easy access by car, bus or taxi. The house (non-smoking throughout) has five letting bedrooms sharing three bathrooms and one bedroom en suite. The rooms, open year round except for the Christmas/New Year period, are bright and attractive, well furnished and very comfortably equipped, with independently controlled heating, remote-control tv, hairdryer and tea/coffee-making facilities. The en suite room is of family size, with its own front door and access for guests in wheelchairs. A comfortable residents' lounge looks out over the garden. Breakfast is a meal really worth getting up for here, as Kathy makes her own bread and preserves with fruit from the garden. The city of Winchester has an almost limitless supply of things to do and places to see, and the surrounding countryside is full of scenic delights - Farley Mount Country Park in particular offers great walking, wonderful views and an abundance of wildlife to spot.

GIFFARD HOUSE HOTEL

50 Christchurch Road, St Cross, Winchester, Hampshire SO23 9SU
Tel: 01962 852628 Fax: 01962 856722

Situated in a leafy suburb just ten minutes' walk from the centre of this ancient city, **Giffard House Hotel** provides exceptional decor, comfort and service. The house has recently been completely refurbished whilst retaining many original features including fireplaces in the reception rooms and a fine stained glass window over the main staircase to recreate the atmosphere of a prosperous Victorian family home while providing all the modern comforts and amenities.

Traditional English breakfast is served in the magnificent dining room where there are lighter alternatives on offer. There is a no-smoking policy throughout the building but guests can smoke in the garden. All 14 bedrooms have en suite facilities, TV, telephone and tea and coffee making facilities and are furnished with impeccable taste and attention to detail. There is a comfortable residents' lounge, cosy bar and ample parking. Guests are assured of a warm welcome from Brian and Lesley Husband.

A more extended stroll can take in the major sights of one of the country's most historic cities; King Alfred made it his capital at a time when his kingdom included a large part of southern England. The chief glory of the city is the magnificent Cathedral, whose treasures include the Winchester Bible and a wealth of the finest wooden carvings and stone monuments. Almost as renowned as the Cathedral is Winchester College, founded in 1382 by Bishop William of Wykeham to provide education for 70 'poor and needy' scholars. Close to the College is an altogether less grand, even austere Georgian House where Jane Austen spent the last months of her life. It was while John Keats was staying in Winchester that he wrote his *Ode to Autumn* - 'season of mist and mellow fruitfulness'. The daily walk that inspired the lines took him past the Cathedral and the College to the meadows beside the River Itchen, on a trail that today's visitors can follow step by step.

Closer to the hotel is the Hospital of St Cross, the oldest almshouse in the land, founded in 1132 and still home to 125 Brothers. The Hospital traditionally provides refreshment for the traveller, including the historic Wayfarers Dole. After a day spent walking and sightseeing, the lounge and bar of Giffard House beckon guests for a relaxing drink and a chat about the day's experiences.

in 1382 by Bishop William of Wykeham to provide education for 70 'poor and needy scholars': motto 'Manners Maketh Man'; and **Wolvesey Castle**, the chief residence of the medieval Bishops of Winchester. Here it was in 1554 that Queen Mary first met Philip of Spain: the wedding banquet was held in the Castle the very next day.

Other parts of this wonderful city are no less fascinating. In and around the historic High Street are the 15th century Buttercross and the nearby little Church of St Lawrence in the Square; the City Museum; the 16th century God Begot House, where a curfew bell tolls every evening at 8 o'clock; and a fine bronze of Horse and Rider by Elizabeth Frink. King Alfred's statue dominates the Broadway, and in nearby Bridge Street the **Winchester City Mill** is a fine example of the industrial past preserved for posterity. In the care of the National Trust, this is an 18th century water-powered corn mill

King Arthurs Round Table, Winchester Castle

Westgate Museum, Winchester

with a working water-wheel, mill races and island garden. The only surviving part of the old **Winchester Castle** is the Great Hall, once the centre of court and government life, where hangs the renowned Round Table, long associated with King Arthur but perhaps dating only from Tudor times. Behind the Hall, Queen Eleanor's Garden is a faithful representation of a medieval garden. The castle grounds are the site of the historic **Peninsula Barracks**, now the site of several

AVINGTON PARK

Winchester, Hampshire SO21 1DB
Tel: 01962 779260 Fax: 01962 779864
e-mail: sarah@avingtonpark.co.uk
website: www.avingtonpark.co.uk

One of the finest stately homes of England, Avington Park is a family home of great distinction that is open to the public at certain times for visits and is also available for hire as the perfect atmospheric setting for a grand event - reception, wedding, private party - or a conference. William Cobbett, author of *Rural Rides*, called it 'one of the prettiest places in the county', an assessment that still holds true. The site of the original building goes back many centuries, perhaps even to Roman times, as Roman wine jars were found during work on the old cellar in 1927.

The banqueting hall, of which little survives, was built in the 16th century where the Orangery now stands; under the auspices of Charles ll, a frequent visitor to Winchester, the building was enlarged in 1670 by the addition of two wings and a classical portico and by enclosing the earlier part with a facade of the same brickwork. The State Rooms on view include the Ballroom, the Red Drawing Room and the Library, and each has its own unique attractions and points of interest. The main hall was decorated by Clermont in about 1780, and at the foot of the main staircase is a memorial to the Hon. Charles Rolls, who was killed in a ballooning accident in Bournemouth in 1911. The Ballroom, or Great Saloon, has a truly magnificent gold plasterwork ceiling, painted wall panels depicting the four seasons and many other remarkable paintings, as well as some imposing mirrors. In the striking Red Drawing Room are more marvellous panels, friezes and cornices, pelmets and especially fine mirrors. Among the features in the Library are original Delft tiles, painted panels of centaurs, a George lll round table, an 18th century samovar and a Dutch model of a man-of-war - and about 2,000 books. In the grounds, the iron bridge over the River Itchen is a rare feature dating from the 18th century.

Avington Park is usually open 2.30 to 5.30 on Sundays and Bank Holidays from May to September. St Mary's Church, one of the finest Georgian churches in Hampshire, replaced a Saxon church that stood on the site and may be visited. For private functions, the Library can be transformed into an intimate dining room for 90 diners or a reception room for 175 buffet-style. For more information about visiting times and private hire contact Sarah Bullen. Avington Park is located a short distance northeast of Winchester: leave the B3047 opposite the Trout In at Itchen Abbas and turn right through the iron park gates after the hump bridge. Closed Tuesdays.

military museums, among them the Gurkha Museum; the King's Royal Hussars Museum, whose displays include the Charge of the Light Brigade; the Light Infantry Museum, telling the story of a modern regiment and featuring the Fall of the Berlin Wall and the Gulf War; and the **Royal Green Jackets Museum**, whose nine battle models include one of Waterloo with 22,000 model soldiers and horses, plus a sound and light commentary. The regiments combining to make the Royal Green Jackets have won no fewer than 55 Victoria Crosses, many of which are displayed here in their campaign cases. **The Balfour Museum** on Stockbridge Road tells the story of the Red Cross in Hampshire, and the **Historic Resources Centre** in Hyde Street offers access to collections of historic records for the area; it is located near the site of **Hyde Abbey**, which recent excavation has revealed as the probable site of King Arthur's final burial place. Visitors can study new information panels in the old abbey gateway.

Two years after Jane Austen was buried in the Cathedral, the poet John Keats stayed in Winchester and wrote his ode *To Autumn*. The inspiration for the *Season of Mist and Mellow Fruitfulness* was a daily walk past the Cathedral and College and through the water meadows beside the River Itchen. A detailed guide allows visitors to follow this walk, one of many marked walks in and around the city. A mile south of the Cathedral across the meadows is the oldest and one of the loveliest almshouses in Britain. The **Hospital of St Cross** was founded in 1132 by Henri du Blois, grandson of William the Conqueror, and extended in 1446 by Cardinal Beaufort, son of John of Gaunt, Chancellor of England and successor to William of Wykeham. Many original features survive in the Hospital, where pilgrims would meet and crusaders gather

on the eve of sailing from Southampton. The tradition of hospitality lives on in the restored Hundred Men's Hall, and the Wayfarer's Dole is still given at the porter's gate to all travellers who request it.

AROUND WINCHESTER

CRAWLEY
7 miles NW of Winchester off the B3049

A pretty village with a duck pond and an interesting social history: it is a possibly unique example of an early 20th century model village. The estate was bought in 1900 by the Philippi family, who set about adding faithful fakes to the village's store of traditional cottages. They also thought modern by providing the villagers with a state-of-the-art bath house and a rollerskating rink, but had the sensitivity not to touch the Church of St Mary, whose roof was, and still is, supported by mighty wooden columns.

ITCHEN ABBAS
4 miles NE of Winchester on the B3047

On the north bank of the River Itchen, this is the village where Charles Kingsley is believed to have written *The Water Babies*. One of the gravestones in the churchyard is in memory of John Hughes, who died in 1825 aged 26, thought to be the last person to be hanged for horse-stealing. In the nearby hamlet of **Avington**, John, the brother of the poet Shelley, is remembered in a monument in the 18th century Church of St Mary, which was built by Margaret, Marchioness of Carnarvon(see panel opposite for **Avington Park**).

MICHELDEVER
6 miles N of Winchester off the A33

The church here has an unusual octagonal

Orchard Close

The Highways, Micheldever, Hampshire SO21 3BP
Tel: 01962 774470

Jean Holmes retired three years ago after a lifetime in the nursing profession - practising and teaching - and now devotes most of her energies to running her Bed & Breakfast business at **Orchard House**. This striking modern house, which stands by the A33 between Winchester and Basingstoke, has three letting bedrooms, two doubles and a twin, all comfortable and spacious, with easy chairs, tv, radio-alarm and hairdryer. They are located end to end on the ground floor overlooking the garden. One has a bathroom en suite, the others share a bathroom; all are wheelchair accessible. Guests can relax

in a warm, welcoming lounge, and the day starts with hearty breakfast. Winchester is a 12-minute drive away, Basingstoke about the same, and there are several places of interest nearby. The Jane Austen connection is strong in this part of the world, and she was born and lived for 25 years in a house at Steventon; the house no longer stands, but the village church is well worth a visit. Also within a short drive is Whitchurch Silk Mill, a working mill that provided some of the silk for the costumes in the BBC's *Pride and Prejudice*. Orchard House has off-road parking for six cars.

nave designed by the Regency architect George Dance, who was also responsible for the pairs of thatched cottages in the neighbouring village of East Stratton.

TWYFORD
5 miles S of Winchester on the B3335

Hampshire churchyards are well known for their splendid old yew trees, and the tree that shelters Twyford's church is a particularly fine specimen. The Victorian church of striped brick and flint was designed by Alfred Waterhouse, architect of the Natural History Museum in London. There are pleasant walks on Shawford Down and along the Itchen Navigation, an early 18th century canal that runs from Winchester to Southampton. An interesting piece of industrial heritage is **Twyford Pumping Station**, a late 19th century waterworks with a working steam engine and boiler, water softening plant and lime kilns, and

a regular programme of special steam open days.

OTTERBOURNE
7 miles S of Winchester off the A33

Otterbourne was the home of the Victorian novelist Charlotte Young, whose best known work is *The Heir of Redcliffe*. She was a friend and publicist of the churchman and poet John Keble, sometime vicar of nearby Hursley. The two are buried in the churchyard of St Matthew's, Otterbourne. Charlotte Young is commemorated by an ornamental screen in the Lady Chapel of Winchester Cathedral.

ROMSEY

A prosperous market town on the River Test, with many historic buildings. **Romsey Abbey** was founded as a nunnery

Romsey Abbey

the Romsey Rood, which shows Christ with arms spread and the hand of God descending from the clouds. The memorials include a floor plate in honour of Lord Mountbatten (see under Broadlands below). At the time of the Dissolution of the Monasteries, when so many ecclesiastical buildings were destroyed, the people of Romsey, who had always used part of the Abbey as their parish church, managed to make an agreement with Henry VIII to purchase the Abbey. The price was £100 and the bill of sale, signed and sealed by Henry, is displayed in the south choir aisle. Close by the Abbey, in Church Court, stands the oldest secular building in Romsey, **King John's House**. Built probably around 1240 and therefore not for King John, it nonetheless served royalty in its time, including Edward I and his retinue, who

in 907 by Edward the Elder, son of Alfred the Great, and later in the same century King Edgar established the Benedictine Order here. The present building dates from between 1120 and 1230 and contains some of the very finest architecture of the period. The most spectacular feature is the nave, which soars to over 70 feet and extends for 76 feet. The Abbey's many treasures include

BROADLANDS

Romsey, Hampshire SO51 9ZD
Tel: 01794 505010 Fax: 01794 505040
e-mail: admin@broadlands.net
website: www.broadlands.net

One of the finest stately homes in the country, this gracious Palladian mansion was built by Henry Holland for an ancestor of Lord Palmerston.

It stands by the River Test in lovely grounds landscaped by Lancelot 'Capability' Brown. The elegant interior houses important collections of furniture, porcelain, sculpture and paintings (including several Van Dycks) acquired by the Palmerstons. The house passed to the

Mountbatten family and it was Lord Louis Mountbatten who first opened it to the public in 1979, shortly before his tragic death.

The present owner, Lord Romsey, carrying on the tradition started by his grandfather, established the Mountbatten Exhibition, which follows Lord Louis' remarkable career as sailor, commander, statesman, diplomat and sportsman. An audio-visual film is supported by a display of uniforms, decorations, trophies and mementoes. Open daily in summer.

Broadlands

scratched their coats of arms on to the plaster walls. The house is open for guided tours during the summer.

A surprise for railway fans stands behind the infants' school in Winchester Road. This is **Romsey Signal Box**, a preserved vintage signal box in working order, with signals, track and other artefacts. It is open for visits on the first Monday of each month (not January).

Romsey's most famous son is undoubtedly Lord Palmerston, three times Prime Minister during the 1850s and 1860s. A bronze statue in the Market Place honours this flamboyant statesman, who lived just south of town at the family home, **Broadlands**. One of the finest stately homes in the country, this gracious Palladian mansion by the River Test was built for an earlier member of the Palmerston family by Henry Holland and is set in lovely grounds landscaped by the ubiquitous Lancelot 'Capability' Brown (see panel on page 37).

AROUND ROMSEY

AMPFIELD
3 miles NE of Romsey on the A3090

Once a centre of the pottery industry, bricks made from local clay were used to build the Church of St Mark in the 1830s. One of the vicars was the father of Thomas the Tank Engine's creator the Rev W Awdry, who spent his childhood here. The chief attraction in the vicinity is the **Sir Harold Hillier Gardens & Arboretum**, begun by the renowned eponymous gardener. He started the unique collection in 1953 and the 180-acre site is now home to the greatest assembly of hardy trees and shrubs in the world. Justly billed as 'a garden for all seasons', it features among its 40,000 plants 11 National Plant Collections, including quercus and hamamelis, champion trees and the largest winter garden in Europe.

MOTTISFONT
4 miles N of Romsey off the A3057

Mottisfont's little Church of St Andrew boasts a wealth of 15th century stained glass, including a superb Crucifixion, and should not be overlooked on a visit to **Mottisfont Abbey**. Built as an Augustinian priory in the 12th century, the building was adapted to a country mansion after the Dissolution and further much modified in the 18th century. Some parts of the priory survive, including the monks' cellarium, an undercroft with vast pillars, but the main attraction inside is the drawing room decorated as a Gothic trompe l'oeil fantasy by Rex Whistler. He was also to have designed the furniture, but World War ll intervened and he was killed in action. The superb grounds contain the National Collection of old-fashioned roses, established in 1972, a lovely pollarded lime walk designed by Sir Geoffrey Jellicoe and some superb trees, including what is thought to be England's largest plane tree.

BRAISHFIELD
4 miles NE of Romsey off the A3090

A scattered village in open country, almost in the shadow of Farley Mount. This country park covers 1,000 acres and from its top, just under 600 feet, the views are superb. The park abounds in wildlife and supports a wide variety of trees. Braishfield's **All Saints Church** (1885) is notable for the coloured bricks that are a signature of the architect Butterfield.

EAST WELLOW
3 miles W of Romsey off the A27

The **Church of St Margaret** is the burial place of Florence Nightingale, who lies

FARLEY FARM COTTAGE HOLIDAYS

Braishfield, Nr Romsey,
Hampshire SO51 0QP
Tel: 01794 368265 Fax: 01794 367847

Wendy Graham's **Farley Farm** is a 400-acre beef and arable farm set in really beautiful countryside three miles from Braishfield and four miles from Hursley. It's a lovely setting for a holiday, with stunning views and exhilarating walks, and Wendy welcomes all ages to the self-catering accommodation within the farm grounds.

Meadow Cottage and Rosie's Cottage, built in the early years of the last century, have been carefully modernised to meet today's requirements while retaining plenty of character. Both are semi-detached cottages with kitchen, cloakroom, living room and dining room on the ground floor and two bedrooms and a bathroom on the first floor. A cot and high chair are available free of charge, and arrangements can be made for a baby-sitting service. Guests can bring a well-behaved pet and a horse or pony, for which a small charge includes stabling and grazing. The cottages have lawned gardens with garden

furniture and a barbecue area, and each has its own carport and covered store.

The large grass paddock and the adjoining downs and woodland provide peaceful walks, with abundant wildlife to be seen, while local places within a short drive which should not be missed include the Sir Harold Hillier Gardens and the National Trust's Mottisfont Abbey. Still closer are the attractive Farley Mount Country Park and the fine Church of St John in Farley Chamberlain.

CRANFORD FARM

Rudd Lane, Braishfield, Nr Romsey, Hampshire SO50 1OU
Tel: 01794 368216

Much-travelled owner Brian Brooks offers a choice of accommodation to the many guests who stay at Cranford Farm, his home set in four acres of farmland. In the main house are five comfortable rooms for Bed & Breakfast visitors, whose day starts with an excellent breakfast, either traditional English or lighter continental, with all the options.

In the grounds of the house are self-catering lodges, where families are especially welcome. The lodges are centrally heated, with comfortable bedrooms and lounges, fully-fitted kitchens and everything needed for a relaxing, do-as-you-please break. Guests in the main house and in the lodges will find ample car parking space and have free rein in the garden, patio, paddocks and swimming pool.

The Test Valley location between Romsey and Winchester puts many towns, villages and places of interest within easy reach. Romsey itself boasts one of the very finest Norman buildings in the country in its remarkable Abbey dating from the 12th and 13th centuries. The National Trust's Mottisfont Abbey, a 12th century Augustinian priory by a tributary of the Test, is a short drive away, and even nearer are the Sir Harold Hillier Gardens & Arboretum, which house the greatest collection of wild and cultivated woody plants in the world.

beneath the family monument. The simple inscription is FN 1820-1910. The church has many interesting features, including 13th century wall paintings and Jacobean panelling. Florence's family home was the nearby country mansion Embley Park.

OWER

5 miles SW of Romsey off the A31

Paultons Park is a leisure park with over 40 attractions ranging from thrilling rides and a Rio Grande railway to bird gardens, museums and dinosaurs.

This part of England's fifth most populous county is an area of contrasts: the coastal crescent that stretches from Southampton through Fareham to Portsmouth and Havant is busy, bustling and built up, while inland there are parts of the South Downs that are as scenic and peaceful as anywhere in the county. Southampton boasts one of the finest natural harbours in the world and has been the leading British deep-sea port since the days of the Norman conquest. It will be forever associated with the glamour of the transatlantic liners, which had their heyday in the 1920s and 1930s. The massive docks were large enough to berth eight of the largest liners at the same time, and the old Terminus Station was a scene of constant activity. The greatest days of the liner may have passed, but there are still several sailings every week, and the sight of the modern Queens of the Sea is still a stirring one. The associations of Portsmouth are not with the liners but with fighting ships such as the *Mary Rose*, *HMS Victory* and *HMS Warrior*. Portsmouth is also a popular seaside resort providing, with its neighbour Hayling Island, seven miles of sandy beaches.

HMS Victory

Sailing for pleasure is a major interest all along this part of the coast, and the fleet of yachts and powered craft berthed in and around the Solent, with Hamble as its 'capital', is one of the largest and most concentrated in the world. Amidst all the maritime activity the natural world has not been forgotten, and there are important nature reserves at Langstone Harbour and Titchfield Haven. This is also a great area for walking as well as sailing, and the 60-mile Solent Way runs from Milford-on-Sea by way of Southampton and Portsmouth to Langstone Harbour and Emsworth.

Southsea Castle and the massive Portchester Castle have fascinating historical associations, and the ruins of Netley Abbey and the Bishop's Palace at Bishop's Waltham are both picturesque and evocative.

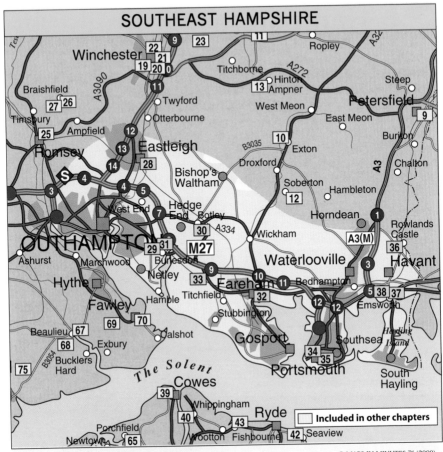

SOUTHEAST HAMPSHIRE

Winchester

Braishfield

Timsbury

Ampfield

Romsey

Eastleigh

Bishop's Waltham

West End

Hedge End

Botley

SOUTHAMPTON

Ashurst

Marchwood

Netley

Hythe

Hamble

Titchfield

Fawley

Stubbington

Beaulieu

Exbury

Calshot

Gosport

Bucklers Hard

The Solent

Cowes

Whippingham

Porchfield

Newtown

Wootton

Fishbourne

Seaview

Ropley

Titchborne

Hinton Ampner

West Meon

East Meon

Steep

Petersfield

Droxford

Exton

Buriton

Chalton

Soberton

Hambleton

Horndean

Rowlands Castle

Wickham

Waterlooville

Havant

Fareham

Bedhampton

Emsworth

Southsea

Hayling Island

Portsmouth

South Hayling

Ryde

Included in other chapters

© MAPS IN MINUTES ™ (2000)

PLACES TO STAY, EAT, DRINK AND SHOP

28	Eastleigh Museum, Eastleigh	Museum	Page 45
29	The Vine Inn, Old Bursledon	Pub, food and accommodation	Page 46
30	The Brewery Bar, Botley	Pub and restaurant	Page 46
31	Bursledon Windmill, Bursledon,	Windmill & nature trail	Page 47
32	Gordon Arms, Fareham	Pub with food	Page 48
33	The Bold Forester, Sarisbury Green	Pub and restaurant	Page 48
34	Flagship Portsmouth, Portsmouth	Naval museum	Page 50
35	Aspex Gallery, Portsmouth	Art gallery	Page 52
36	The Fountain Inn, Rowlands Castle	Pub, restaurant & accommodation	Page 54
37	The Ship Inn, Emsworth	Pub and restaurant	Page 56
38	The Blue Bell Inn, Emsworth	Pub with food	Page 56

SOUTHAMPTON

From this historic port Henry V set sail for Agincourt in 1415, the Pilgrim Fathers embarked on their voyage to the New World in 1620, and in 1912 the great liner the *Titanic* steamed majestically into the Solent on her first and last journey. As a major sea port, Southampton was an obvious target for enemy bombing, and indeed suffered greatly, but a surprising number of ancient buildings survive the bombardment, including about half of the one-mile circuit of the medieval town walls; visitors can follow the Walk the Walls signposts and panels to guide them round the walls. Perhaps the most impressive feature of the walls is **Bargate**, one of the finest medieval city gates in the country. From its construction around 1200 until the 1930s Bargate was the principal entrance to the city. Its narrow archway is so low that Southampton Corporation's trams had to be specially modified to allow them to pass through. Inside the arch stands a statue of George lll dressed as a Roman emperor. Bargate now stands in a pedestrianised area and its upper floor, the former Guildhall, is now a museum of local history and folklore. The **Museum of Archaeology** is

housed in God's House Tower, a massive stone building that was also part of the medieval town defences. It contains one of the most important archaeological collections in the country, with fascinating displays of Roman, Saxon and medieval objects excavated from local sites. The story of Southampton as seen through the eyes of residents is told in the **Tudor House Museum**, a 500-year-old building which has been a family home, artist's studio, dye house and bookbinder's premises. The garden is an authentic reconstruction of a 16th century knot garden with herbs and flowers of the period, a fountain and bee skeps. The lifestyle of the wealthy is the theme of the **Medieval Merchant's House**, which has been restored inside and out to appear just as when it was built in about 1290. The days of the luxury liner have not quite passed, and watching big ships like the *Aurora*, *Oriana* or *Queen Elizabeth ll* from Western Esplanade and Town Quay is still a thrilling experience. The story of the liners and the port is told in the **Maritime Museum**, which is located on the corner of historic Bugle Street and Town Quay in a medieval wool house that once saw service as a prison for Napoleonic soldiers. Southampton was also at the centre of the developing aircraft industry, and in the **Southampton Hall of Aviation** visitors learn about the numerous local aircraft companies, including the Supermarine works where the aircraft designer RJ Mitchell created the legendary Spitfire and the S6 Seaplane that was a winner of the coveted Schneider Trophy. A Spitfire is among the aircraft on show, the largest of which is the four-engined Sandringham flying boat,

Ocean Village Marina

whose flight deck is accessible to visitors on a guided tour. At Totton, in a neck off Southampton Water, **Eling Tide Mill** is probably the only surviving tide mill in the world still producing flour on a daily basis. A mill has stood on the site since Domesday, but the present building dates from the 18th century. Abandoned in the 1940s and opened again after restoration in the 1980s, it takes advantage of the renowned double tide to stage milling demonstrations - and the flour it produces is for sale. It also serves as a museum, combining history, science and technology under one roof. Notable natives of Southampton include Izaak Watts (the hymnologist who wrote '*O God our Help in Ages Past*'), the composer Charles Dibdin and the painter Sir John Millais. Though rich in history Southampton moves with the times; major developments include the enhancement of its impressive central parks, the superbly appointed Leisure World, a state-of-the-art three-pool swimming and diving complex and Ocean Village, a waterfront complex with a 450-berth marina, undercover shopping, restaurants and a multi-screen cinema.

Ocean Village Marina

barbecue areas, children's play areas and an adventure playground. High Wood Barn Visitor Centre contains all the information about the 440-acre park, plus hands-on exhibitions and an aquarium. In the old fire station on the main street is a local history museum whose exhibits include the story of Arthur Henry Rostron, captain of the Cunard liner *Carpathia*, which rescued over 700 passengers from the *Titanic*. Captain Rostron became Commodore of the line, was knighted and retired to the village. His grave is in the old burial ground near the museum.

EASTLEIGH
4 miles NE of Southampton on the A335

A Saxon settlement mentioned in a charter of 932, Eastleigh waited 900 years before expanding rapidly with the arrival of the railway from London. In the heart of town, in an old Salvation Army building, EAstleigh Museumlooks at the town in the 1930's (see panel opposite).

The railway connection (Eastleigh Works were among the largest in the country) is commemorated by Jill Tweed's sculpture *The Railwayman* in the town centre. Just outside town, **Lakeside**

AROUND SOUTHAMPTON

WEST END
3 miles NE of Southampton off the A27

On the northern outskirts of Southampton, **Itchen Valley Country Park** is a great place for a family outing, with miles of waymarked trails, picnic and

Country Park is home to a variety of wildlife and a great place for sailing and fishing; its miniature steam railway is a popular family attraction.

BISHOPS WALTHAM
10 miles NE of Southampton on the B3335/ B2177

A charming and historic small town that from 900 to 1869 was the country residence of the Bishops of Winchester. The sumptuous palace entertained many monarchs, among them Richard the Lionheart returning from the Crusades, Henry V mustering his army before sailing for Agincourt and Henry VIII entertaining Charles V of Spain to a feast fit for a king (or even two kings). The palace, which was erected by the serial builder Henry (Henri) de Blois in 1136, was enlarged by William of Wykeham, who died at the palace in 1404. The palace was largely destroyed in the Civil War, but the ruins are impressive, especially the Great Hall with its three-storey tower. A mile or so out of town, on the B2177, **Waltham Chase Mill** is a 19th century watermill being restored to full working order. Between the town and the mill is the Moors Nature Reserve, where a source of the River Hamble rises through bubbling sand.

The village of **Swanmore**, with its neo-Norman Church of St Barnabas, lies in the Meon Valley just below Bishops Waltham.

NETLEY
4 miles SE of Southampton off the A3025

A Victorian town on the shores of the Solent, Netley was brought into prominence by the vast military hospital built here after the Crimean War. The designer of **Netley Hospital** was EO Mennie and the foundation stone was laid by Queen Victoria in 1856. The chapel, with its distinctive 100' tower, now houses an exhibition about the hospital, but the rest of the buildings were demolished after a fire in the 1960s. The hospital, which became known throughout the world, also found fame in fiction as the place where Conan Doyle's Dr Watson trained as an army doctor. Netley Cemetery is the final resting place of many nationalities, both of servicemen and of the civilian staff who worked at the hospital. The site of the hospital has been developed as the **Royal Victoria Country Park**, with 100 acres of woods and coastline offering pleasant walks and splendid views over Southampton Water. A miniature steam railway runs for a mile round the park.

Netley Abbey, founded in the 13th century, is an extensive and imposing ruin in a quiet setting among lawns and trees. Jane Austen was a frequent visitor to this romantic spot, and Horace Walpole, writing in the mid-18th century, declared that *'these are not the ruins of Netley but of Paradise'.*

EASTLEIGH MUSEUM

25 High Street, Eastleigh, Hampshire SO50 5LF
Tel: 023 8064 3026 e-mail: musmst@hants.gov.uk
Fax: 023 8065 3582 website: www.hants.gov.uk/museum/eastlmus/index

Right in the heart of town, **Eastleigh Museum** is the ideal place to take a break from shopping and discover what life was like in the town in the past. Visitors can meet Mr and Mrs Brown, a local engine driver and his wife, and see the re-creation of their home including the living room, scullery, back yard and outhouse. Also re-created is part of the Southern Railway locomotive works and a steam engine footplate. The museum always offers something new to see with special exhibitions, including art, crafts, photography, local history and natural history, as well as the work of local artists and societies. In the local studies area visitors can dig deeper into the area's past and even do some family history research. Tea, coffee and snacks are served in the Whistle Stop Café.

THE VINE INN

The High Street, Old Bursledon, Hampshire SO81 8DJ
Tel: 02380 403836

The Vine Inn is located on the southeastern fringes of Southampton, but the big city could be miles away at this unspoilt pub. The 'High Street' in the address is in fact a quiet loop off a main road, and the countryside around is both peaceful and attractive. The pub's low beamed ceilings create a delightfully traditional ambience, assisted by plates and porcelain and old prints of local scenes. Darts, bar billiards and dominoes are played in the games area.

The tenants, Margarette and Ray Standing, generate a genuine, friendly atmosphere as well as a great sense of community - they and the pub support a number of worthy causes. Hot and cold bar snacks are served, and Sunday lunch has become a very popular occasion. Evening meals can be ordered only by residents, for whom three well-appointed bedrooms over the pub provide comfortable overnight accommodation.

Southampton has a great deal to offer the visitor, and the maritime connection naturally remains strong. The Pilgrim Fathers set sail from here in 1620 and in more recent times the great passenger liners started their transatlantic crossings from the docks. The River Hamble, one of the country's foremost yachting centres, is within very easy reach of the inn, and nearby Hamble Common is an area rich in history and teeming with wildlife; it has been designated a Site of Special Scientific Interest (SSSI). Bursledon itself has a number of attractions, including the only working windmill in the county and the imposing Bursledon brickworks.

THE BREWERY BAR

Winchester Street, Botley, Hampshire SO30 2AA
Tel: 01489 799991

There is an exceptionally warm and friendly feel about the **Brewery Bar**, a convivial hostelry in 17th century premises that were for many years precisely what the name suggests - a brewery. Ken and Sue Parslow are the welcoming tenants, and the appeal of their pub extends beyond the loyal local clientele to tourists, passing trade and lovers of traditional jazz: music nights are a popular regular feature. The public bar has 60s juke box music, darts and bar billiards, and is also the practice ground for the dominoes team, which has seen success in several national championships.

The beamed, carpeted lounge bar sports pictures of the brewery in the old days; in the dining area, where small screens separate the tables, food is served every lunchtime from a menu that encompasses snacky 'lite bites', grills, main dishes and desserts.

Among the many local places of interest is the 13th century Netley Abbey, a glorious ruin which captivated Horace Walpole and Jane Austen and now provides an evocative backdrop for open-air theatrical performances. William Cobbett, author of *Rural Rides*, lived for some years in Botley, and his memorial can be found in the Market Square. The Brewery Bar has plenty of off-road parking.

BURSLEDON
4 miles SE of Southampton on the A3025

A village that, like its neighbours, is linked inextricably with ships and shipbuilding. Twenty Viking longships were sunk by King Alfred's men in a battle on the river here, and many of the sailors who were killed are buried beneath the Church of St Leonard. Nelson's flagship at the Battle of Copenhagen, The *Elephant*, was built in a yard that is still in the business.

Just off Junction 8 of the M27, Manor Farm Country Park is a working farm of a bygone age on the banks of the Hamble river. Among its many attractions are a Victorian schoolroom, vintage machinery, traditional farm animals and demonstrations of Victorian farm activities.

In a magnificent hilltop setting, **Bursledon Windmill** is the only one surviving in Hampshire; it was built by a Mrs Phoebe Langtry in 1814 at a cost of £800. Inactive from the time of depression in the 1880s, the tower mill was restored to full working order between 1976 and 1991 (see panel below).

The village has another relic of the county's industrial heritage in the shape of **Bursledon Brickworks**, the last surviving example in the country of a steam-driven brickworks. Built in 1897, the works closed in 1974 but have been lovingly restored and are open to the

public. Among the special features are displays on the history and technique of brickmaking, and visitors can buy traditional building products in the shop.

BOTLEY
4 miles SE of Southampton on the A334

This attractive village of redbrick houses on the Hamble is as pleasant now as when William Cobbett, the 19th century writer and political commentator, described it as *'the most delightful village in the world....it has everything in a village I love, and none of the things I hate'*. The author of *Rural Rides* lived a very comfortable, well-to-do life in Botley between 1804 and 1817 and is honoured by a memorial in the Market Square. **Botley Mills**, on a site mentioned in the Domesday Book, consist of an 18th century water mill and an early 20th century roller mill; the mills are being restored as a museum of flour milling.

Halfway between Botley and the pretty village of **Wickham**, on the A334, **Wickham Vineyard** was established in 1984, and its original six-acre planting had expanded to 18 acres of vines. The vineyard and the modern winery are open for visits, as is the adjacent nature reserve, where the sparrowhawk and the great spotted woodpecker can be seen, along with a wealth of meadow flowers. Wickham was the home of William of Wykeham, Chancellor of England, Bishop of Winchester and founder of Winchester

BURSLEDON WINDMILL

Windmill Lane, Bursledon, Southampton, Hampshire SO31 8BG
Tel: 023 8040 4999

The last surviving working windmill in Hampshire was built by a Mrs Phoebe Langtry in 1814 at a cost of £800. Inactive from the time of the depression in the 1880s, the tower mill was restored to full working order between 1976 and 1991. Its sails - a fine sight on a hilltop setting - revolve whenever a good northerly or southerly wind blows, producing stoneground flour for sale.

Next to the mill is the Windmill Wood Nature Trail, a woodland habitat supporting a wide range of wildlife including woodpeckers.

GORDON ARMS

Gordon Road, Fareham, Hampshire PO16 7TG
Tel: 01329 280545

Diana Valance, who worked for the previous tenants, has known the **Gordon Arms** for 20 years, and now runs it with her daughter. This friendly, welcoming team have made the pub very much a focal point for the local community, with all ages and a number of sporting and social groups among the regulars. Flower baskets adorn the Victorian facade in spring and summer, and at the back, accessed through the pub, is a garden where children can play in safety. The two bars are bright and modern and usually buzzing with the cheerful crowd. Darts and cribbage teams have their home here, and quiz nights have become a popular regular attraction.

The food on offer ranges from sandwiches and filled baguettes to hearty home-made soups and classics such as gammon or steak & kidney pudding, with roasts on Sunday and real ales to accompany. The Gordon Arms is located in a mainly residential side street a short walk from the centre of Fareham, which Thackeray, who often stayed here during his school holidays, described as 'a dear little old Hampshire town'. That description could still apply to the High Street, which presents the visitor with a delightful mix of architectural styles.

THE BOLD FORESTER

120 Bridge Road, Sarisbury Green, Nr. Fareham,
Hampshire SO31 7EL
Tel: 01489 576400

Tenants Sue and Stuart Banger pride themselves on the home-cooked food served at their mid-Victorian pub set back from the main road (A27) close to Junction 9 of the M27. Behind the long white-painted frontage, a large part of the interior is given over to eating, with chairs set at neat round or square tables between open-brick or half-panelled walls.

There are seats for about 100, but such is the pub's popularity that booking is recommended for all sessions. Traditional home-cooked dishes, including fresh fish and succulent steaks, make up a varied menu, which is supplemented by a specials

board. Children are welcome, and some of the tables are designated non-smoking. Tables and chairs are set outside on a small green in front of the pub, and at the back there is a large beer garden with a patio, barbecue area and children's adventure playground. **The Bold Forester** has a great atmosphere that makes it a popular venue for business lunches, weddings, anniversaries and other special occasions. This part of Hampshire was once renowned for the cultivation of strawberries, and Parkgate, a little way east along the A27, was the main distribution centre, with scores of special trains commissioned to transport the fruit to London and beyond.

College and New College, Oxford. The mill by the bridge over the River Meon is of particular interest to American visitors as it contains beams from the American frigate *Chesapeake*, captured in 1813 off Boston by the British frigate *Shannon*.

HAMBLE
6 miles SE of Southampton on the B3397

Hamble was a major trading post in the 14th century and an important centre of the shipbuilding industry. Famous now as a yachting centre, the village takes its name from the river, just ten miles in length, that flows past on its way to Southampton Water. Some 3,000 craft have berths in the Hamble Estuary, and in the high season there's an amazing variety to be seen, from vintage barges to the sleekest modern vessels. The area south of the village is **Hamble Common**, 55 acres of

Sailing, Hamble Estuary

coastal heath with a wide range of habitats and a correspondingly extensive variety of flora and fauna. Along the shore are the remains of Iron Age settlements, a Tudor castle and a Napoleonic gun battery. The castle was built on the orders of Henry VlII in 1543 as part of a defence against a feared French invasion; it has disappeared apart from a few foundation stones which can be seen at low tide. At the eastern tip of the Common is a Bofors anti-aircraft gun, installed in 1989 to replace the gun that helped to protect the docks and oil terminals during World War ll.

FAREHAM
10 miles SE of Southampton on the A27

Much expanded since Thackeray described it as a 'dear little old Hampshire town', Fareham still has considerable charm, and the handsome houses on the High Street reflect the prosperous days as a shipbuilding centre. Many aspects of the town's history are exhibited in **Westbury Manor Museum**, located in a large 17th century farmhouse on the outskirts of town. Also nearby are the Royal Armouries at **Fort Nelson**, whose displays of artillery dating from the Middle Ages form one of the finest collections of its kind in the world. Among the 300 guns on display are a wrought-iron monster of 1450 that could fire a 60kg granite ball almost a mile, Flemish guns captured at Waterloo and bits of the notorious Iraqi supergun. Daily gun firings take place at noon and 3pm, and the dramatic interpretations include accounts of the defence of Rorke's Drift, experiences under shellfire in the World War l trenches and a Royalist eyewitness account of the execution of Charles l. The fort was built on the orders of Lord Palmerston as part of the defences of the Royal Dockyards against a possible French invasion. The French attack never

FLAGSHIP PORTSMOUTH

Porters Lodge, Building 1/7, College Road,
HM Naval Base, Portsmouth, Hampshire PO1 3LJ
Tel: 023 9286 1533 Fax: 023 9229 5252
e-mail: enquiries@flagship.org.uk
website: www.flagship.org.uk

Flagship Portsmouth, in the historic dockyard, is home port to three of the greatest ships ever built, but has many other attractions. The latest of these is the blockbusting Action Stations, where visitors can test their skills and abilities through a series of high-tech interactive displays and simulators.

The most famous of the ships is undoubtedly *HMS Victory*. From the outside it's a majestic three-master, but inside it's creepily claustrophobic except for the Admiral's and Captain's spacious, mahogany-panelled quarters. Visitors can pace the very same deck from which Nelson masterminded the decisive encounter with the French navy off Cape Trafalgar in 1805. Standing on the deck arrayed in his Admiral's finery, Nelson was an easy target for a keen-eyed French sniper; the precise spot where he fell and the place on the lower deck where he later died (knowing that the battle was won) are both marked by plaques.

The *Mary Rose*, the second largest ship in Henry VIII's fleet, was putting out to sea, watched proudly by the King from Southsea Common, when she suddenly heeled over and sank. All 700 men on board lost their lives. More than 400 years later, in 1982, the ship was raised in an amazingly delicate operation from the seabed. The impressively preserved remains of the ship are now housed in the timber-clad Mary Rose Museum. (One of the tombs in Portsmouth Cathedral is that of one of the Mary Rose's crew.) *HMS Warrior* was the Navy's first iron-clad warship and the most formidable fighting ship the world had seen in 1860: bigger, faster and more heavily armed than any warship afloat, built of iron and powered by both sail and steam. Her size and might proved to be a deterrent to potential enemies and she never actually had to go to war.

Boat trips round the harbour give a feel of the soul of the city that has been home to the Royal Navy for more than 800 years, and the most attractive part, picturesque Old Portsmouth, can be seen to advantage from the little ferry that plies the short route to Gosport.

The Royal Naval Museum is the most fascinating of its kind, with a marvellous exhibition of the life and deeds of Nelson, and the interactive Dockyard Apprentice Exhibition explains the skills and crafts of 1911 that went into the building of the world's finest fighting ships, the Dreadnoughts.

materialised, but the fort saw service in World War ll as part of Britain's anti-aircraft defences as an enormous ammunition depot. Abandoned in the 1960s, it has subsequently been restored by Hampshire County Council. Most of it is now open to the public, and visitors can take a guided tour round the ramparts, the tunnels and underground ammunition stores, the barracks and the Victorian kitchen.

TITCHFIELD
8 miles SE of Southampton on the A27

Two miles west of Fareham stands the village of Titchfield, where the ruins of a 13th century abbey can be seen. The abbey reflects the former prominence of Titchfield, which was an important market centre and thriving port on the River Meon. The parish church contains a notable treasure in the shape of the **Wriothesley Monument**, carved by a Flemish craftsman in 1594. This remarkable and massive piece is a triple tomb chest depicting Thomas Wriothesley, the 1st Earl of Southampton, with his wife and son. The Earl it was who converted part of the abbey into a house, in which the 3rd Earl, Henry Wriothesley, entertained William Shakespeare.

GOSPORT
12 miles SE of Southampton
on the A32

Gosport is the site of another of Palmerston's forts - the circular **Fort Brockhurst**, in virtually original condition, is open for visits - and of the **Royal Naval Submarine Museum**. Located at *HMS Dolphin*, the museum has many exhibits relating to the development of submarines and submarine warfare, and visitors can look over *HMS*

Alliance, a submarine built towards the end of World War ll. Another, much earlier submarine, known as *Holland 1*, is also on display. Gosport's splendid **Holy Trinity Church** contains an organ that was once played by Handel when he was music master to the Duke of Chandos at Little Stanmore in Middlesex. The town of Gosport bought the organ when the Duke died. Gosport's original railway station still stands, a fine colonnaded building of 1842.

PORTSMOUTH

Loacted at Portsmouth is the country's leading naval base where, at **Flagship Portsmouth**, people come from all over the world to see the historic ships in the naval dockyard (see panel opposite). The most famous of all is **HMS Victory** and visitors can pace the very same deck from which Nelson masterminded the decisive encounter with the French navy off Cape Trafalgar in 1805. The **Mary Rose**, the second largest ship in Henry Vlll's fleet, was putting out to sea when she suddenly heeled over and sank. More than 400 years later, in 1982, the ship was raised and the impressively preserved remains

HMS Victory

are now housed in the timber-clad Mary Rose Museum.

Built in 1860, **HMS Warrior** was the Navy's first ironclad warship and the most formidable fighting ship the world had seen. The **Royal Naval Museum** has a marvellous exhibition of the life and deeds of Nelson, and the Dockyard Apprentice Exhibition explains the skills and crafts that went into the building of the world's finest fighting ships, the Dreadnoughts.

Other museums (there are at least a dozen in the city) that should not be missed are the **City Museum & Record Office**, with period room settings from the 17th century to the 1950s; the **Industrial Heritage Museum** of WM Treadgold & Co; and the **City of Portsmouth Preserved Transport Depot** with 21 vintage and veteran passenger vehicles on show. Portsmouth's literary connections include Jane Austen and Charles Dickens. Jane Austen mentions Portsmouth in her novel *Mansfield Park*, and while living in Southampton she visited the town to see her brothers Francis and Charles, both of whom reached very high rank in the Navy. Charles Dickens was born in Portsmouth in 1812, the second of seven children, and the house of his birth is now a museum.

Portsmouth Guildhall

Some of his personal belongings, from a paperweight to the couch on which he died at his last home, in Kent, are on display in the museum. A large collection of Dickens memorabilia is kept in the City Library, and the Tourist Information Centre will supply details of **Dickens Celebrity Guide Walks**. Two of Dickens' mistresses - Maria Sarah Winter (née Beadnell) and the actress Ellen Walton-Robinson (née Ternan) are buried in Highland Road cemetery in Southsea. Other distinguished sons of Portsmouth include Isambard Kingdom Brunel and the yachtsman Alec Rose.

Port Solent Marina, Portsmouth

Like Southampton, Portsmouth suffered badly during World War ll, losing the majority of its fine 17th and 18th century buildings. **St George's Church**, a handsome Georgian building of 1754, was damaged by a bomb but has been splendidly restored, and the barn-like Beneficial Boys School, built in 1784, is another survivor. In the **Royal Garrison Church**, Catherine of Braganza married Charles ll in 1662. The major art gallery in Portsmouth is the Aspex Gallery (see panel opposite).

Southsea, the southern section of the city, also offers much to interest the visitor. The **D-Day Museum** commemorates the Allied invasion of Europe in 1944; pride of place among the many evocative exhibits must go to the remarkable 83-metre Overlord Embroidery. The **Royal Marines Museum** highlights some of the Marines' outstanding achievements throughout the world and is home to a world-famous collection of medals, including the ten Victoria Crosses awarded to Royal Marines. The Museum is housed in Eastney Barracks, and also at Eastney is a

splendid old engine house with a pair of magnificent James Watt beam engines. One of the engines is in steam when the house is open, on the last complete weekend of every month. **Portsmouth Sea Life Centre**, on Clarence Esplanade at Southsea, reflects the city's rich maritime history with a themed interior that includes lifeboats, a ship's bridge, a tropical reef observatory and close encounters with all sorts of sea creatures, from shrimps to sharks.

Southsea Castle was built in 1545 by Henry Vlll to protect Portsmouth against the French; in the early 19th century it was altered to accommodate extra guns and men, and a walk through the tunnels that surround the moat is one of the highlights of a tour of the castle. A little way out to sea from the Hovercraft Terminal on Clarence Esplanade stands **Spitbank Fort**, a monumental Victorian fort with 50 rooms and a maze of passages. Four of these forts were built offshore, part of a later defence against the French threat. This one can be reached by ferry from Southsea Pier.

At the head of Portsmouth Harbour,

Southsea Beach

Porchester Castle

Portchester Castle is not only the grandest medieval castle in the county but also stands within the best-preserved site of a Roman fort in northern Europe. Sometime around 280AD the Romans enclosed eight acres of this strategic headland and used it as a base for ships clearing the Channel of pirates. The original walls of the fort were 20ft high and 10ft thick, though their depth was much reduced down the years by local people pillaging the stone for their own buildings. The castle dates back to 1120, though the most substantial remains are those of the royal palace built for Richard ll at the very end of the 14th century. Also within the walls of the Roman enclosure is Portchester Church, a superb Norman building that was part of an Augustinian Priory. The priors for some reason moved inland, leaving the church in disuse; it remained thus for more than 550 years until Queen Anne personally donated £400 for its restoration. One of the glories of the church is a 12th century font of carved Caen stone.

THE FOUNTAIN INN & THAI RESTAURANT

34 The Green, Rowlands Castle, Hampshire PO9 6AB
Tel: 02392 412291

Herbie Armstrong, one-time member of Van Morrison's band, and his Swedish-born wife Elizabeth combine their talents in running one of the best eating places in the area. Two eating places, in fact. **The Fountain Inn** is a cheerful, sociable pub serving traditional bar food at lunchtime (ploughman's, ham, egg & chips, home-made pie of the day); it's also a popular spot for get-togethers and for its Tuesday evening live music sessions. The style of the open-plan bar and lounge areas is Regency, with deep-red upholstered seating and darkwood stools, and a collection of prints and photographs.

Across the courtyard of this village-centre site opposite the green the couple have won acclaim with their authentic Thai restaurant, **Thaiger on the Green**, with colonial-style decor and furnishings and a mouthwatering evening menu prepared by Thai chefs that spans the classic Thai repertoire, from fish cakes and fragrant soups to rich, satisfying curries, crunchy stir-fries and tangy salads.

Above the restaurant are five elegant en suite letting bedrooms, doubles or twins, with televisions and hospitality trays; like the restaurant, they showcase the impeccable style and taste of interior designer Elizabeth. One room has a four-poster bed.

AROUND PORTSMOUTH

BEDHAMPTON
3 miles NE of Portsmouth off the B2177

This charming little village in a conservation area has a Norman church and a house - Old Mill House - where Keats once stayed.

ROWLANDS CASTLE
5 miles N of Portsmouth off the A3

A small village with a long green and the remains - largely obscured by the railway - of a medieval castle. Roland was a local hero who slew a foreign giant.

One of the south of England's most elegant stately homes is nearby **Stansted Park**, a fine example of Caroline Revival architecture. The first house on the site was an 11th century hunting lodge, and Stansted House was built on the present site in 1688. Much altered and extended over the next two centuries, the house was burnt down in 1900 and rebuilt to the same blueprint. Set in 1,750 acres of lovely park and woodland, the house is full of treasures, among them 18th century Brussels tapestries, fine English furniture and a collection of bird paintings by Dutch Old Masters. The servants' quarters, kitchen and wine cellars provide a fascinating insight into life below stairs. The grounds include a beech avenue, an arboretum, Ivan Hicks' 'Garden in Mind', a garden centre and an exquisitely decorated secluded chapel.

HORNDEAN
5 miles N of Portsmouth off the A3

A busy village that has a long association with the brewing industry. The company of **George Gale**, founded at Horndean in 1847, opens its doors to visitors for a guided tour that includes the techniques of brewing and the opportunity to taste prize-winning ales and country wines.

Queen Elizabeth Country Park, at Gravel Hill, Horndean, is part of the landscape of the South Downs and is located in an Area of Outstanding Natural Beauty. Open throughout the year, its 1,400 acres include walking and cycle trails, adventure play trails, horse riding, and picnic and barbecue areas. It's a naturalist's paradise, with many species of butterflies and wild orchids, and a large area is designated as a National Nature Reserve. The many Roman and Iron Age sites in the Park are preserved as Scheduled Ancient Monuments. The Park is dominated by the three hills of **Butser, War Down** and **Holt Down**, which provide a contrast between the dramatic downland and beautiful woodland.

EMSWORTH
6 miles NE of Portsmouth on the A27

A picturesque village located in the upper reaches of Chichester Harbour, Emsworth is a popular spot with sailors, walkers, birdwatchers and artists. In the 18th century it was the main port in the harbour, and was later important for the production of oysters, but the main maritime activity now is yachting. **Emsworth Museum** is filled with exhibits reflecting the history of the village, particularly from the great fishing days. One of the many model ships on display is the *Echo*, which was the largest sailing fishing vessel to work out of any British port. The author PG Wodehouse lived in Record Road, where a blue plaque marks his house.

A short distance to the west is the Saxon village of **Warblington**, of which little survives but the ruins of a 16th century castle and the **Church of St Thomas à Becket**, with its little tower and timbered spire, which has some Roman bricks, Saxon archways, medieval floor tiles and, in the churchyard, a pair of

The Ship Inn

24 High Street, Emsworth,
Hampshire PO10 7AW
Tel: 01243 377151 Fax: 01243 389163
e-mail:
mailbox@theshipemsworth.co.uk
website: www.theshipemsworth.co.uk

Young and not so young alike are guaranteed a good time at **The Ship Inn**, where licensees Jane and Mark Smith are the most cheerful and sociable of hosts. Everyone is greeted with open arms, and even dogs are welcome - provided they are accompanied by well-behaved owners!

The pub dates back to its time as a coaching inn almost 300 years ago, when the regulars no doubt included a few smugglers, and the bar has a comfortably traditional look that's assisted by wood panelling, period prints and several snug little corners. The front part of the open-plan public area is the liveliest - especially when the pub's rugby league team is celebrating - while in the quieter dining section (some non-smoking tables) food is served all day every day (Tuesday 12.00-15.00 only).

Linda's Galley offers something for all appetites, from sandwiches, jacket potatoes and burgers to traditional Sunday roasts and favourite main meals such as lasagne, chilli with rice or steak & Guinness casserole. Serious walkers on the Solent Way will particularly appreciate the hearty all-day breakfasts.

The Blue Bell Inn

29 South Street, Emsworth,
Hampshire PO10 7EG
Tel: 01243 373394

Born and bred in Hayling Island, Tom Babb brings 35 years of experience in the licensed trade to the **Blue Bell Inn**, which stands on the edge of town near the Mill Pond Promenade. He also brings a great sense of humour, a quality, shared by his staff, that creates a cheerful ambience among the customers. These include regulars from the locality, yachtsmen and walkers - the 60-mile Solent Way starts here and runs by way of Langstone Harbour, Portsmouth and Southampton to distant Milford-on-Sea.

The pub was rebuilt in traditional style after the Second World War, and among the bricks and beams in the open-plan bar-lounge are naval memorabilia and a series of lithographs depicting England's history through Roman eyes. Thirsts are quenched by real ales and appetites satisfied by home-cooked food that runs from sandwiches to steaks by way of soups, cottage pie and Emsworth cockles. Live music nights are held once a week.

Emsworth was once a thriving port, and the narrow streets and alleys of the old port are well worth exploring. The oyster trade which brought it fame is still thriving , but Emsworth has also found a new role as a yachting centre complete with a marina.

stone grave-watchers' huts. From these huts men could guard the graves from body-snatchers - a group of criminals who did a lot of body-snatching until it was officially outlawed by the Anatomy Act of 1832. There are some interesting gravestones in the cemetery, some to drowned sailors, one to Augustus Short, the first Bishop of Adelaide. The cemetery is on the path of the long-distance Solent Way, one of many marked walks in the county.

HAVANT
6 miles NE of Portsmouth off the A27

The town of Havant developed from a network of springs and a Roman crossroads into a leading centre for the manufacture of leather goods, gloves and parchment. Its modern leisure and recreation facilities are extensive, but for a feel of the history of the place a visit to **Havant Museum** is rewarding. Special exhibitions cover arts, crafts, local and social history, and natural history, and three rooms are given over to an important collection of firearms.

HAYLING ISLAND
4 miles S of Havant on the A3023

With its five-mile sandy beach, Hayling Island has been a traditional family seaside holiday resort for 150 years, but one that manages to retain much of its rural character, particularly in the northern part. The island lies between **Langstone** and **Chichester Harbours**; much of the former is given over to an RSPB reserve which in winter is home to up to 20,000 migrant wading birds as well as year-round residents. The **Hayling Billy Coastal Path**, once the old Hayling Billy railway line, provides access for walkers, cyclists and horse-riders, and there are excellent views over the harbour for birdwatching. At South Hayling stands the parish church of St Mary, which combines formal Early English and the freer Decorated styles. The southern part of the island is more developed as a resort, with arcades, beach huts and houses from the 1930s, which is when the island really began to boom as a holiday destination. Hayling is something of a mecca for board sailors. Not only does it provide some of the best sailboarding in the country for beginners and experts alike, it is also the place where the sport was invented. Many places claim that honour but Peter Chilvers has a High Court ruling to prove it. In 1982 a judge decided that Mr Chilvers had indeed invented the sailboard at Hayling in 1958. As a boy of ten, he used a sheet of plywood, a tent fly sheet, a pole and some curtain rings to make his conveyance and sail up one of the island's creeks.

4 Isle of Wight

The largest island off the English coast covers an area of 147 square miles, half of which is designated an Area of Outstanding Natural Beauty. The 67 miles of coastline include chalk and sandstone, sandy beaches, marshes and estuaries, while inland are ancient forests, farmland, downs and river valleys. Excavation sites have revealed more than 120 million years of history, with visible evidence of occupation by Stone Age, Bronze Age and Iron Age communities. The Romans were here in some force - they called the island Vectis - and for many centuries after them the islanders lived

Compton Bay

isolated lives, disturbed occasionally by French raiders but largely cut off from the mainland. That state of isolation changed dramatically in the 1840s, when Queen Victoria and Prince Albert bought an estate near East Cowes and built Osborne House. Poets, authors and artists followed, and before long the world at large came to enjoy the peace, the scenery and the wide-ranging appeal of the island, an appeal that has endured to this day. The Isle of Wight is a paradise for walkers, with hundreds of miles of footpaths and trails, and in 1999 the Walking Festival was launched to commemorate the island becoming the first county to achieve the Countryside Commission's National Target for Rights of Way. It's also a popular place for cyclists, while for those who

Sailing at Cowes

want to do little but laze and bathe and comb there are no fewer than 23 major beaches. Many of the island's towns and villages hold carnivals and festivals in the summer; the Tourist Information Centres (see the list at the back of the book) will supply dates and details.

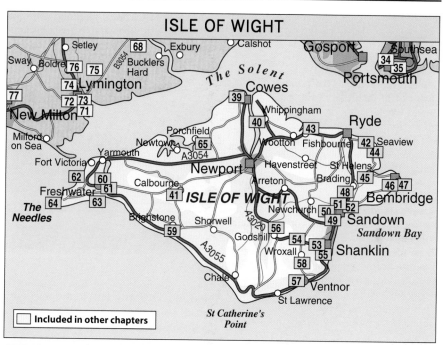

ISLE OF WIGHT

Included in other chapters

St Catherine's
Point

PLACES TO STAY, EAT, DRINK AND SHOP

© MAPS IN MINUTES ™ (2000)

COWES

A chain ferry links the two parts of Cowes across the River Medina. West Cowes is renowned as the home of the Royal Yacht Squadron, and **Cowes Week** is a rendezvous for sailors from all over the world and a firm fixture in the social calendar. The Prince Regent, later George IV, was the senior flag officer of what was originally the Yacht Club for 20 years, and the 'Royal' was added when he became King in 1820. His brother William IV renamed it the Royal Yacht Squadron in 1833. On a platform at the Squadron's headquarters, previously one of Henry VIII's castles, stand 22 brass cannon from William's yacht the *Royal Adelaide*. Shipbuilding was for centuries the main

Sailing off Cowes

industry of East Cowes, spanning ships for the Royal Navy, lifeboats, flying boats and seaplanes. Many of the seaplanes took part in the Schneider Trophy races which brought great excitement to the Solent in the inter-war years. Sir Donald Campbell's *Bluebird* was built here, and the hovercraft

ALAMO

15 Shooters Hill, Cowes, Isle of Wight PO31 7BG
Tel: 01983 298754 Fax: 01983 281966
e-mail: doug@alamo.demon.co.uk website: www.alamo.demon.co.uk

American-born Doug Peterson and his enthusiastic partners and staff run one of the liveliest eating places on the island. Behind a red-painted shop-window frontage in a town-centre precinct, **Alamo** has considerable character, with a stained-wood floor, cane-backed seating, seascapes and yachting prints. The ground floor has seats for 40, with a further 30 down in the basement and 30 outside in the beer garden. Jazz and swing plays in the background, giving way from time to time to live sessions. The menu is mainly American-inspired, with steaks and burgers among the all-time favourites. Other popular orders include Texas spare ribs, nachos and buffalo-style chicken wings, all available in either starter or main course portions, chilli, rotisserie chicken and seafood pasta. The Sunday roast, served from 1 o'clock till 3, is a weekly treat not to be missed.

Alamo is open from noon to 11pm, with food served from 12 to 3 and from 7 to 10.30. Outside meal times you can drop in for a cup of coffee or tea or a glass of something. When you're in Cowes - remember the Alamo!

Sunset at Cowes

had its origins in what is now the home of Westland Aerospace. Westland's factory doors were painted with a giant Union Jack to mark the Queen's Jubilee in 1977 - a piece of patriotic paintwork that has been retained by popular demand. Two museums in Cowes have a nautical theme. The **Sir Max Aitken Museum** in an old sailmaker's loft in West Cowes High Street houses Sir Max's remarkable collection of nautical paintings, instruments and artefacts, while the **Cowes Maritime Museum** charts the island's maritime history and has a collection of racing yachts that includes the Uffa Fox pair *Avenger* and *Coweslip*. On the Parade, near the Royal Yacht Squadron, the **Isle of Wight Model Railways Exhibition** has for almost 20 years been one of the most admired attractions of its kind in the country. The displays include models spanning the whole history of railways, from the *Rocket* to *Eurostar*. Some are set in a British landscape, others against a stunning Rocky Mountains backdrop, and there is even a low-level layout which small children can operate and see without being lifted.

A romantic landmark on the east bank of the Medina is Norris Castle, built in the 18th century for Lord Henry Seymour. The 12-year-old Princess Victoria stayed here and was so charmed that when she returned as Queen with Albert to look for a retreat she tried to buy it. She failed, and instead made plans for the construction of **Osborne House** a mile south of East Cowes. Designed in the style of an Italian villa by Thomas Cubitt with a little help from Albert, the new Osborne House was built as 'a modest country home' between 1845 and 1850. If it was modest, it was modest only by royal standards. The scale and grandeur of what became Victoria's favourite country house are impressive, and the interior decor has recently been restored in the original colours. Visitors can admire the Indian Room, the marbled pillars and the magnificent paintings, look in on the Queen's private study and bedroom, or take a peek below stairs at the recently restored Table Deckers rooms where the staff prepared the royal meals. The landscaped gardens are no less majestic than the house, and there are dazzling views from the terrace. A short stroll or a carriage ride away is the delightful Swiss Cottage, originally the royal children's playhouse, where refreshments and souvenirs are on sale. On view in the Swiss Cottage chalet are the royal children's gardening tools and Queen Victoria's bathing machine. Osborne House and its grounds were, not surprisingly, the setting for some of the scenes in the film *Mrs Brown* with Judi Dench and Billy Connolly.

AROUND COWES

WHIPPINGHAM
3 miles S of Cowes on the A3021

The Queen also acquired **Barton Manor** at nearby Whippingham, a peaceful retreat whose grounds are occasionally open to the public. The present owner is a keen conservationist, and the gardens contain the National Collections of red hot pokers and watsonias. He has recently added a splendid hedge maze (see panel below). Prince Albert had a hand in the design of the ornate Church of St Mildred, where the contractor and co-designer was AJ Humbert, who was also responsible for Sandringham. The royal family regularly worshipped at St Mildred's, which is predictably full of royal memorials, including a monument to Victoria's son-

in-law Prince Henry of Battenberg, who succumbed to malaria in Africa. Alfred Gilbert's wonderful art nouveau screen in the chancel arcade is a unique work of art, and other notable pieces are a bronze angel and the font, both of them designed by Princess Louise, a daughter of the Queen.

WOOTTON
3 miles SE of Cowes on the A3054

Wootton is the western terminus of the **Isle of Wight Steam Railway**, with an old wooden booking office and signal box moved from elsewhere on the island. It is also the home of **Butterfly World & Fountain World**. This complex comprises a sub-tropical indoor garden with hundreds of exotic butterflies flying free; a colourful Italian garden with computer-controlled fountains; a Japanese garden with Oriental buildings and a koi carp

BARTON MANOR
Whippingham, East Cowes,
Isle of Wight PO32 6LB
Tel: 01983 292835 Fax: 01983 293923

The estate of Barton is first mentioned in the Doomsday Book of 1086, and later an Augustinian oratory was founded. That fell into gradual decline, and from the 15th to the 19th centuries the estate was run as a farm. When Queen Victoria and Prince Albert bought Osborne House, **Barton Manor** and its estate became their home farm and the Prince has a new set of farm

buildings erected. In 1902, after the Queen's death, King Edward VII made a gift of Osborne to the nation and kept Barton Manor for himself. It was eventually sold by the Crown in 1922 and has been in private hands ever since. Today the property is owned by the film and stage entrepreneur Robert Stigwood, who is also a keen conservationist. The gardens are a real delight, with many treasures and surprises including the rhododendron walk, the splendid rose maze, a water garden, a secret garden and the national collections of Watsonia and red hot pokers. The estate is open on four special days in the year in aid of the local Earl Mountbatten Hospice.

lake; and a five-acre garden centre.

HAVENSTREET
4 miles SE of Cowes off the A3054

Headquarters and nerve centre of the **Isle of Wight Steam Railway**. Havenstreet has a small workshop and museum, gift shop and refreshment room. The locomotives working the line date back as far as 1876 and include a tiny A1 class engine acquired from the London, Brighton & South Coast Railway in 1913, and a W14, named *Calbourne*, which was built in 1891 and came to the island in 1925.

Isle of Wight Steam Railway

The road south from Cowes to Newport (A3020) passes by the edge of **Parkwood**

Forest, 1,000 acres of ancient royal hunting forest now managed by the Forestry Commission. From the car park and picnic area a waymarked trail leads through the forest, which is one of the few remaining 'safe houses' for the red squirrel.

NEWPORT
5 miles S of Cowes on the A3020

The island's capital, Newport was once a busy shipping centre on the Medina, and many of the old riverside warehouses are still standing. One of them houses the important Quay Arts Centre and another the **Classic Boat Museum**. Beautifully restored sailing and power boats, along with engines, equipment and memorabilia, are all under cover, and there's also a café, shop and chandlery on the premises. Among the highlights are a 1910 river launch and *Lady Penelope*, a fabulous speedboat once owned by the fabulous Lady Docker. Alongside this museum is another, equally fascinating, the **Isle of Wight Bus Museum**, which houses an impressive line-up of island buses and coaches and a former Ryde Pier tram. The buses include a 1920s Daimler and a Bristol Lodekka that recently carried

Isle of Wight Steam Railway

tourists on a trip to Nepal. There are several fine old buildings in the High Street, the most renowned and distinctive being the porticoed **Guildhall**, designed by John Nash in 1813. It stands on the site of an earlier building where Charles l met the Parliamentary Commissioners in 1648 in an attempt to keep the throne. The Guildhall now houses an exciting new museum where classic displays combine with the latest in computer technology to bring alive the history of the island.

In **St Thomas' Church** is the tomb of the tragic Princess Elizabeth, daughter of Charles, who died of a fever at the age of 14 while a prisoner at Carisbrooke Castle (qv). Her brother Henry was also imprisoned at Carisbrooke but he lived and was allowed to go into exile. Elizabeth's grave was discovered during building work on a new church, whose foundation stone was laid by Prince Albert in 1854. Queen Victoria ordered that a memorial be erected in her honour, and another fine memorial honours Sir Edward Horsey, who governed the island from 1565 to 1582.

A monument to Queen Victoria stands in St James' Square, and opposite it a bronze bust of Lord Mountbatten, who was Governor of the island until his death in 1979. In 1926 a **Roman Villa** was discovered in Avondale Road, and subsequent excavations and reconstructions have produced an exhibition that gives an accurate insight into how the occupants of a late Romano-British villa lived and how sophisticated and ingenious were the villa's designers and builders. The

narrow streets and passageways of old Newport were the scene of many hauntings and dastardly deeds down the years and visitors can see the sights and hear the tales on the **Newport Ghost Walk**, organised every Wednesday night.

A mile or so southwest of Newport, **Carisbrooke Castle** is one of the most impressive in England. Standing high on a ridge overlooking **Carisbrooke**, once the island's capital, the castle is a beautifully preserved Norman fortress on the site of a Roman fort. It is best known as the place where, in 1647, Charles l sought refuge and a passage to France from the castle's governor, Colonel Hammond. The Colonel imprisoned the King before sending him back to the mainland and the scaffold. Visitors with a head for heights can walk the ramparts and admire the view; see traces of the bowling green constructed for the King's amusement; look around the 800-year-old Great Hall and the museum and see the window

Carisbrooke Castle

Castle Entrance

William Montacute, son of the Earl of Salisbury. The most enchanting part of the village is Barrington Row, usually known as Winkle Street, a row of charming old cottages opposite the village stream (Caul Burn) and an ancient sheepwash.

The grandest building in the neighbourhood is historic Swainston Manor, now a luxurious hotel. Earlier buildings on the site were owned by royalty and by Bishops of Winchester; the 12th century Bishops Chapel still stands next to the hotel.

On the B3401 between Newport and Freshwater, the **Water Mill** is just one of many attractions on an 11-acre landscaped valley site which no visitor to the island should miss (see panel on page 66).

which Charles tried to squeeze through in a bid to escape. A well at the end of the courtyard is worked by donkeys, who are splendidly looked after at a centre in the castle grounds. Concerts and plays are performed in the castle during the summer months.

Well worth a visit in Carisbrooke itself is **St Mary's Church**, which contains the elaborate canopied tomb of Lady Wadham, an aunt of Jane Seymour. The Perpendicular tower is covered with carvings, including a clearly discernable group of singers.

AROUND NEWPORT

CALBOURNE
5 miles SW of Newport on the B3401

In the picturesque village of Calbourne, All Saints Church is a remarkably original 13th century building whose treasures include a handsome 16th century brass of

ARRETON
3 miles SE of Newport on the A3056

Probably the most beautiful historic house on the island is **Arreton Manor**. There was a house on this site long before Alfred the Great mentioned Arreton in his will of 885, and the manor was owned by successive monarchs from Henry Vlll to Charles l. It has recently been sold and is no longer open to the public. The Norman church at Arreton was rebuilt in the 13th century; one of its most prized possessions is a 15th century brass - headless, alas- of Harry Hawles, who was killed fighting with Henry V at the Battle of Agincourt. A more modern treasure is the Burma Star window. In a coach house next to the church is the **Island Brass Rubbing Centre**, where visitors can learn the simple craft of brass rubbing and create their own rubbing of a knight, or

The Water Mill & Museum of Rural Life

Calbourne, Isle of Wight PO40 3JN
Tel: 01983 531227

On the B3401 between Newport and Freshwater, the **Water Mill** is just one of many attractions on an 11-acre landscaped valley site which no visitor to the island should miss. A mill on this site was mentioned in the Domesday Book and a fine example of a 17th century Water Mill is still working today. In 1963 it was opened as

a tourist attraction by the family that had owned the mill since 1878. The present owners, Sally & Tony Chaucer have continued to develop the sites historic importance.

The Domesday Book records 34 water-powered mills on the island, and the Calbourne Mill is the last survivor. For centuries it used the traditional stone grinding process, but modern technology caught up with it in the late 19th century, when an additional roller plant was constructed in 1894 by Henry Simon. The plant was driven by a portable steam engine which was replaced in 1970 by a suction gas engine that gave reliable service for the remainder of the mill's working life. Milling takes place every day at 3pm except Saturday, producing flour for the bread and cakes which are on sale in the café and shop.

The café is open from 10am to 7pm, and apart from the terrific cakes and pastries sells sandwiches and floured baps, filled jacket potatoes, miller's (ploughman's) platters and main meals such as burgers, deep-fried plaice or chicken breast with a wild mushroom sauce. At teatime, the clotted cream tea is a treat that should not to be resisted.

The mill is only one of many fascinating features on the site, which also incorporates the Museum of Rural life. Here the visitor can see a fine collection of agricultural implements and machinery and other vintage exhibits - there's even a classic fire engine. Some of the items on display are impressive in their size, none more than the enormous gun that guards the entrance to the mill. Originally intended to protect the Needles approach to Portsmouth, the gun, one of four built in the 1870s, weighs 38 tons and is almost 20 feet in length. Grandma's Kitchen contains an expanding collection of domestic bygones, and there's a fascinating assembly of washing machines down the years. Traditional skills are practised in the wheelwright's shop and in the smithy. The grounds around the mill stream and pond provide picturesque walks, and a picnic area has been set aside in a quiet spot.

buy something ready rubbed from the stock. One of the knights is friend Harry Hawles, whose head has been restored for rubbing purposes. Oliver Cromwell's grandson William is buried in the churchyard.

A mile southeast of Arreton stands the oldest grand house on the island, **Haseley Manor**, with a history that traces back to around 1300. This, too, was recently sold and has passed into private hands, so, sadly, the two most distinguished properties in the area can no longer be visited by the public. Very much still open is **Robin Hill**, an adventure park at Downend with a head-spinning variety of rides and slides and runs and trails.

NEWCHURCH
7 miles SE of Newport on the A3056

Amazon World is a popular family attraction that tells the story of the rain forest with the help of a large number of exotic animals and birds. Conservation is the name of the game. One of the highlights in Newchurch is the annual Garlic Festival, held on a weekend in August. The date for 2001 is August 18-19. The village church and its steeple are clad in wood.

RYDE

For many visitors to the island (residents call them Overners), Ryde is the arrival point. Foot passengers on the ferry from Portsmouth disembark at the end of Ryde Pier, which was one of the first to be built; the coast shelves very gently at this point, and before the construction of the pier passengers had an inconvenient cart ride from ferry to shore. The half-mile long pier is served by an electric railway that runs to Sandown and Shanklin. Steam locomotives gave way in 1967 to a small fleet of electric trains (1938 stock) recently

retired from duty on London Transport's Northern Line. The line connects with the Isle of Wight Steam Railway at Smallbrook Junction. Ryde is blessed with a five-mile sandy beach, which, along with all the usual seaside attractions and a marina, makes it a popular holiday spot. Reminders of its Georgian and Victorian heyday are still there in abundance, among them a fine arcade in Union Street opened in 1837, the year of Queen Victoria's accession. The town has some important churches: **All Saints**, designed by Sir George Gilbert Scott, the Roman Catholic **St Mary's** with a Pugin chapel, and **St Thomas**, which is now a heritage centre featuring an exhibition of memorabilia associated with the transportation of convicts to Australia - many of the convicts left these shores in ships moored off Ryde.

In the middle of **Appley Park** stands **Appley Tower**, built as a station for troops guarding Spithead and now open to the public as a centre for fossils, crystals, natural gems, oracles and rune readings. Another public space is **Puckpool Park**, a leisure area behind the sea wall between Ryde and Seaview. It surrounds what was once a battery, built in the 19th century; its last gun was removed in 1927. At the Westridge Centre, just off the A3055 road to Brading, **Waltzing Waters** is an indoor water, light and music spectacular performed several times daily in a comfortable modern theatre.

AROUND RYDE

FISHBOURNE
2 miles W of Ryde on the A3054

Fishbourne is the port where the car ferry from the mainland docks. Nearby **Quarr Abbey** is a handsome redbrick

HOLIDAY HOME SERVICES (SEAVIEW)

Madeira Road, Seaview, Isle of Wight PO34 5BA
Tel: 01983 811418 Fax: 01983 616900
e-mail: holidayhomes@ic24.net website: www.seaview-holiday-homes.co.uk

Seaview is a village of unspoilt charm, a seaside location with safe, sandy beaches, a place for swimming, sailing or windsurfing - or relaxing totally and enjoying the escape from the mainland bustle. The narrow streets are a picturesque mixture of little whitewashed cottages and grand Edwardian and Victorian houses, and many of the properties - more than 60, in fact - are available for hire throughout the year on a self-catering basis through Holiday Home Services (Seaview).

The service is run by Diana Stansfield, who brings warmth, charm and great professionalism to the business of managing her client's properties. The range of the properties is impressive, the smallest offering a cosy little nest for two, the largest catering for families or groups of up to a dozen.

At the smaller end of the scale are a number of compact one-bedroom flats, while typifying the largest and grandest is a six-bedroom Edwardian house with gardens and off-road parking. Some of the properties have a ban on

pets and/or smoking, so be sure to ask when you book. All are fully equipped with all the necessities for an independent, go-as-you-please holiday.

Most are very close to the amenities of the village and some enjoy sea views. Cleaning and babysitting services can be provided on request, and cots and high chairs are either available for hire or already supplied.

The delights of Seaview are on the doorstep, and many other attractions and places of interest can be reached easily and quickly by car or public transport. Notable among these are two unmissable family treats. Flamingo Park, on the B3330 between Seaview and Ryde, is home to flamingos, penguins, swans, cranes and many other birds. Visitors can join in the fun by helping to feed the penguins, macaws and parrots as well as the koi carp and giant carp. Waltzing Waters, just off the main Ryde-Sandown road, is billed as the world's most elaborate water, light and music production. In a recent excellent move Holiday Home Services have linked up with Red Funnel and Wight Link Ferries so now all your accommodation and travel arrangements to the Isle of Wight can be arranged with just one telephone, fax or e-mail contact to Holiday Homes.

Benedictine monastery built around 1910 near the ruins of a 12th century Cistercian Abbey. The old abbey, founded by a certain Baldwin de Redvers, enjoyed 400 years of prestige and influence, owning much of the land and many of the grand houses, before its destruction in 1536.

The stone for the original Quarr Abbey at Fishbourne came from the quarries at nearby **Binstead**, where a major family draw is **Brickfields Horse Country**, a centre that is home to more than 100 animals, from magnificent shire horses to miniature ponies, farm animals and pets. Open daily throughout the year, the numerous attractions include racing pigs (the Lester Piglet Derby!), wagon rides, a parade of Cowboys and Indians, a blacksmith's forge and museums focusing on carriages, tractors and many aspects of farm life. The shire horses are the particular pride and joy of the centre's owner Phil Legge, whose Montgomery and Prince won him top honours in a recent All-England ploughing match. A new inmate is the former high-class racehorse Carisbrooke, who has taken up duties as a stallion.

SEAVIEW
2 miles SE of Ryde off the B3330

A pleasant village, and one that is aptly named, as it commands fine views of Spithead, the open sea and the Napoleonic forts that were built to defend the Solent and Portsmouth from the marauding French. Once a haunt of smugglers and a centre of the island's important salt industry, it is now a favourite holiday base, with a gently sloping sandy beach and a calmer air than the bustling major resorts.

A short distance west of Seaview lies **Flamingo Park** Waterfowl & Water Gardens, whose colonies of flamingos, penguins, macaws and waterfowl are

THE FISHBOURNE INN

111 Fishbourne Inn,
Fishbourne, Isle of Wight
PO33 4EU
Tel: 01983 882823

On the edge of Fishbourne village a short walk from the beach, the **Fishbourne Inn** is a very handsome and substantial 1930s' brick building with a Tudor-look black-and-white facade and a good covering of creeper. The open-plan interior is roomy and traditional, with exposed beams, open fires, small-paned windows, cane-backed chairs and upholstered bench seating, and lots of brassware, china ornaments and local prints of the area in days gone by.

The tenant, Keith Terrill, has wide experience in running public houses and brings with him a fine reputation as something of a seafood specialist. Certainly the Fishbourne Inn continues to enhance this reputation, and in the 50-cover restaurant locally caught fish and shellfish are always at the head of the popularity stakes. There's plenty of other choice, too, from sandwiches and light snacks to steaks and interesting daily specials. The restaurant is a popular venue for functions and business lunches and is also an ideal spot for a first taste of Island food for tourists arriving from Portsmouth at the car ferry terminal, which is only 200 yards away. Places of interest in the vicinity include Osborne House, holiday home of Queen Victoria, and Quarr Abbey.

Flamingo Park

Wildlife Encounter, Springvale, Seaview, Isle of Wight PO34 5AP
Tel: 01983 612153 Fax: 01983 613465
e-mail: flamingo.park@virgin.net
website: www.isle-of-wight.uk.com/flamingo-park

A unique wildlife encounter awaits visitors to **Flamingo Park**, set on the B3330 in beautifully landscaped gardens overlooking the Solent. The stunning waterfalls and water displays make a splendid backdrop for the resident wildlife.

This nature haven specialises in hands-on feeding, which encourages everyone to participate in feeding the abundant wildlife including Humboldt penguins, macaws and parrots, koi and giant

mirror carp plus thousands of domestic and exotic water fowl tame enough to feed by hand. The 100+ flamingos in residence include three flocks of Chilean, Caribbean and Lesser flamingos.

Exciting new projects for 2001 include Beaver Island, Pelican Bay, Owl Country, Red Squirrels and the Rainbow Experience where visitors can step inside a world of colour and surround themselves with a dazzling display of free-flying birds in every colour of the rainbow. Open from 10 to 5 April to October, the Park has a restaurant, gift shop and picnic/patio area.

Old Mill Holiday Park

Mill Road, St Helens, Isle of Wight PO33 1UE
Tel: 01983 872507

The Stephens family, here for more than 30 years, run **Old Mill Holiday Park**, which stands in a picturesque, peaceful location overlooking Bembridge Harbour and the National Trust Common. Winner of numerous awards, and ranked among the very best holiday parks in the country, Old Mill offers a wide variety of accommodation. Thirty-five top-of-the-range quality caravans, all maintained to the highest standards, provide roomy, stylish quarters for up to six visitors. Glade House, a modern purpose-built brick house, comprises two holiday apartments, each sleeping 4-5 in two bedrooms. 9 Port (Marina House) has spectacular views overlooking the River Yar, St Helens Marina and Harbour sleeping 6 in three bedrooms. Marina House

has off street parking and a garage. Three Pine Cabins with 2 or 3 bedrooms, again have spectacular views of the harbour. Most accommodation is open all year complete with central heating and other essential comforts.

Facilities include launderette, games room and a good play area. The surroundings are particularly beautiful and peaceful, and visitors can be equally happy relaxing in the gardens or watching the passing shipping. The harbur attracts a variety of birds and the area is ideal for natural beaches, walking, cycling and fishing. The Park is four and a half miles from Sandown and Ryde with a bus service available. St Helens has a choice of restaurants and shops.

among the largest in the country. Visitors are encouraged to join in feeding the birds and also the giant carp and koi carp (see panel opposite).

ST HELENS
4 miles S of Ryde on the B3330

A small village with a very large green that was once dotted with open wells and is now used as a cricket and football ground. There are some excellent walks in the area, both on the common and on the Duver (it rhymes with lover), an expanse of grass and dunes reaching down to the harbour at Bembridge. The stretch of water off the coast, known as St Helen's Roads, has seen some significant moments in history, notably as the point from which, in 1346, Edward lll launched his invasion of Normandy, and as an assembly point for part of the D-Day landing force in the Second World War.

BEMBRIDGE
5 miles SE of Ryde on the B3395

Once a thriving fishing village, Bembridge is now a popular sailing centre and a holiday base. The maritime connection remains strong, and visitors can take a guided tour round the lifeboat station or spend a fascinating few hours in the **Maritime Museum and Shipwreck Centre**. Open every day from March to October, the centre is overflowing with relics and objects recovered from the sea, including pirate gold and silver. Also on display are antique and modern diving equipment and model ships (see panel below).

Art lovers should find time to visit the **Ruskin Gallery**, where an impressive collection of paintings and manuscripts of the 19th century artist are housed, and Bembridge Gallery in the High Street,

THE SHIPWRECK CENTRE & MARITIME MUSEUM
Sherborne Street, Bembridge, Isle of Wight PO35 5SB
Tel: 01983 872223 Tel/Fax: 01983 873125

Open every day from March to October, the centre is overflowing with relics and objects recovered from the sea and shipwrecks, including pirate gold and silver. The setting is Providence House, a mid-18th century building which was a bakery until 1973 and opened as a museum in 1978.

Special exhibits include Diver's Corner, charting the history and development of diving equipment from the 1840s; a fine collection of model ships; Bembridge Lifeboat Past & Present, detailing the background of the local lifeboat from 1867 to the present day; photographs of Bembridge village as it used to be; and the sad story of the disappearance of the submarine *HMS Swordfish* in 1940.

The most macabre and unusual exhibit is the 'merman', a gruesome-looking creature that is actually a Victorian trick by sailors in the Far East by grafting the mummified head of a monkey on to the body and tail of a dead fish. These 'mermen' were popular attractions at Victorian fairs, and this one never fails to intrigue visitors to this fascinating place.

The Museum, which has a shop selling gifts and souvenirs, was founded and is still owned by Martin Woodward, a renowned diver who started salvage diving on shipwrecks in 1968. He is the present coxswain of the Bembridge lifeboat.

THE WINDMILL INN,

1 Steyne Road, Bembridge, Isle of Wight PO35 5UH
Tel: 01983 872875 Fax: 01983 874760
e-mail: info@windmillhotel.co.uk website: www.windmill-inn.com

A programme of total refurbishment has transformed the **Windmill Inn**, which stands in the centre of Bembridge on the island's most easterly headland. Owners Graham & Liz Miles offer 15 beautifully appointed bedrooms, all with en suite facilities, ranging from singles, doubles and twins, to family rooms, and a delightful honeymoon suite with a four-poster bed. All the rooms (no smoking; no pets) have remote T.V., clock radio, hairdryer and direct dial telephones. The major programme of works included a new state-of-art kitchen and a stylish function room for up to 100 for parties or wedding receptions (the hotel is actually licensed for the performance of the ceremony).

There's parking space for up to 60 cars, and a south-facing rear garden with patio which gets plenty of sun. The warm and friendly bar and dining areas have a wood-burning stove with cane-backed chairs and tables or a snug bar to relax in front of the open fire. The Windmill Inn has earned a good reputation for its cooking, and the menus are full of tempting dishes. The specials board always includes the pick of the day's catch, and the dessert list keeps up the enjoyment level with such delights as bread and butter pudding with creme anglaisse or apricot parfait with plum compote. With notice, the kitchen can cater for special dietary needs. For lighter appetites, sandwiches and light bites are available, while afternoon tea in the bar or on the patio is a leisurely, civilised treat.

Bembridge, formerly a fishing port and now an internationally renowned yachting centre, is a place of wide appeal. The fine sandy beach and the charming harbour are a gentle stroll from the hotel, as is the famous windmill from which the hotel takes its name. In the care of the National Trust, the windmill, the only one still in existence on the island, is a stirring sight. Dating from about 1700, it is open to visitors throughout the summer. The coastal path from Bembridge to Sandown offers fine walking and great views, and after an invigorating walk or a day's sightseeing (everywhere on the island is within easy reach by car, bus or rail) the Windmill Inn beckons with its comfortable, convivial surroundings and its delicious homecooked food.

featuring the work of island artists. Half a mile south of Bembridge on the B3395 stands one of the island's best known landmarks, **Bembridge Windmill**. In the care of the National Trust, it is the last surviving windmill on the island, dating from about 1700 and last used in 1913. Much of the original wooden machinery is still in place, as are the sails, and there are spectacular views from the top floor. In common with many parts of the island, this is excellent walking land, and the coastal path from Bembridge to Sandown has the bonus of fine sea views. On top of Bembridge Down stands the Victorian Fort Bembridge.

BRADING
5 miles S of Ryde on the A3055

One of the oldest towns on the island, Brading was granted its first Royal Charter by Edward 1 in 1285. But its history goes back a good deal further, certainly to the Bronze Age. The Romans were here, too, and the **Roman Villa** discovered here in 1880 is one of the most complete in Britain. Among the many other interesting buildings in the town is the

12th century **Church of St Mary**, whose features include a processional passage under the west tower and wooden monuments to the Oglander family, who for 800 years were the most important family on the island. There is a particularly poignant monument, sculpted in great detail, to Elizabeth Rollo, who died in 1875 at the age of one. The church is said to stand on the spot where St Wilfrid converted the islanders to Christianity in 680 (another source has it that Christianity came to the island by way of King Caedwalla of Wessex, who put to death the majority of the islanders when they refused to take up the faith he sought to impose). Next to the church is the diminutive town hall, where stocks and a whipping post are reminders of how justice was summarily dispensed.

The **Isle of Wight Wax Works** presents 2,000 years of local history with sound, light and animation, along with animal exhibits from around the world, a chamber of horrors, a haunted mansion, an exhibition of oddities and a display of candle carving. The **Lilliput Museum of Antique Dolls & Toys**, in the High Street,

THE LILLIPUT MUSEUM OF ANTIQUE DOLLS & TOYS
High Street, Brading, Isle of Wight PO36 0DJ
Tel: 01983 407231
e-mail: lilliput.museum@btconnect.com
website: www.lilliputmuseum.com

This cottage museum in the High Street contains one of the finest collections of old and antique dolls and toys in the country, with over 2,000 exhibits on display dating from c2000BC to approximately 1945, and a couple more recent items. There are examples of almost every seriously collectable doll together with a number of dolls houses; rocking horses; tinplate toys; trains; bears; soft toys and many other unusual playthings.

Among the many exhibits can be found, for example, a wax doll made circa 1790 and dressed by a lady-in-waiting to Princess Caroline of Brunswick - the material used was a remnant of the Princess's wedding dress. Next to her is the modern equivalent: one of only two contemporary dolls in the Museum, this is a portrait doll of Diana, Princess of Wales, produced by a member of the British Doll Artists Association in 1981. Like the wax doll, this exhibit is also dressed in a remnant of the original wedding gown. Most of the dolls and toys have been acquired from the first owners or their descendants, so there is a fund of stories about them. Adjoining the Museum is a specialist shop stocking a variety of collectable dolls houses and furniture, china dolls, limited edition bears and traditional toys.

THE TIGER & BIG CAT SANCTUARY

Yaverland Seafront, Sandown,
Isle of Wight PO36 8QB
Tel: 01983 401685/403883
Fax: 01983 407049
website: www.isleofwightzoo.com

A unique attraction on the seafront at Sandown. Judith and Jack Corney's **Tiger & Big Cat Sanctuary** specialises in breeding and caring for some of the planet's most severely threatened creatures. The Corneys and their staff are completely devoted to their charges, as any visitor will quickly see from the wonderful conditions in which the animals live. The stars of the show are the beautiful and dangerous Big Cats - Royal and White Bengal Tigers, Chinese Tigers, Siberian Tigers, Lions, Leopards, Jaguars, Black Panthers.

But other creatures are equally fascinating, including lemurs, monkeys, reptiles, birds, insects and spiders. A day spent here is both entertaining and educational, and anyone can adopt (sponsor - not take away!) any animal in the Sanctuary. Sponsors will receive an adoption certificate with a photograph of the adopted animal. The friendly, expert staff are always more than happy to answer questions about the animals in their care. Here are a few facts which visitors will learn: 3 of the original 8 subspecies of tiger have lost their fight for survival in the last 60 years; only 32 species of lemur remain out of the original 50, the largest of which was the size of a fully grown gorilla; only South American monkeys have prehensile tails - the Sanctuary's spider

monkeys use their tails as an extra limb for movement and collecting food.

The Sanctuary has a snack bar, a children's play area, a gift shop and a large car park that's also ideal for visits to the beach. Route 1 Vectis Bus passes the gates, or visitors can ride on the Sanctuary's own seafront road train. Sanctuaries such as these are among the last hopes for many of the world's endangered species. They are sometimes called modern-day Noah's Arks, though in the wild their inhabitants would be threatened by much more than floods. It is thanks to people like the Corneys and their devoted staff that some of the world's most beautiful creatures still have a future. David Taylor, the distinguished wild animal vet, paid this tribute to the enterprise: 'Jack Corney's Tiger Sanctuary is not only the best in the UK, it is the best in Europe.' Who would disagree?

is home to an impressive collection of exhibits dating from around 2,000BC to 1945. The 2,000 items include tin toys, model trains, teddy bears, dolls houses and dolls, among them some very rare German and French bisque dolls (see panel on page 73).

Two notable houses with long and distinguished histories are close to the town. **Nunwell House**, set in five acres of lovely gardens, is the former home of the Oglander family. Guided tours take in an old kitchen exhibition and a military collection assembled by the family. The six acres of grounds include a rose garden (originally a bowling green) and an arboretum. It was in Nunwell House that Charles 1 passed his last night of freedom. **Morton Manor** dates back as far as 1249, with major rebuilding carried out in 1680. It stands in the most exquisite gardens, frequent winner of the "Isle of Wight in Bloom" awards. Features include an Elizabethan sunken garden surrounded by a 400-year-old box hedge, dazzling herbaceous borders, ponds and waterfalls and 90 varieties of Japanese maples. In 1981 the Trzebski family added a vineyard, which visitors are welcome to include in a tour of the house and gardens.

Just outside Brading is another vineyard: Adgestone Vineyard is the oldest on the island, having been established in 1968. Guided tours take place daily, and pony and trap rides are an added attraction.

SANDOWN

'A village by a sandy shore' was how a guide book described Sandown in 1870. Since then it has grown into the island's leading holiday resort, with miles of flat, safe sands, a traditional pier, abundant sports and leisure facilities and a number of attractions for all the family.

ST MORITZ HOTEL

9 Culver Parade, Sea Front, Sandown,
Isle of Wight PO36 8AS
Tel: 01983 403687 Fax: 01983 407536
e-mail: arul@lineone.net website: www.stmoritz.co.uk
Jay, Theresa and their staff put out the welcome mat at the **St Moritz Hotel**, which occupies an enviable position right on the seafront. Built in traditional style in the 1920s, the hotel has a patio at the front and an ample private car park. It's a very cheerful, convivial place with live entertainment or some other activity most evenings in the comfortable bar and lounge that overlook the sea.

Overnight accommodation comprises 26 well-appointed modern bedrooms, all centrally heated, with en suite facilities, televisions, hair dryers and tea/coffee-makers. Rooms at the front enjoy direct sea views. The 60-cover non-smoking restaurant specialises in good, generous portions of traditional English dishes. The St Moritz is in a very central position, with all the town's amenities within an easy walk: a pitch and putt course almost on the doorstep, the beach and the sea across the road, the pier, the shops and the railway station a short stroll away.

The owners came to the island three years ago after many years on the mainland, and they cater admirably for guests of all ages. Their hotel is open all year round for short breaks, long breaks and weekend breaks. Bed & Breakfast terms are available in the off season.

THE OLD MANOR HOUSE

Lake Hill, Sandown, Isle of Wight PO36 9EH
Tel: 01983 401239

The Old Manor House is a friendly, cheerful family pub at the heart of a small village on the main road between Sandown and Shanklin. It's very much the social hub of the hamlet, thanks to the efforts and enthusiasm of tenants Mark Silk and Heather Wilkinson. Born and raised on the island, they have breathed new life into the old place, and a warm welcome awaits all who set foot inside the door. The rear bar is a favourite local meeting place, with Sky television for sporting events, a pool table, popular quiz nights and regular evenings for live performances of jazz and folk music.

At one end of the open-plan area is a snug, at the other a 20-cover dining room with beamed ceiling and attractive small-paned windows. The food is an important side of the business at the Old Manor House, with menus that cater for appetites large and small. Baguette sandwiches, baked potatoes and burgers make satisfying snacks, while for full meals there's a good variety of familiar favourites - starters such as prawn cocktail or garlic mushrooms could precede lasagne, chicken kiev, a tasty curry or something from among the daily specials chalked up on the blackboard. To round things off, how about an ice cream sundae or a toffee and butterscotch sponge pudding. Accompanying the food are well-kept real ales and a dozen well-chosen wines from around the world. And if the mood is for pushing the boat out, the house champagne is an excellent choice!

The pub, which dates from the end of the 18th century, has a patio at the front and a garden at the back. It is ideally placed for all the attractions on the east side of the island: the beaches and the sea, the historic sites, all the holiday amenities of Sandown and Shanklin.

The whole of the island is great for walking and cycling. It was the first county in the British Isles to be given national recognition by the Countryside Commission for the maintenance and signposting of its footpaths and bridleways, of which there are no fewer than 500 miles. The walking and the cycling and the sightseeing are guaranteed to generate a thirst and an appetite which everyone at the Old Manor House looks forward to dealing with!

John Wilkes, sometime Member of Parliament and Lord Mayor of London, was one of the first celebrities to be taken with the village, and as a town Sandown was host to many other distinguished visitors, including Lewis Carroll, Charles Darwin, George Eliot and Henry Wadsworth Longfellow. Above the library, the **Museum of Isle of Wight Geology** offers an insight into millions of years of fossil history, with special displays relating to ammonites and dinosaurs. A new attraction, a Dinosaur Museum, will be added to the tourist trail in 2001.

Two miles west of Sandown, near Apse Heath, is a National Trust area known as **Borthwood Copse**. The trees there range from coppiced chestnut and hazel to ancient oaks, and in spring the bluebells blossom into a colourful carpet.

Shanklin Beach

AROUND SANDOWN

SHANKLIN
1 mile S of Sandown on the A3055

Shanklin is Sandown's more sedate neighbour, sharing the same sweeping bay but differing in many respects from its brasher brother. The old village stands on

HAZELWOOD PRIVATE LICENSED HOTEL

19 Carter Street, Sandown, Isle of Wight PO36 8BL
Tel: 01983 402536

Hazelwood is a small, friendly and relaxed family hotel with a warm and genuine welcome for visitors of all ages. It's a Victorian town house with a garden at the back and private off-road parking, close to the town centre and just a short stroll from the seafront.

The accommodation comprises seven bedrooms with traditionally-styled furnishings and fittings; there is a television set in the residents' lounge and a bar in the dining room. The friendly ambience is apparent the moment guests walk through the front door, and resident owner Pauline Wright is the most sociable and attentive of hostesses. She is always busy organising something special for her guests, many of whom have become firm friends over the years. The special events often include a super lunch or dinner prepared and cooked by Pauline using the best produce from local suppliers.

A hearty breakfast provides fuel for a day sporting on the beach or exploring the island - on foot, by cycle, in a car or on one of the island's two railway systems.

Sandown Railway Station is a short walk from the hotel. There are many activities to be enjoyed on the 'Garden Isle'. Pauline also grows an array of fuschias for your delight.

BURLINGTON HOTEL

6 Chine Avenue, Shanklin,
Isle of Wight PO37 6AG
Tel: 01983 862090 Fax: 01983 862190
e-mail: m.tulett@zoom.co.uk
website: isleofwighthotels.org.uk

Built in the reign of Queen Victoria as a gentleman's residence, **The Burlington** is now a comfortable family hotel of wide appeal. Resident owners Mark and Jane Tulett are always on hand to look after their guests, who include all ages, families and singles, walkers and tourists.

The hotel, which stands in its own grounds overlooking the sea, has 22 letting bedrooms, all with en suite facilities, television and tea/coffee-making kit, and the residents' lounge is a comfortable, relaxing place to enjoy a drink and to chat with fellow guests. In the dining room, Mark oversees the menus, which offer an interesting range of dishes and excellent value for money. Typical choices on the fixed-price menu include deep-fried brie with raspberry vinaigrette, grilled salmon with a lemon and mushroom sauce and a very tasty home-made red Thai chicken curry. Rounding off a meal are some wicked-sounding desserts such as 'death by white and raspberry' or hot chocolate fudge cake with whipped cream.

With its high levels of sunshine, Shanklin is an ideal place for a traditional seaside family holiday and the hotel is just yards from the cliff path that runs down to the beach; the town, an appealing blend of the modern and the old-world, is also a good base for exploring the many places of interest on the island. Almost on the Burlington's doorstep is the famous Shanklin Chine, a historic and

spectacular gorge that is a rich haven of rare plants and wildlife. It's a place where the visitor could easily spend the whole day admiring the wealth of natural beauty and the enchanting waterfall, looking round the Heritage Centre and taking in the exhibition of a century of Solent Sea and Sail that includes a display about PLUTO, the renowned Pipeline Under the Ocean. It is reached either from the Esplanade or from the delightful Old Village, which has strong connections with Charles Darwin, Longfellow and John Keats, who wrote some of his best-known poems while staying here. The grassy open space known as Keats Green commemorates his stay. Keats was very impressed with the island and particularly with the Chine, which moved him to write in 1819:

'The wondrous Chine here is a very great lion:
I wish I had as many guineas as there have been spyglasses in it.'

Shanklin Chine

a 150ft cliff from which the ground slopes gently down to the safe, sheltered beach with its long seafront esplanade. With its scenic setting, numerous public gardens and healthy climate, Shanklin has had wide appeal down the years. Charles Darwin and Longfellow were great fans, and John Keats wrote some of his best-known poems while staying here. The grassy open space known as Keats Green commemorates his sojourn. The village has survived largely intact at the head of one of the island's most renowned landmarks, **Shanklin Chine**. First opened in 1817 and a former refuge of smugglers, this 300' deep wooded ravine, mysterious and romantic, has long fascinated visitors with its waterfalls and rare flora. In the Heritage Centre at the top of the chine a special millennium exhibition **A Century of Solent Sea & Sail 1900-2000** has joined the PLUTO display: during the Second World War a vast tank, part of the

VILLAGE WAY CARAVAN & CAMPING PARK

Newport Road, Apse Heath, Sandown, Isle of Wight PO36 9PJ
Tel: 01983 863279 mobile: 077132 84395

Village Way Caravan & Camping Park enjoys a picturesque setting of trees and lawns among gently rolling hills. For visitors without their own tourers or tents the site has ten fully equipped, modern 4-6 berth static caravans, each with two bedrooms, shower and toilet, lounge with television, kitchen with fridge, cooker and sink, and a dining area.

Pets are welcome, but dogs must be kept on a lead. Carp fishing is available on site, so anglers should remember to pack their rods! Other on-site facilities include a modern toilet block with showers, a laundry room and a dishwashing room. A superstore is located less than half a mile away, and a little further afield the Heights Leisure Centre has swimming pools and a gym.

The Park is an ideal base for exploring the island, whether it's a day spent on the beach (Sandown and Shanklin are a few minutes away by car) or a leisurely tour of the many attractions and places of interest, some historic - Osborne House, Morton Manor, Carisbrooke Castle - others with a family theme, such as Amazon World or the Tiger & Big Cat Sanctuary.

THE EMPRESS OF THE SEA

10 Luccombe Road, Shanklin, Isle of Wight PO37 6RQ
Tel: 01983 862178 Fax: 01983 868636
e-mail: empress.sea@virgin.net

Elegance....comfort....tranquillity - these are just a few of the many outstanding qualities that describe the **Empress of the Sea**, a totally charming hotel standing in landscaped gardens that run down from the cliff almost to the water's edge. The American mother and son owners have taken over the hotel, bringing years of professional experience and an unerring sense of style to a major renovation programme that has transformed the Victorian building.

The 15 en suite bedrooms represent the epitome of gracious living: each has its own highly individual appeal, with superb classical furnishings and delightfully different decor, and most enjoy spectacular sea views. The owners offer both standard and superior rooms, and one room is fully equipped for disabled visitors; two others have been adapted for the semi-disabled. All the bedrooms have telephones, tea/coffee-makers and televisions with satellite channels. The day rooms are equally appealing, and the beautiful lounge overlooking the sea is a civilised spot for enjoying a quiet read, tickling the ivories on the grand piano or sipping a drink while watching the big ships setting out into the English Channel.

In the spacious dining room, where the tables are set with the finest linen and crystal, chef Terry Overton regales residents with a fine variety of dishes, some traditional English in style, others with

more adventurous Continental or American leanings. Evening meals can be served by candlelight, adding a further touch of romance to the delightful surroundings, or room service is available. The garden is the perfect place for quiet contemplation or enjoying afternoon tea in the sun, and in the warmer months the outdoor heated swimming pool is a boon - a quick dip is a great way to start the day before tucking into a splendid breakfast.

Shanklin Old Village and the famous Chine are a few minutes' walk away, and the beach is accessible by steps or by lift. The hotel welcomes guests of 16 years and over. Special dinners and functions are a regular feature, along with courses in such subjects as needlework or fine arts, and themed events including murder mystery weekends. Keats fell in love with this part of the island: had he had the good fortune to stay at the Empress of the Sea who knows to what further heights his poetry might have soared!

PLUTO (**Pipe Line Under the Ocean**) project for pumping fuel across the Channel to supply the troops involved in D-Day, was hidden in Shanklin. The Chine also has a memorial to the Royal Marines of 40 Commando who used the Chine as an assault course before the disastrous assault on Dieppe in 1942.

GODSHILL
4 miles W of Shanklin on the A3020

A short drive inland from Shanklin leads to the charming village of Godshill, which with its stone-built thatched cottages and its medieval **Church of All Saints** is one of the most popular stops on the tourist trail. The double-naved church, whose 15th century pinnacled tower dominates the village, contains some notable treasures, including a 15th century wall painting of Christ crucified on a triple-branched lily, a painting of Daniel in the Lions' Den and many monuments to the Worsleys and the Leighs, two of the leading island families.

Godshill has much to entertain visitors, including the magical **Model Village** with its 1/10th scale stone houses, trains and boats, even a football match taking place on the green (see panel below),and the **Natural History Centre** with its famed shell collection, minerals and aquarium. Also in Godshill is the **Nostalgia Toy Museum**, where 2,000 Dinky, Corgi and Matchbox toys and 1960s dolls bring back childhood memories.

Someone who likes to shout about Godshill is Shirley Ballard, the village's town crier, who has been involved in organising town crying events since 1987.

VENTNOR

With its south-facing aspect and the protection of St Boniface Down, Ventnor

THE MODEL VILLAGE

High Street, Godshill, Isle of Wight PO38 3HH
Tel/Fax: 01983 840270
e-mail: isleofwight.uk.com/model village

Island life in miniature is portrayed in the magical **Model Village** located in the Old Vicarage Gardens on the main street of Godshill. The original owner built his model of Shanklin with the help of model-makers from Elstree film studios and local people, and after two years' preparation the model was opened to the public in 1952. The present owners purchased the model village in 1969, by which time it was in a state of disrepair. Major repairs and rebuilding, together with a new project Godshill Main Street and Church Hill have filled the subsequent years, with all the work done in the workshop on site.

The 1/10 scale models are made of coloured cement and the detail is quite incredible. Real straw is prepared in the correct way for the thatching; the church on the hill took 600 hours of work before being assembled in its position; each house has its own tiny garden with miniature trees and shrubs chosen for their ability to respond to and withstand the bonsai-without-a-pot treatment. The airfield is in the style of small landing strips of the 1920s and 1930s, and the little railway is modelled on the older Island systems. Cricket, football, croquet and show-jumping are among the sports taking place on the beautifully tended lawns, and the sea is represented by a delightful pond complete with beach huts and fishermen's cottages. Things get even smaller in the model garden of the model Old Vicarage, where there is another (1/100 scale) model village with yet another Old Vicarage, and within its garden another (1/1,000 sale) model village - a model of a model of a model! This irresistible attraction is open daily from March to October.

enjoys a particularly mild climate. A series of terraces rises from the sandy beach, and most of the houses were built with balconies and large windows to make the most of the generous rations of sunshine.

Before the 1830s Ventnor had been a small, remote fishing village with something of a reputation for smuggling, but after a famous doctor, Sir James Clarke, reported the virtues of its climate, the visitors started to arrive. The railway, which came in 1866, assisted the boom, and soon the village of 300 became a town of 5,000. Much of its Victorian charm remains intact (partly because of the limited geographical scope for expansion) and the meteorological advantages allowed the development of one of its chief attractions, **Ventnor Botanic Garden**, which stands a mile west of town on the site of the former Royal National Chest Hospital. Many

DARENA

Bellevue Road, Ventnor, Isle of Wight PO38 1DB
Tel: 01983 853159
e-mail: darena@netguides.co.uk
website: www.netguides.co.uk/wight/darena.html

Standing above Ventnor, with views out to sea, **Darena** is a large, semi-detached Victorian house with a small front and rear garden. Owners Mr and Mrs Landon, who live next door at Somerford, offer excellent self-catering accommodation for 2-8 guests, let normally from Saturday to Saturday - but that's negotiable.

Darena's ground floor comprises hall, lounge with television, piano and sea view, dining room and fully equipped kitchen; on the first floor are four bedrooms and a bathroom. The tariff includes

all electricity and gas, linen and duvets, towels (not beach towels) and teacloths. There is a parking bay at the front of the house, and secure bike storage and hose-down facilities. Pets are permitted by arrangement, but smoking is not.

Ventnor town is a five-minute walk from the house, the seafront and the beach a ten-minute stroll, and the Botanic Garden (compete with spectacular Visitor Centre), cricket ground, park and downs are all within easy walking distance. Motorists can journey quickly and easily to many other places of interest, including the theme park at Blackgang Chine, the Coastal Visitors Centre and the Isle of Wight Donkey Sanctuary.

APPULDURCOMBE HOUSE

Wroxall, Nr. Ventnor, Isle of Wight PO38 3EW
Tel: 01983 852484 Fax: 01983 840188
website: www.appuldurcombe.co.uk

Appuldurcombe House was once the grandest and most striking house on the Island, and its 18th century baroque elegance is notable still in the partly restored building (it suffered bomb damage in 1943 and has not been lived in since). Visitors can stroll in the 11 acres of grounds designed by Capability Brown and maybe enjoy a picnic. The Owl & Falconry Centre is set up in the imaginatively restored servants' quarters and brewhouse. It puts on daily flying displays, featuring owls and other birds of prey from around the world. There is an excellent shop, a café for light refreshments, a photographic exhibition of the history of the house and a newly restored barn for indoor flying displays in poor weather. Open daily.

hundreds of rare and exotic plants flourish in the temperate surroundings, and the centre received a huge boost in the spring of 2000 with the opening of an exciting new **Visitor Centre** whose exhibits include an interactive display called The Green Planet - the Incredible Life of Plants. Snuggling in the Garden is the **Smuggling Museum**, whose 300 exhibits illustrate 700 years of smuggling lore.

Back in town, the **Coastal Visitor Centre** provides a fascinating and educational insight into the island's coastal and marine environment, with special features on animal and plant life, coastal defences and living with landslides - a problem very familiar to the island as well as to many parts of England's south coast. Two museums that tell of local life are the **Longshoreman's Museum** and the **Ventnor Heritage Museum**. One of the highlights of the year is the Crab Fair, held annually just outside Ventnor. The date for the 2001 renewal is May 28.

Outside town, St Boniface Down is a must for the serious walker, and a climb to the top of the highest point on the island (almost 800 feet) is rewarded with stupendous views. On nearby Bonchurch Down wild goats were introduced to control the holm oaks, while New Forest ponies live on Luccombe Down, the site of several Bronze Age burial mounds.

A little way east of Ventnor, the quiet village of **Bonchurch** stands at the start of the six-mile strip of land called the Undercliff. This remarkable feature, which runs along the coast to Blackgang, is marked by towering cliffs that offer protection from the elements and have also inspired poets and artists with their rugged, romantic beauty. The poet Algernon Swinburne spent some of his childhood in Bonchurch, and Charles Dickens wrote part of *David Copperfield* while staying here.

AROUND VENTNOR

WROXALL
2 miles W of Ventnor on the B3327

Owls, falcons, vultures and donkeys all call Wroxall their home! **Appuldurcombe House**, once the grandest mansion on the whole island with gardens laid out by Capability Brown, was badly bombed in 1943 and has never been lived in since. The **Owl & Falconry Centre**, in what used to be the laundry and brewhouse, stages daily flying displays with birds of prey from around the world and holds courses in the centuries-old art of falconry (see panel opposite).

Heaven for 200 donkeys and many other animals is the **Isle of Wight Donkey Sanctuary** at Lower Winstone Farm. The rescue centre is a registered charity relying entirely on donations, and visitors have several ways of helping, including the Adopt a Donkey scheme.

ST LAWRENCE
1 mile W of Ventnor on the A3055

Nestling in the heart of the Undercliff, the ancient village of St Lawrence has a 13th century church that once laid claim to being the smallest in Britain. It was extended in 1842 but remains diminutive, measuring just 20' by 12'. Close to the village is the **Rare Breeds Waterfowl Park** set in 30 acres by the coast. The park includes one of the largest collections in Britain of rare farm animals, plus animals and birds from all over the world. The meerkats who arrived in 1999 have been so successful at breeding that their quarters have had to be extended. Other new arrivals for the millennium are the first litter of Kune Kune pigs from New Zealand. Not far away, old farm buildings were converted into **Isle of Wight Studio Glass**, where skills old and new produce

Lighthouse, St Catherine's Point

The coast road continues through the village of Niton to **St Catherine's Point**, the wildest part of the island, from where steps lead down to St Catherine's lighthouse. A path leads up to the summit of St Catherine's Hill, where the remains of a much older lighthouse, known as the Pepperpot, can be seen.

Blackgang Chine, at the most southerly tip of the island, has been developed from an early Victorian scenic park into a modern fantasy park with dozens of attractions for children. Also inside the park are two heritage exhibitions centred on a water-powered sawmill and a quayside, with displays ranging from cooper's and wheelwright's workshops to a shipwreck

glass of the highest quality. Lord Jellicoe, hero of Jutland, lived for some years in St Lawrence and often swam in Orchard's Bay, a small cove where Turner sketched.

DINOSAUR FARM MUSEUM

Military Road (A3055), Nr Brighstone, Isle of Wight PO30 4PG
Tel/Fax: 01983 740844

Dinosaur Farm Museum came into being following the unearthing in 1992 of the skeleton of a brachiosaurus, the island's largest and most spectacular dinosaur discovery. Billed as 'The Working Museum in the Heart of Dinosaur Country', this unique attraction follows the tale - still unfolding - of the original skeleton and of the exciting fossil discoveries that are still being made on the island. It is the only museum in Britain where visitors can see the bones of giant dinosaurs in the process of being identified, preserved and catalogued. Visitors are invited to bring their own fossils for identification, and to chat to the resident experts about dinosaurs and fossils. Dinosaur Farm also organises guided fossil hunts, held at various locations on the island, which can be pre-booked when visiting the museum. The museum shop is stocked with dinosaur-themed souvenirs and locally collected fossils, and

refreshments are provided in an attractive tea room housed in a converted 17th century farmhouse. This fascinating museum is open Sundays and Thursdays from mid-April to the end of September, also Tuesdays and Fridays in July and August. The owners of the site, Barbara and Geoff Philips, offer accommodation in a number of modern 5- and 6-berth caravans standing in a secluded part of the farm grounds.

collection, a huge whale skeleton and a 19th century beach scene complete with a bathing machine. The coastline here is somewhat fragile, and a large slice of cliff has been lost to storms and gales in recent years.

SHORWELL
7 miles S of Newport on the B3399

An attractive village of thatched stone cottages. South of the village, just off the Newport-Brighstone road, is **Yafford Mill**, an 18th century water mill restored to working order. Also on the site are a farm park with rare farm animals, owls, monkeys and Sophie the seal; nature walks; a narrow gauge railway; a tea room and a gift shop. The **Church of St Peter** is notable for its ornate decor, its 500-year-old stone pulpit, the many monuments to the Leigh family and a carefully restored 15th century wall painting of St Christopher with all his usual travelling paraphernalia.

BRIGHSTONE
8 miles S of Newport on the B3399

One of the prettiest villages on the island, Brighstone was once notorious as the home of smugglers and wreckers. But in the late 19th century the villagers assembled a lifeboat crew; its first skipper was a certain James Buckett, a former smuggler who was forced to serve five years in the Navy as punishment for his crimes. The National Trust runs a shop in a picturesque row of thatched cottages, and a little museum depicting village life down the years - including some relics of the lifeboat.

The island has long been known for its fossil finds, especially relating to dinosaurs. Brighstone recently came into the news when on a clifftop near the village the bones of a completely new species of predatory dinosaur were unearthed. The 15ft carnivore, which

lived in the cretaceous period about 120million to 150 million years ago, has been named *cotyrannus lengi* after Gavin Leng, a local collector who found the first bone. Parts of the skeleton are on display in the museum of the Isle of Wight Geology at Sandown.

A mile or so west of Brighstone, the National Trust is also responsible for **Mottistone Manor Garden**, a charming hillside garden alongside an Elizabethan manor house. The Mottistone estate extends from Mottistone Down in the north to the coast at Sudmoor. On **Mottistone Common**, where New Forest ponies graze, are the remains of a neolithic long barrow known as the Longstone. There are two stones, one standing upright, the other, smaller, on its side. A local story has it that the first stone was thrown there by St Catherine in a contest with the Devil for control of the island. The second stone, thrown by the Devil, fell just short of the first, so the upright stone thrown by St Catherine represents the triumph of good over evil. Back on the coast road, Compton Bay (excellent surfing) and Compton Down (National Trust) is a wild area rich in wildlife and affording superb views. On top of nearby Brook Down is a group of Bronze Age barrows known as the Five Barrows.

FRESHWATER
8 miles W of Newport on the A3055

A bustling town with good shopping and a village atmosphere. It was put on the map by Alfred, Lord Tennyson, who lived at Farringford House (now a hotel) and later bought the house with the money he made from his poem *Maud*. A dedicated walker, Tennyson was often to be seen on the dramatic High Down in his cloak and wide-brimmed hat. After his death the area was renamed Tennyson Down and a cross erected high on the cliffs in his

THE RED LION

Church Place, Freshwater, Isle of Wight PO40 9BP
Tel: 01983 754925

Discerning diners come from all over the island and from well beyond to enjoy the superb cuisine that has earned the **Red Lion** many accolades from top publications like the Good Pub Guide and the

Egon Ronay Pub Guide. The origins of the pub go back to the 11th century - though the handsome redbrick building we see today is somewhat more recent - and the open-plan bars have a pleasingly traditional look, with flagstone floors, scrubbed pine tables and a variety of seating, some of it rescued from churches.

Many of the photographs that hang on the walls have a cricketing theme, reflecting the passion of owner Michael David Mence, who used to play professionally for Warwickshire, and who, with only the slightest twisting of an arm, will talk with great authority on the subject. He runs the pub with his wife Lorna, who will talk with equal authority on the subject of cooking and who oversees the three chefs in the kitchen.

The Red Lion's regularly changing menus are a world away from typical pub fare, and the mouthwatering choice makes ordering a real problem! Locally caught crab is always a favourite - with a plain salad, au gratin, chilli Singapore-style, with Stilton for a mushroom stuffing - and other options run from herring roes on toast or bacon and lentil soup to grilled plaice, tuna steak with lime and

coriander butter, Thai chicken curry, baby leg of lamb for two or a traditional steak and kidney pie. Few of the regulars even think about saying no to one of the terrific puddings - perhaps whisky and walnut trifle or chocolate roulade with mint cream. All the herbs used in the cooking come from the herb garden that is lovingly tended by Roly the gardener. Sandwiches and lighter snacks are also available, but those in the know save plenty of time and settle down to a meal to remember.

The Red Lion is located on the eastern edge of town next to the parish church, where Lady Tennyson, wife of the poet who lived on the island for 40 years, is buried. Freshwater is not lacking in places to visit, among them Dimbola Lodge, where the work of the eminent Victorian photographer Julia Margaret Cameron is displayed. To build up an instant appetite, there are many lovely walks in the vicinity, including Freshwater Way, a 3.5 mile walk along the Western Yar, following the route of an old railway track.

THE TUDOR LOUNGE

17 School Green Road, Freshwater, Isle of Wight PO40 9AJ
Tel: 01983754901

Value for money is high on the list of priorities at the **Tudor Lounge**, which is run in fine style by Mr and Mrs Smith, who were both born on the Island. They have been here for six years, having previously been hoteliers elsewhere on the island. Mr Smith was a builder by profession, and he is responsible for the interior design of what
was originally a small cinema
and is now a tearoom-cum-
restaurant that has become
one of the favourite meeting
places of local community.

Behind the small
windowpanes of the glass
frontage all is spick and span,
with oak tables and cane-
backed chairs, wall lighting,
prints and photographs, and
everywhere the expert's eye
for colour co-ordination is
apparent. A terraced garden
at the back, with patio-style
tables and chairs, is a safe
place for children, with
access only through the
tearoom.

There's something to enjoy throughout the day: English breakfast, morning coffee, homemade cakes and sandwiches, savoury snacks and cream teas. Traditional home-cooked lunches with a selection of roasts, pies, fresh fish etc. are served with *fresh* vegetables, in a menu changed daily.

Sunday lunch is always a treat to look forward to, with a fine variety on all courses. The owners have the friendliest of welcomes for everyone who comes through the door, be they loyal regulars or

first time visitors. Opening times at the Tudor Lounge are 8.30am till 5pm in the summer, 8.30am till 4pm in the winter.

It's the perfect place to start the day before a tour of the island, or to pause for a break between trips.

The little town of Freshwater is a rewarding place for a stroll or a shop. It is the major shopping centre in West Wight but remains largely unspoilt, with something of a village atmosphere; indeed, it claims to be England's largest village. A mile away, Freshwater Bay a cove cut into chalk cliffs, is a delightful place to visit, and the countryside at this western end of the island is particularly attractive. The poet Alfred Lord Tennyson lived at nearby Farringford House (now a hotel) for 40 years, and the walk from the Bay to the glorious Tennyson Down, is named in his honour and is one of the most scenic and popular walks on the island. Lady Tennyson is buried in the churchyard at Freshwater, and a touching memorial inside the church commemorates their son Lionel, who died at the age of 32 while returning from India.

THE COUNTRY GARDEN HOTEL

Church Hill, Totland Bay, Isle of Wight PO39 OET
Tel/Fax: 01983 754521
e-mail: countrygardeniow@cs.com
website: thecountrygardenhotel.co.uk

The superb garden setting is just one of the many attractions of the **Country Garden Hotel**, an elegant boutique hotel whose resident owners Pat and Pauline Burton have 30 years experience in leading hotels in five countries. The gardens are a riot of colour at most times of the year, and the

bedrooms make the most of the delightful setting, which also affords views of the nearby Solent.

There are 16 centrally heated bedrooms - singles, doubles, twins and a lovely suite - all of them with bath and shower facilities en suite. Television, radio, telephone, fridge and hairdryer are standard in all rooms. One ground-floor room is specially adapted for less able visitors, and all the ground-floor rooms and public areas are wheelchair accessible.

The elegant restaurant (non-smoking) has built up a fine reputation under long-serving Executive Chef Brian O'Reilly, whose daily changing table d'hote and à la carte menus feature the best and freshest produce, much of it local. Crab, lobster, sole and sea bass are usually available, and other typical choices could include local game, veal medallions with sauce bordelaise or saddle of lamb for two. The bar, lounge and restaurant all look out over the gardens, which are prettily floodlit in the evening.

The Solent is a five-minute stroll away, and for more serious walking there's easy access to established

walking routes such as the Tennyson Trail and The Needles. Also nearby is Alum Bay, renowned for its coloured sands and pleasure park. The busy port town of Yarmouth is only eight minutes away by car, and among its many attractions is the Tudor Yarmouth Castle, which Henry Vlll built in 1547 as his final fortress.

And when the walking is done, the sightseeing is over for the day and the thirst and appetite return, this hotel of unique delights beckons the most discerning of adult guests with its civilised ambience, its lovely gardens and its fine food - a combination that explains the fact that more than 70% of its guests return for more of the same! Reservations may be made from any day to any day, and a free ferry crossing is included in the rate for a double occupied room for guests staying two nights or more between October and April.

Freshwater Bay

memory. There are more remembrances of the great poet in the **Church of All Saints** on a hill high above the River Yar. Lady Emily Tennyson is buried in the churchyard and there is a touching memorial to their son Lionel, 'an affectionate boy' who died at the age of 32 while returning from India. The town has gradually spread southwards towards **Freshwater Bay**, where Julia Cameron, the pioneer photographer, was persuaded by her friend Lord Tennyson to settle. Her home was **Dimbola Lodge**, which now attracts thousands of visitors with its permanent exhibition of her work and changing exhibitions of the work of other distinguished photographers (see panel below).

DIMBOLA LODGE

Terrace Lane, Freshwater Bay, Isle of Wight PO40 9QE
Tel: 01983 756814 Fax: 01983 755578
e-mail: administrator@dimbola.co.uk
website: www.dimbola.co.uk

Dimbola Lodge, sometime home of the pioneering photographer Julia Margaret Cameron, and later a hotel, was saved from demolition in 1991 by the Julia Margaret Cameron Trust to become a museum, photographic study centre and gallery. Julia was born in Calcutta in 1815, one of seven daughters of James Pattle, an official in the British East India Company, and his French wife Adeline de l'Etang, a couple noted for their hospitality and joie de vivre. Sent to England and France for her education, Julia returned to Calcutta in 1838, where she married Charles Hay Cameron, a widower 20 years her senior whom she had met two years earlier at the Cape of Good Hope.

When Charles retired in 1848 the Camerons moved to London into an artistic community at Little Holland House, Kensington, that included Poet Laureate Alfred, Lord Tennyson, the painter GF Watts and other artists who would later influence her photographic style - Dante Gabriel Rossetti, John Everett Millais, William Holman Hunt. In 1860 Mrs Cameron visited Farringford House, the Tennysons' home on the Isle of Wight, and immediately bought two nearby adjacent cottages which she linked with a Gothic tower and named Dimbola Lodge after the family tea estates in Ceylon.

The gilt of a camera as a Christmas present from her daughter and son-in-law in 1863 sparked an immediate enthusiasm in Julia for this new art form and soon she was welcoming and photographing the cream of Victorian society. Tennyson, Thackeray, Darwin, GFWatts and his wife the actress Ellen Terry lived locally, and frequent guests included Lewis Carroll, Robert Browning and Edward Lear. The poet Henry Taylor wrote of Dimbola Lodge: '....a house indeed to which everyone resorted for pleasure and in which no man, woman or child was ever known to be unwelcome.'

Permanent exhibitions at the Lodge of her work include 'Famous Men and Fair Women', reflecting her life on the island, rare images of her time in Ceylon and a section of her work illustrating Tennyson's poetry. A new room has displays concerning the history and natural history of the area, and throughout the year there are changing exhibitions and photographic workshops. The Lodge and its vegetarian restaurant are open Tuesday to Sunday and Bank Holiday Mondays.

Freshwater Bay

Two miles west of Freshwater, **Alum Bay** is famous for its multi-coloured sand and its spectacular chair lift. The Bay is the site of the **Needles Park**, with children's entertainment, a sand shop, sweet factory and glass blowing studio (see panel below). Here, too, are **The Needles**, the island's best-known landmark. A continuation of the cliffs at the western

Freshwater Bay is the start point of the 15-mile Tennyson Trail, which ends at Carisbrooke.

Totland, on the coast west of Freshwater, is a popular holiday spot with safe bathing in **Totland Bay**. Just outside Totland is Headon Warren, from where the coastal path runs to Alum Bay. On a hill a little way inland is the Victorian Gothic Christ Church with a massive lych gate made from timbers from *HMS Thunderer*, which saw action at the Battle of Trafalgar.

Alum Bay

THE NEEDLES PARK

Alum Bay, Isle of Wight PO39 0JD
Tel: 0870 458 0022 Fax: 01983 759079

Set above the world-famous sand cliffs, overlooking The Needles Rocks and Lighthouse, the Park offers a range of attractions for all the family including Alum Bay Glass Studio, Isle of Wight Sweet Manufactory and the popular chairlift to the beach to view the Island's most dramatic landmark.

Special events include 'Magic in the Skies' fireworks finale very Thursday throughout August.

The Needles

attractive old houses. It has had its ups and downs - up in the heady days when it returned two Members of Parliament to Westminster, down when it lost both and was declared a rotten borough. In the mortuary chapel of the 13th century **Church of St James** is an intriguing statue on the tomb of Governor Holmes. During one of the many conflicts with the French, he captured a ship on board which was a sculptor with an unfinished statue of Louis XIV. He was travelling to Versailles to model the King's head from life. The Governor thought that the statue of the King, even though it was in full French armour, would be just right for his own tomb, and he ordered the sculptor to model his head instead of the King's. One of the most interesting buildings, but one that is easy to miss down by the ferry, is **Yarmouth Castle**, built by Henry VIII in 1547 after the town had been sacked by the French. This was the final fortress in his coastal defence system, and a climb to the battlements provides the best views of the comings and goings of ships in the Solent. The estuary of the River Yar is rich in wild life, especially bird life.

tip of the island, they comprise three jagged slabs of rock, with a striped red-and-white lighthouse at the end of the most westerly. The sea has gouged deep caves out of the stacks, which are a particularly spectacular sight when viewed close up from a pleasure boat. Two of them are known as Lord Holmes' Parlour and Kitchen, named after a 17th century Governor of the Island who once entertained his guests in the Parlour and kept his wine cool in the Kitchen. in the car park at Alum Bay is a monument to Marconi, who set up the first wireless station here in 1897. A clifftop walk leads to the **Needles Old Battery**, one of many forts built under the direction of Lord Palmerston against the threat of a French invasion. Two original gun barrels are mounted in the parade ground, and there are various displays explaining the battery's function. A 200ft tunnel with a spiral staircase leads down to a searchlight position with dramatic views.

YARMOUTH
10 miles W of Newport on the A3054

A fascinating, picturesque little place with old stone quays, narrow streets and

FORT VICTORIA
1 mile W of Yarmouth off the A3054

Another of the forts built by Lord Palmerston as a defence against a feared French invasion. They were never used in active service and became known as Palmerston's Follies. The area around the fort has been converted into one of the island's major leisure complexes, with unspoilt beaches, walks and tours and a wide range of attractions including a sunken history exhibition, an aquarium, a planetarium and the largest model railway layout in Britain. The trains, points, signals, sound effects and level crossings are controlled by computers, using two PCs and over 40 microprocessors. The scale is HO and the setting is Germany.

NEWTOWN
5 miles E of Yarmouth on the A3054

Founded in the 13th century by a Bishop of Winchester, Newtown once had a large, busy harbour, but silting led to its decline as a maritime centre and the harbour is now a nature reserve. The town's most notable building is the **Old Town Hall**, erected in 1699 and now in the care of the National Trust. A small, unassuming building of brick and stone, it contains many interesting documents and memorabilia.

PORCHFIELD
2 miles E of Newtown on the A3054

Fun in the country for the whole family is promised at **Colemans Animal Farm**, where visitors are encouraged to stroke and feed the animals. Children will also love the huge wooden play area, the sandpit, the straw maze and the mini-farm with pedal tractors.

BETHEL COTTAGE

New Road, Porchfield:
enquiries to Bridget Lewis, Blackbridge
Brook House, Main Rd, Havenstreet,
Isle of Wight PO33 4DR
Tel: 01983 884742
e-mail: bridget-lewis@talk21.com

Bridget Lewis and her husband offer self-catering accommodation of great character in **Bethel Cottage**, a charming stone building set well back from the road in a large garden. The cottage, which has been sympathetically restored and modernised, is decorated and furnished to a very high standard. It can sleep up to four guests (plus a cot for a small child) in a double bedroom and a twin which share a shower-bathroom. The lounge-dining room is particularly attractive with its original oak beams and beautiful old brick and stone fireplace. The kitchen is equipped with everything needed for a comfortable stay, right down to a CD player and a microwave. Electricity, bed linen and towels are all included in the letting price, and a cot and high chair will be loaned free on request. The cottage has a large garden with mature trees, a favourite visiting place for a variety of wild birds. The patio area is supplied with a picnic bench, barbecue and sun loungers.

The village of Porchfield is small and quiet, an ideal spot for a break from the hustle and bustle of city life yet within easy reach of Newport and the sailing resorts of Cowes and Yarmouth. Porchfield's pub is just round the corner from the cottage, and nearby Parkhurst Forest offers some lovely walks.

5 The New Forest

One of the country's great treasures, the New Forest has remained a very special part of rural England ever since William the Conqueror set it aside as his private hunting ground more than 900 years ago. Seizing some 15,000 acres that the Saxons had laboriously reclaimed from the heathland, he began a programme of planting thousands of trees. To preserve the Forest against any threat to the wildlife he would hunt (especially deer) he adopted all the rigorous hunting laws of the Saxons and introduced many of his own. Anyone who killed a

Autumn in the Forest

deer would himself be killed. If he shot at a deer and missed, his hands were cut off; and anyone who disturbed a deer during the breeding season had his eyes put out. There are still plenty of deer roaming in the 145 square miles of the Forest. They number about 2,000; fallow deer make up the majority, but there are also small numbers of red and roe deer, along with some sika deer which were first introduced at the end of the 19th century. Visitors are more likely to

The New Forest

see the famous wild New Forest ponies, and the signs that warn against feeding or even approaching them should be taken very seriously: they can be very dangerous and do not need feeding - the Forest provides everything they need. The keen-eyed bird-watcher might be rewarded with the sight of a tiny Dartford warbler or the spectacular hobby, a small type of predatory falcon. The Forest, less than half of which is actually wooded, is of great importance in terms not only of recreation and conservation but also of commerce: the Forestry Commission maintains an annual production of 36,000 tonnes of timber from the mainly conifer plantations. The Forest is ideal walking country, with vast tracts virtually unpopulated but criss-crossed by hundreds of footpaths and bridleways. The Commission has also established a network of waymarked cycle routes which make the most of the scenic attractions and are also designed to help protect the special nature of the Forest.

THE NEW FOREST

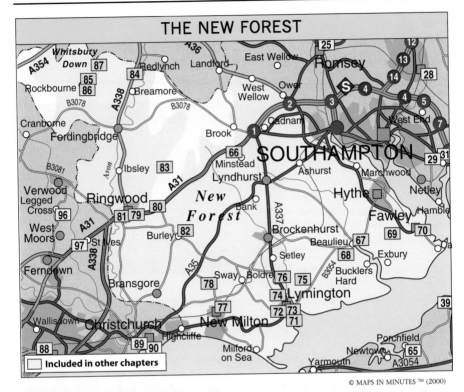

© MAPS IN MINUTES ™ (2000)

PLACES TO STAY, EAT, DRINK AND SHOP

LYNDHURST

The only town of any size in the New Forest, Lyndhurst was the administrative centre of William's Forest. The most striking building in this compact little town is the **Church of St Michael and All Angels**, rebuilt in the mid-19th century in what Sir John Betjeman described as 'the most fanciful, fantastic Gothic style that I have ever seen'. The rebuilding, the work of George Gilbert Scott's pupil William White, coincided with the heyday of the Pre-Raphaelite movement, and the church contains some fine stained glass by Burne-Jones from the firm of William Morris. The most famous work of all is the huge mural by Lord Leighton depicting the parable of the wise and foolish virgins. In the churchyard is the grave of Alice Liddell, who, as a young girl, was the inspiration for Alice in Lewis Carroll's *Alice in Wonderland*. As Mrs Reginald Hargreaves, Alice lived all her married life in Lyndhurst and lost two sons in the First World War. Next to the church is the Queen's House. Originally built as a hunting lodge, and still showing medieval and Tudor elements, it has been host to many sovereigns (and changes its name to King's House when the monarch is male). The last monarch to stay was George lll, who graciously allowed loyal villagers to watch through the window as he ate dinner. The house is now the Headquarters of the Forestry Commission and is also home to the **Verderers' Court**, an institution dating back to Norman times which still deals with matters concerning the Forest's ancient commoning rights. The verderers sit in public ten times a year, working in close partnership with the Forestry Commissioners in managing the Forest and reconciling the needs of the commoning system (the right to rent land and graze livestock) with the demands concomitant with the Forest being a major recreational and tourist attraction. Another duty of the verderers is to appoint five agisters, stockmen who are responsible for the day-to-day supervision of the 5,000 ponies and cattle roaming in the Forest. The main car park in the High Street is the location of the **New Forest Museum & Visitor Centre**, where many aspects of the Forest - the development of the trees, the ponies, the deer, the human inhabitants - are covered in detail by audio-visual shows, exhibits and interactive displays. Animals of a more reclusive kind are the theme of the **New Forest Reptile Centre** situated two miles west of town and open every day from Easter to October. Here visitors can be sure to see the reptilian inhabitants of the Forest that might otherwise elude even the most observant traveller in the Forest itself, including the sand lizard and the rare smooth snake. Lyndhurst's High Street, an attractive thoroughfare of mainly Edwardian buildings, slopes down to Bolton's Bench, a tree-crowned knoll where

New Forest Ponies

ponies can often be seen grazing. At the other end of town Swan Green, surrounded by picturesque cottages, is a much-photographed setting for summer cricket matches.

AROUND LYNDHURST

MINSTEAD
3 miles NW of Lyndhurst off the A337

A village of picture-postcard appeal, looked over from a hill by the 13th century **Church of All Saints**, which has almost a cottagey appearance. It features an unusual triangular nave, a triple-decked pulpit and an open fireplace. During the 18th century, the gentry of Minstead regarded attending church as a duty that should be made as agreeable as possible. Three of the most affluent residents paid to have the church fabric

altered so that they could each have their own entrance door leading to a private parlour complete with the fire and comfortable chairs. The squire of Minstead even installed a sofa on which he could doze during a sermon, which at the time would normally last a minimum of an hour. Sir Arthur Conan Doyle, the creator of Sherlock Holmes, and his wife are buried in the churchyard. Though the detective, with his pipe and deerstalker, is the best-known of the author's creations, he actually preferred to write historical novels, some of which were set in Hampshire. His own favourite among these novels was *The White Company*, which is set in part in the New Forest.

Conan Doyle loved the New Forest and had a home near Cadnam, a short distance northwest of Minstead. Minstead's other main attraction is **Furzey Gardens**, eight acres of delightful woodland gardens laid out by Hew

ACRES DOWN FARM

Minstead, Nr. Lyndhurst, Hampshire SO43 7GE
Tel: 02380 813693
e-mail: annie-cooper@talk21.com

Acres Down Farm enjoys a delightful setting in the heart of the New Forest, but is easily reached from the main A31 and A35. This New Forest Commoner's farm comprises 38 acres which Annie Cooper farms with the added benefit of her New Forest Commoners rights, whereby her animals graze and browse the whole of the forest woods and open heathlands. Visitors have a number of possibilities in terms of accommodation. Three rooms in the redbrick and tiled modern farmhouse are available for Bed & Breakfast, while the two 19th century cottages on the farm, one with three bedrooms, the other with two, are let on a self-catering basis - all available throughout the year. Another option is the basic camping site close to the farmhouse with toilet and shower facilities, where you can enjoy a full farmhouse breakfast if requested. There is a caravan site with water and diposal point situated on the top of Acres Down with views as far as the Isle of Wight. Families are very welcome at all amenities - the house, the self catering cottages, camp and caravan sites. As there are a large number of farm animals - sorry no pets.

An overnight stay is not the only reason for visiting Annie's farm, as people return time after time in the summer to enjoy her superb cream teas - glorious, indulgent mini-feasts of home baking with a choice of preserves and lashings of cream served in the spacious garden and conservatory. The farm is situated on the western side of Minstead with lovely old thatched cottages and a historic church (also originally thatched) with some remarkable features - a triple pulpit, two family pews one with a fireplace, a balcony and a gypsy gallery. Sir Arthur Conan Doyle, author of the Sherlock Holmes books, is buried in the churchyard. A great place for exploring and what better treat after an invigorating walk or cycle ride than one of Annies cream teas.

Minstead, New Forest

Cathedral without ceremony and almost without mourning.

ASHURST
3 miles NE of Lyndhurst on the A35

Ther are a number of family attractions here. The **New Forest Butterfly Farm** in Langley Wood houses butterflies, birds and insects in a garden and jungle setting. **Longdown Dairy Farm** shows the workings of a modern dairy farm and is home to the **National Dairy Council Museum Collection**. The **Otter, Owl and Wildlife Conservation Park**, set in 25 acres of ancient woodland, contains Europe's largest gathering of multi-specied otters, owls and other indigenous wildlife. Ashurst Lodge, now a private house, contains the remains of an Elizabethan industrial site

Dalrymple in the 1920s. The informal landscape enjoys views over the New Forest towards the Isle of Wight. Beautiful banks of azaleas and rhododendrons, heathers and ferns surround a picturesque water garden, and among the notable species to be found are spectacular Chilean fire trees and the strange Bottle Brush tree.

Just north of Minstead, across the A3 at Canterton Glen, stands the **Rufus Stone**, said to mark the spot where William Rufus (William ll, son of William the Conqueror) was killed by an arrow while hunting. His entourage sped off in all directions to report the event and William's body was carried on the cart of Purkis the charcoal-burner to Winchester, where William's brother Henry had already arrived to proclaim himself King. Rufus, the most unpopular of monarchs, was buried in the

The Rufus Stone

BEAULIEU NATIONAL MOTOR MUSEUM

Beaulieu, Brockenhurst,
Hampshire SO42 7ZN
Tel: 01590 612345
Fax: 01590 612624
e-mail: info@beaulieu.co.uk
website: www.beaulieu.co.uk

The **National Motor Museum**, in the grounds of Lord Montagu's estate, houses over 300 vehicles covering all aspects of motoring. Among the exhibits - the oldest dates from 1896 - are world landspeed record-breakers *Bluebird* and *Golden Arrow*, Damon Hill's championship winning Formula 1 Williams Grand Prix car, an Outspan Orange car, Ariel and Vincent motorcycles and a large number of commercial vehicles.

Special attractions for 2001 include a fabulous collection of over 2,000 toy vehicles in the Motoring Through Childhood Exhibition, and the exhibition of James Bond cars, including the Aston Martin from *Goldeneye* (the earlier ejector-seat Aston is in a museum in Amsterdam), the BMW 7 Series from *Tomorrow Never Dies* and Goldfinger's Rolls-Royce. The exhibition also includes examples of Q's gadgetry and some of the villains' trademarks, notably Jaws' steel teeth.

One of the many permanent displays is an accurate reconstruction of a 1938 garage complete with forecourt, servicing bay, machine shop and office.

Many Montagu family treasures are now on display in **Palace House**, formerly the Great Gatehouse of Beaulieu Abbey, where visitors can meet characters from Victorian days, among them the butler, housemaid and cook, who will talk about their lives. The old monks' refectory houses an exhibition of monastic life, and embroidered wall hangings designed and created by Belinda, Lady Montagu, depict the story of the Abbey from its earliest days. The glorious gardens are an attraction in their own right, and there are plenty of rides and drives for young and old alike - including a monorail that runs through the roof of the Museum in the course of its tour of the estate.

where saltpetre was mined. The Forestry Commission offers visitors the opportunity of camping in the heart of the Forest, and the site at Ashurst is one of three offering full facilities.

MARCHWOOD

6 miles E of Lyndhurst on the A326

A community with strong links with both woodland and water. Ships of the Royal Fleet Auxiliary are based at the military port, which was built in 1943 for the construction of the Mulberry Harbours. On the western edge of the village, the woodland of Crookedhays Copse is a haven of wildlife.

HYTHE

8 miles SE of Lyndhurst off the A35

This is one of the very best places to watch the comings and goings of the big ships on Southampton Water, and no visit

Beaulieu Abbey House

here is complete without taking a ride up the pier on the quaint little electric train, the oldest electric pier train in the world; from the end of the pier a ferry plies the short route across to Southampton. Hythe is the birthplace of the Hovercraft - its inventor Sir Christopher Cockerell lived in the village. In the 1930s Hythe was the home of the British Powerboat Company and of T E Lawrence (Lawrence of Arabia) while he was testing the RAF 200 series powerboats.

BEAULIEU

7 miles SE of Lyndhurst on the B3056

This historic settlement on the banks of the Beaulieu river has been a popular place to visit for many centuries - it was here in 1202 that King John gave an area then known as Bellus Locus (Beautiful Place in Latin, Beaulieu in French) to the Cistercian monks. The **Abbey** passed into the ownership of the Earl of Southampton in 1538; he pulled most of it down, and used some of the stones in the construction of Calshot and Hurst Castles. But many parts survive, and a stately

Beaulieu Abbey

THE TURFCUTTERS ARMS

Main Road, East Boldre, Nr. Beaulieu,
Hampshire SO42 7WL
Tel: 01590 612331 Fax: 01590 612003

A picturesque New Forest village off the B3054 a couple of miles south of historic Beaulieu is the setting for an outstanding hostelry. **The Turfcutters Arms**, smartly modernised from its 17th century origins, is a handsome redbrick building standing in ample grounds, and behind the immaculate facade the scene is delightfully traditional. The pub, which is run by Saxon Irving and her son James French, is open every lunchtime and evening throughout the year, and its popularity has been greatly enhanced since they took over two years ago. Quality real ales - three in winter, four in summer - include the local Ringwood brew, and there's a good choice of draught lagers and a draught cider. Food is a key part of the business, and the menu runs from snacks, grills and fish dishes to seasonal

game and all-time favourites such as roast lamb or pork, Cajun chicken, chilli served with rice and tortillas, and steak & kidney pie. The pub has seats for 60, but it fills up quickly at busy times - booking is recommended for Saturday night and Sunday lunchtime. Happy night on Wednesday sees selected drinks at reduced prices. An old thatched barn next to the main building is a popular venue for parties and functions. The Turfcutters has one letting bedroom - an en suite double room - for overnight accommodation, at a very reasonable price that includes a fine breakfast.

THE BRIDGE TAVERN

Ipers Bridge, Holbury, Hampshire SO45 2HD
Tel/Fax: 02380 892554

The A326 from Southampton or the B3056 and B3055 from Lyndhurst will bring the visitor to Ipers Bridge and the **Bridge Tavern**, run by Jean and Bill Galbraith for the past six years. Their 17th century pub has spacious gardens, with the little River Darkwater running alongside. Inside, the open fire, cane-back chairs and darkwood furniture provide an inviting setting for enjoying the Galbraiths'' good wholesome food served lunchtime and evening every day - best to book for a table in the separate dining area. Main courses could include home-made steak & kidney pie, a hearty mixed grill, a good choice of fish

dishes and always a choice for vegetarians. There's a mini-menu for younger members of the family (high chairs available), daily specials - usually about 30 - and a wide selection of starters and snacks such as omelettes, ploughman's and jacket potatoes. Be sure to leave room for a splendid old-fashioned dessert, perhaps steamed suet pudding or fruit crumble. And Sunday would not be Sunday without the traditional roasts. The Bridge Tavern also offers an extremely well-chosen and realistically priced wine list with European and New World vintages available by glass or bottle, along with a wide range of real ales and other beers and lagers.

home grew up around the Abbey's imposing gatehouse. In the grounds of Lord Montagu's estate is the **National Motor Museum**, one of the country's premier attractions, with over 300 vehicles covering all aspects of motoring and glorious gardens which are worth a visit in their own right (see panel opposite).

FAWLEY
12 miles SE of Lyndhurst on the A326

Oil is king here, and the terminals and refineries of what is probably the largest oil plant in Europe create a science fiction landscape; standing bravely apart is the village church, a link with earlier days, looking out over Southampton Water. Fawley is where some islanders from Tristan da Cunha settled after fleeing a volcano that threatened their island in 1961; a model of one of the boats they used for their escape can be seen in the

chapel. Also of note in Fawley is **Cadland House**, whose garden was designed by Capability Brown. It houses the national collection of leptospermums. Beyond the refineries a road leads off the B3053 Calshot road to **Ashlett Creek** and another world, the natural, unrefined world of creeks, mud flats and bird-haunted marshland.

CALSHOT
14 miles SE of Lyndhurst on the B3053

The RAF were based in both World Wars at Calshot, where seaplanes were prepared and tested for the Schneider Trophy races. The hangars once used by the RAF are now the Calshot Activity Centre, whose many activities include an artificial ski slope. At the very end of a shingle spit stands one of Henry VIII's coastal defence castles. This is **Calshot Castle**, which is now restored as a pre-World War I garrison. Visitors can admire the view

THE FALCON HOTEL

The Square, Fawley, Hampshire SO45 1DD
Tel/Fax: 02380 891005

The Falcon Hotel is a distinctive brick building standing in the centre of Fawley, which lies on the B3053 on the western edge of Southampton Water. The premises date back to the end of the 18th century, and behind the frontage on the square the bar is bright and welcoming, with a striped pattern for the chairs and wallpaper and a number of prints and little ornaments.

Di and Andy Buckle, managers here since 1999, have many years experience in the trade and welcome visitors with an excellent selection of food and drink. There's always a choice of three real ales, with several other beers and lagers and a cider on draught, and Andy keeps the inner man happy with his first-class cooking. Many of his dishes are served on sizzling platters, with stir-fries a speciality, and booking is necessary for Friday dinner and also for Sunday lunch, when an organist performs

from 1 o'clock till 4. Food is not served on Sunday evening or on Monday, and the Falcon is closed Monday lunchtime except when it's a Bank Holiday. Fawley is close to the sea and to the Forest, and within a short drive there is plenty to interest the visitor, including Calshot Castle and the motor museum at Beaulieu. The Falcon provides an excellent base for touring the area with three en suite bedrooms which are available throughout the year. Children are welcome, whether eating or staying the night. There is ample off-road parking at the side of the hotel, which has a little garden with picnic benches.

from the roof of the keep, walk round the barrack room looking like it did before World War 1 and see the exhibition of the Schneider air races. A little way to the west is **Lepe**, one of the major embarkation points for the 1944 D-Day invasion. The area at the top of the cliffs at Lepe is now a country park, and there's safe swimming off the beach.

EXBURY
10 miles SE of Lyndhurst off the B3054

Created by Lionel de Rothschild in the 1920s and still run by members of the family, **Exbury Gardens** fully justify the reaction of one visitor, who described them as 'Heaven with the gates open'. The displays of rhododendrons, camellias and azaleas are renowned the world over, and the 200-acre grounds are a delight to visit in spring, summer or autumn, with May perhaps the best time of all. Many varieties of the Exbury specialities are on sale in the plant centre, where there's also a gift shop, tea room and restaurant.

Exbury's **Church of St Catherine** is best known for its moving, lifelike bronze memorial to two brothers who were killed in action in World War 1. The work was commissioned by the brothers' parents and executed by Cecil Thomas, a gifted young sculptor who was a friend of the brothers. The area around Exbury and Lepe is featured in Nevil Shute's sad story *Requiem for a Wren*, which describes the preparations made in the New Forest for the D-Day landings. Shute himself was an aero-engineer as well as a writer, and for a time worked here on a top-secret pilotless plane.

BUCKLER'S HARD
10 miles SE of Lyndhurst off the B3056

Across the river from Exbury, Buckler's Hard is a popular spot for berthing yachts and cruisers and has a long and distinguished history of shipbuilding. Many fighting ships were built here, including one of London's favourites, *HMS Agamemnon*, which saw service at both Copenhagen and Trafalgar. It was a ship Nelson loved in spite of the fact that it was while he was in command, in a battle off Corsica, that he lost an eye. The village was created by the 2nd Duke of Montagu in the early 1700s for the main purpose of receiving and refining sugar from his estates in the West Indies. His grand plans involved the building of a number of broad streets but in fact only one was ever constructed, grass-verged and running down to the water's edge.

One of its buildings is now a Maritime Museum which tells the story of Buckler's Hard from the earliest sugar cane days.

Buckler's Hard

Displays include models of ships, among them *Victory, Agamemnon* and the yacht *Bluebottle*, which Prince Philip raced with success. A special display recounts the exploits of Sir Francis Chichester, who sailed round the world in *Gypsy Moth* from his home port of Bucklers Hard.

A lovely riverside walk passes through **Bailey's Hard**, a former brickworks where the first naval vessel built on the river was completed in 1698. Henry Adams, the most distinguished of a family of shipbuilders, lived in the village in what is now the Master Builders Hotel. In the summer, half-hour cruises on *Swiftsure* depart from the pier at Buckler's Hard.

BROCKENHURST
3 miles S of Lyndhurst on the A35

A large village in a lovely setting in the heart of the New Forest. Forest ponies are frequent visitors to the main street and the village green (they naturally have right of way!). The **Church of St Nicholas** has a vast graveyard with a yew tree that is probably the oldest tree in the whole region. In the graveyard lie many soldiers, many of them from New Zealand, who had died of their injuries in a nearby military hospital. But the best known grave is that of Harry Mills, known as "Brusher Mills", who brushed the New Forest cricket pitch and followed the occupation of snake-catcher (see below). His headstone states that 'his pursuit and the primitive way in which he lived caused him to be an object of interest to many'. The annual **New Forest Show** takes place in New Park, a little way north of the village.

LYMINGTON

An ancient seaport and market town, Lymington was once a major manufacturer of salt, with hundreds of salt pans between the quay and the tip of the promontory at Hurst Castle. **St Barbe Museum**, in New Street, tells the story of the area between the New Forest and the Solent, with special reference to the salt industry (salt was made here beside the sea for hundreds of years), boatbuilding, smuggling and the area at war. There is also a changing exhibition of the work of artists both local and world-renowned - the gallery has in the past hosted works by artists as diverse as David Hockney and Goya. The broad High Street leading up from the quay is a hive of activity on Saturday, when the market established in the 13th century is held. The Isle of Wight ferry runs from Walhampton, just outside Lymington, where a notable building is the Neale Obelisk, a memorial to Admiral Neale erected in 1840.

At **Hordle**, just north of the A337 between Lymington and New Milton, **Apple Court** is a delightful garden with an important collection of hostas.

New Forest Pony Round-up

THE CHEQUERS

Ridgeway Lane, Lower Woodside, Lymington, Hampshire SO41 8AH
Tel: 01590 673415 Fax: 01590 679177
e-mail: enquiries@chequersinn.com website: www.chequersinn.com

A former counting house from the days of the thriving local salt industry is now a delightful country pub and restaurant run by Simon Thoyts. Low beamed ceilings and small-paned windows are clues to the 16th century origins of the building, and the bar area has lots of intimate little nooks and crannies as well as plenty of room to lift a glass of real ale.

There are also discreet alcoves in the panelled restaurant section, where chef Sara produces a fine selection of dishes to suit all tastes and appetites: mushrooms à la grecque, moules marinière, fresh fish from local suppliers, chargrilled steaks, pork with chilli, coriander and lime. There's also a good range of bar snacks, from garlic bread with cheese and prawns to burgers, scampi, lasagne and Thai curry, and barbecues are held on the front patio at weekends - weather permitting.

A woodburning stove keeps things cosy in winter, and when the sun shines, tables and chairs are set out in the walled garden. This is sailing territory, and yachtsmen are usually very much in evidence. Simon's pride and joy is a signed photograph of the New Zealand crew who won the Americas Cup a few years ago.

The nautical presence could explain the fact that Mount Gay rum is one of the most popular orders at the bar - Mount Gay promotional nights are always very well attended.

Sailing is by no means the only activity in the area. There are some lovely scenic walks, and Pennington Marshes, designated an area of Special Scientific Interest, is a magnet for bird-watchers. The historic small port of Lymington is well worth exploring on foot, and the pub, on the southern edge of town, is close to Adam & Eve Creek, Moses Dock and the sea wall. A breezy interlude can be enjoyed by taking a trip on the ferry to the Isle of Wight. To find the pub take the A337 towards New Milton. After half a mile turn left at the roundabout by the White Hart pub into Ridgeway Lane. The Chequers is three-quarters of a mile along the lane.

THE HILLSMAN HOUSE

Milford Road, Lymington, Hampshire SO41 8DP
Tel: 01590 674737
e-mail: caroline@hillsman-house.co.uk website: www.newforest.demon.co.uk/hillsman.htm

Caroline Tidbury owns and runs a Bed & Breakfast establishment with unique style and character two minutes drive from the centre of Lymington. **The Hillsman House**, built in 1925, sits in an acre and a half of grounds that provide a quiet, attractive setting for a stay at any time of the year. The outstanding feature of the exterior of the house is a Deep South-style veranda that was actually imported from his homeland by an American owner of the house. Bed & Breakfast accommodation is provided in four

upstairs bedrooms, each with its own personal style and all with full en suite facilities. Mornings get under way with a hearty breakfast, and there are numerous pubs and restaurants in the locality for lunch and dinner. To reach Hillsman House from Lymington take the A337 in the direction of Christchurch. The house is on the brow of a hill a little way beyond the parade of shops at Pennington. Lymington is a delightful place to visit, with plenty to see and do, and a bustling market on Saturdays. Scenic walks and nature reserves are other attractions, and the Isle of Wight is only 30 breezy minutes away on the ferry.

HARPER'S BAR-CAFÉ

Lymington Yacht Haven,
Kings Saltern Road, Lymington,
Hampshire SO41 3QD
Tel: 01590 679971
e-mail: harpersbar@enterprise.net

Without actually taking to the water, this is about as close as you'll get to being a sailor. Frank Hardman opened **Harper's Bar-Café** in March 1997 and has a non-stop success in the four years since. The premises are located right on the quayside within Lymington Yacht Haven, and the floor-to-ceiling windows permit unsurpassed views of the marina and the Solent beyond.

The bar has an on licence, so visitors can pop in just for a drink and a chat, or a quiet contemplation of the beautiful yachts and cruisers on show. But this is really a place to linger longer, as the food is delicious. Open seven days a week, and from 9 o'clock in the morning in the summer, the restaurant section (non-smoking) offers a fine variety of dishes, with real ales and a good selection of wines to accompany. Many of the regulars don't have to think twice before plumping for the mussels, which are the main speciality - steamed in white wine with onions, garlic and a dash of cream. Other popular items on a typical evening menu could include seared tuna, salmon steak, chicken cordon bleu, steaks and mushroom stroganoff. Children are welcome. Booking is essential at the weekend.

THE TOLLHOUSE INN

167 Southampton Road, Buckland, Lymington,
Hampshire SO41 9HA
Tel: 01590 672142

On the northern edge of the bustling yachting town of
Lymington, the **Tollhouse Inn** presents a cheerful white-
painted and red-tiled face to the world by the main A337
road to Southampton. It dates back as far as 1795, and
the bars have traditional charm in abundance. The Inn,
which is run by leaseholders Ivan and Sally Frend, is
open lunchtime and evening Monday to Thursday and all day Friday, Saturday and Sunday. Real ales
from Ringwood and HSB are among the beers served, and traditional pub dishes and fish specialities
can be enjoyed lunchtime and evening anywhere inside the Inn or outside on balmy summer days.
There are special value-for-money deals Monday to Friday lunchtimes; booking is recommended Friday
and Saturday night and Sunday lunchtime. The Tollhouse welcomes visitors not only for a drink and
a meal but for an overnight stop, too. Three guest bedrooms are available all year round, all en suite,

with tv and tea-makers; one of the rooms is a large family
room on the ground floor. There's plenty of off-road parking,
and the Inn has a spacious beer garden and a children's play
area. Notable internal features include some very ornate
woodwork in the beams and ceilings and a large fireplace in
the lounge bar surmounted by a canopy adorned with 15
painted crowns. The Crown was an early name of the pub;
it was later called the Monkey House when the landlord of
the time used to keep monkeys which he trained to steal
things from customers. It then reverted to The Crown, and
has been The Tollhouse for the last ten years.

FLEUR DE LYS

Pilley Street, Pilley, Nr Brockenhurst,
Hampshire SO41 5QB
Tel: 01590 672158

Two lovely thatched cottages with a history
going back 900 years were combined many
centuries ago into the **Fleur de Lys**, one of
the most delightful and photogenic public
houses in the whole county. The white-
painted frontage with its marvellous thatch
topping promises much, and the interior
does not disappoint. Low beamed ceilings,
open fires and a collection of brass and
copper ornaments add up to a setting of
great character and warmth throughout the public areas, which include a children's bar and a non-
smoking bar. Occupying pride of place on one of the walls is a framed, handwritten list of all the pub's
landlords from 1498, to which the name of the present incumbent, Neil Rogers, was added in 1999.

Neil and his wife Lolly, both with many years experience in the licensed trade, keep their customers
very well fed with an exceptional choice of freshly prepared, home-cooked food, from lunchtime
snacks and light bites to the full menu and the daily specials chalked up on the blackboard. Typical
mouthwatering main courses run from super trout fishcakes served on a bed of creamy spinach to
gammon with parsley sauce, long-roasted shoulder of lamb and a scrumptious steak, kidney and
Guinness pie. Booking is advisable, especially at weekends. The fine food is complemented by a
carefully selected wine list, and beer-lovers have a choice of real ales, including local brews. Families
are made very welcome, and there's a children's play area in the garden. Neil and Lolly organise
regular theme nights and quiz nights, and their pub is a popular venue for functions and special
occasions.

THE RED LION

Boldre, Nr. Lymington, Hampshire SO41 8NE
Tel: 01590 673177 Fax: 01590 676403

New tenants Karen and Vince Kernick are maintaining the reputation of the **Red Lion** as one of the very best dining pubs in the whole of Hampshire. Discerning regulars and delighted first-timers are captivated by the highly desirable combination of a quiet, civilised ambience and superb food served with style and panache. The pub dates from the 15th century and was originally two separate cottages and a stable.

There are three bar areas, the Stable Bar with horsy knick-knacks, the Hall Bar with its feature of an old black leaded kitchen range and the Middle Room, with an unusual decor of chamberpots hanging from the beams. Roaring log fires keep the pub cosy in winter, while in summer the lovely floral patio garden comes into its own. There's ample off-road parking.

The French chef (here 4 years) and a local lady (who likes the place so much that she's been here for 20 years!) produce a really splendid selection of dishes to appeal to both traditional and more adventurous tastes. Flying the traditional flag are the likes of scampi, lasagne, liver & bacon and steak & kidney pie made properly with shortcrust pastry, while among the less familiar choices might be pan-fried pigeon breast with a cranberry sauce or grilled bass fillet served with a vegetable stir-fry, drizzled with a honey balsamic sauce. Home-made sweets such as lime tart or whisky bread-and-butter pudding keep the enjoyment level high right to the end.

Well-kept real ales and a varied wine list (lots by the glass, and it's nice to see champagne available in halves) complement the outstanding food at this fine old pub, where Karen, Vince and their three Jack Russells can look forward to many years of success.

AROUND LYMINGTON

BOLDRE
2 miles N of Lymington off the A337

Boldre is a pretty little village on the River Lymington, with a charming square-towered 13th century church. 'The village is here, there and everywhere', wrote Arthur Mee in the 1930s, describing the agglomeration of hamlets - Pilley, Portmore and Sandy Dow - that make up the parish of Boldre. Mee approved of the church and also praised an 18th century rector, the Rev William Gilpin, who found fame with his books describing his travels round Britain. After the Second World War, the church at Boldre became a shrine to *HMS Hood*, sunk by the *Bismarck* in 1941 with the loss of 1,400 lives. A service in memory of the victims is held every year. Figures remembered by memorials in the church include the Rev Gilpin, John Kempe, a 17th century MP for Lymington and Richard Johnson, a vicar who was on the first sailing of convicts to Botany Bay in 1788 and who built the first church in Australia. The interior of the church has been changed very little down the centuries, one exception being some modern windows designed by Alan Younger. In School Lane, **Spinners** is a charming, informal woodland garden with a national collection of trilliums.

SWAY
3 miles N of Lymington off the A337

This rural village and the surrounding countryside were the setting for much of Captain Marryatt's *Children of the New Forest*, an exciting tale set in the time of the Civil War and written a year before Marryatt died in 1848. In Station Road, **Artsway** is a visual arts centre that was originally a coach house; the site contains a garden and a gallery. South of the village

BASHLEY MANOR TEA ROOMS
at Sammy Millers Motorcycle Museum, Bashley Cross Roads, New Milton, Hampshire BH25 5SZ
Tel: 01425 610777 Fax: 01425 619696

Bashley Manor Tea Rooms are housed in a converted farmhouse in a complex that also includes Sammy Millers Motorcycle Museum (see above) and a number of craft and gift shops. The tea rooms are owned and run by Barry Coakley, who has been here for four years and does almost all the food preparation and cooking. Open seven days a week from

10am to 4pm, the tea rooms offer a good range of snacks to enjoy either inside under the beams at one of the neat little round tables, or, if the weather allows, outside at a picnic bench on the paved courtyard. The menu includes granary bread sandwiches plain or toasted, soup, salads, jacket potatoes and hot and cold snacks, and there's a traditional Sunday lunch for which bookings are essential. For the sweeter tooth, a selection of cakes and pastries is on tempting display at the counter, and for a real treat the cream tea, with scones, clotted cream, butter, strawberry preserve and a pot of tea, is a must - but that should be instead of, not in addition to the fruit pies and sundae specials! The room is available in the evenings for special occasions, when it has a table licence. All in all, a splendid tea room in a splendid setting.

is a famous 220ft folly called **Peterson's Tower**. This curiosity was built by a retired judge, Andrew Peterson, in honour of his late wife and as proof of the efficacy of concrete. The tower was originally topped by a light that could be seen for many miles, but it was removed on the orders of Trinity House as a potential source of confusion to shipping. The judge's ashes were buried at the base of his folly but were later moved to be next to his wife in the churchyard at Sway.

MILFORD-ON-SEA
5 miles SW of Lymington on the B3058

An unspoilt resort village with a parish church dating from the 13th century. A shingle spit extends a mile and a half from Milford, and at the end, less than a mile from the Isle of Wight, stands **Hurst Castle**, another in the chain of coastal fortresses built by Henry Vlll. Charles 1 was imprisoned here before being taken to London for his trial and execution. The castle was modernised during the Napoleonic Wars and again in the 1860s, when the massive armoured wings were added. Two of the huge guns installed in the 1870s can still be seen. The castle was used as a garrison during World War ll and is now in the care of English Heritage. Access is either along the beach or by ferry from Keyhaven. Between Milford and Everton are **Braxton Gardens** and Everton Grange Lake, where visitors can tour the walled garden with its beautiful roses, see the knot garden planted with germander and cotton lavender, fish in the lake or buy something in the plant centre or farm shop.

NEW MILTON
4 miles W of Lymington on the A337

A lively little town with a superb stretch of coastline minutes away at Barton-on-Sea. The best-known landmark in the

COTTAGE B&B AT APPLEDORE

Holmsley Road, Wootton,
New Milton, Hampshire BH25 5TR
Tel: 01425 629506

Visitors to the New Forest will find the warmest of welcomes and a relaxed, friendly atmosphere at Mariette and Trevor Jelley's **Cottage** Bed & Breakfast. Beautifully restored throughout, the cottage stands in two acres of quiet, secluded grounds, with chestnut and beech trees lining the drive that leads up to the house and a large garden at the back.

The three bedrooms at Appledore are a sheer delight, combining great charm with abundant comfort. The Thai Room features Thai pictures and craft items gathered from the owners' ventures to Thailand; the Forest Room is done out in greens and autumnal shades; and the Old English Room is in traditional cottage style. All three rooms are appointed and fitted to a very high standard, with plentiful towels and toiletries in the en suite bath or shower rooms, televisions and a thoughtfully provided tray including home-baked biscuits. An excellent breakfast, with free-range eggs from Mariette's 'girls', is served in the conservatory overlooking the garden.

Guests can walk straight out of the cottage and into the forest to wander through the beautiful sylvan landscape and watch the ponies and deer who are never far away. Local pubs and restaurants provide plenty of choice for lunches and suppers, and amenities in the vicinity include horse riding, mountain biking, sailing, fishing and golf. The village of Wootton lies about three miles north of New Milton on the B3058. The A35 road linking Southampton and Christchurch/Bournemouth is just moments away.

PICKET HILL HOUSE

Picket Hill, Ringwood, Hampshire BH24 3HH
Tel: 01425 476173 Fax: 01425 470022

Norman and Audrey Pocock attract a wide cross-section of guests to **Picket Hill House**, their lovely home just off the A31 on the edge of the New Forest. Much travelled, and with an intimate knowledge of the area, Audrey is dedicated to her horses and also really enjoys entertaining.

Guest accommodation here comprises three very comfortable bedrooms (no smoking) with shower rooms en suite. A large, relaxing lounge with television, games and a wide selection of books is set aside for the use of guests. Audrey is also a very good cook, and breakfast is a real feast, with fresh fruits, high-quality preserves and all the best local produce ensuring a memorable start to the day. For other meals there are many good restaurants and pubs in the vicinity.

The garden of Picket Hill House backs directly on to 15 miles of New Forest heathland, where ponies and deer roam free. The house is a perfect base for a holiday that can be as lazy or as active as you like. In addition to the miles of walks, facilities for water-skiing, windsurfing and sailing on lakes are within easy reach, along with a large number of Forest riding centres. The small market town of Ringwood, only minutes away, has an excellent recreation centre, shops and several buildings of historical interest; close by are the Moors Valley Country Park with its charming narrow-gauge steam railway; and the New Forest Owl Sanctuary, home to the largest collection of owls in Europe.

LITTLE FOREST LODGE

Poulner Hill, Ringwood, Hampshire BH24 3HS
Tel: 01425 478848 Fax: 01425 473564

Two and a half acres of lovely secluded grounds make a perfect setting for **Little Forest Lodge**, which lies off the A31 a couple of miles east of Ringwood. The resident proprietors, Cherry and Simon Brittan, could not be more friendly or welcoming, and the atmosphere throughout is wonderfully relaxing. The hotel has six bedrooms, including three family rooms, all with bath or shower en suite and all enjoying garden views.

The Garden Room can be used as part of the hotel or let on a self-catering basis. Its doors open on to a large fenced area of the garden, so it's the ideal room for guests who want to bring a dog. The grounds are a major feature of the hotel, with expansive lawns, woodland a pond and garden games including croquet and clock golf. Simon is a talented chef, so it comes as no surprise that the food at Little Forest Lodge is first-class. Hearty breakfasts and three-course dinners make use of top local suppliers whenever possible. The table d'hote offers a choice of three dishes for each course, and a typical menu could include asparagus quiche, fillets of trout with lemon and capers, braised local venison, beef casserole in Ringwood ale, and fresh mango mousse. Special diets can be catered for with a little notice, and the excellent food is complemented by a good selection of wines. All meals are served in the panelled dining room. The lounge-bar is a comfortable room with log fires in winter, a well-stocked bar, parlour games and a small library. In summer the patio doors open on to the garden.

With its attractive setting, comfortable accommodation, fine food and happy, relaxed atmosphere, the Lodge is an ideal centre for a holiday or short break to explore the forest, at any time of year - and it's the perfect choice for a really special house party, which Cherry and Simon would be delighted to arrange!

town is the splendid **water tower** of 1900. Late-Victorian providers of water services seem to have enjoyed pretending that their water towers and sewage treatment plants were in fact castles, and the specimen at New Milton is particularly striking. Three storeys high, with a castellated parapet, the octagonal building has tall, narrow windows - ideal for water authority archers to see off attackers disputing their water bills! At Bashley Crossroads, west of New Milton, the **Sammy Miller Museum & Farm Trust** is a mecca for motorcycle enthusiasts, with the finest collection of fully restored machines in Europe. The two galleries house over 200 rare and classic models, and the Rocket Gold Star, the 1958 Velocette LE200, the AJS V4, the 1936 Indian Four, the 1951 497cc McCandless prototype Norton Twin and the streamlined Mondial racer are just a few of the machines on display for the bikers to drool over. Special events are held on selected Sundays in the summer months. The 2001 Calendar includes Triumph Day on 27 May; Velocette Club 8 July; Harley Davidson Riders Club 15 July; BSA Day & Honda UK Riders 5 August; Sammy Miller Bike Jumble 30 September. The events run from 10.30 to 15.00.

The village of **Wootton** lies a couple of miles north of New Milton, with forest to the north and west.

RINGWOOD

Situated on the western edge of the New Forest at a crossing point of the River Avon, Ringwood has been modernised and greatly extended in recent years, but its centre still boasts a number of elegant Georgian houses, both large and small. **Ringwood Meeting House**, built in 1727 and now a museum, is an outstanding example of an early Non-Conformist chapel, complete with the original, rather austere fittings. **Monmouth House** is of much the same period and stands on the site of an earlier building in which the Duke of Monmouth was confined after his unsuccessful attempt to oust James ll. The Duke had been discovered hiding in a ditch just outside the town and despite his pleas for mercy to the King he was beheaded at Tower Hill a few days later. The records at Ringwood's parish church tell of a gardener called Bower who used to drink 16 pints of ale a day - a feat of which William Hague would surely be proud! Ringwood was granted its market charter in 1226, and a lively market is still held every Wednesday. Visitors to Ringwood should take time to look round the Bettles Gallery in Christchurch Road (see panel below).

A few miles west of town and into Dorset stretches the mighty Ringwood Forest, which contains the **Moors Valley**

BETTLES GALLERY

80 Christchurch Road, Ringwood, Hampshire BH24 1DR
Tel: 01425 470410

On the southern edge of town, **Bettles Gallery** is housed in a 300-year-old building with oak beams, low ceilings and an inglenook fireplace. The gallery specialises in British Studio Ceramics and Contemporary Paintings and over the years has built up a first-class reputation for the quality of the work on display. The eight or nine solo or group exhibitions which are held each year attract collectors from far afield. Work from leading potters and promising newcomers is always available and as an added dimension interesting ceramic jewellery and carefully selected paintings, mostly by artists from the South of England with leanings towards impressionistic and the abstract, are also on display.

Country Park and its delightful narrow-gauge steam railway (see chapter 6 for Avon Heath Country Park).

In Crow Lane, at **Crow**, just north of Ringwood, is the **New Forest Owl Sanctuary**, with a vast collection of owls, three flying displays every day, lectures and films. The sanctuary is also home to three pairs of breeding red squirrels. Bruce Berry, the founder of the sanctuary, and his dedicated staff have put hundreds of birds back into the wild, often after treatment in the Hospital Unit, which is totally funded by donations and sponsorship.

AROUND RINGWOOD

BURLEY
3 miles SE of Ringwood off the A31

Great walking, cycling and horse riding around an attractive village high above

FOREST TEA HOUSE & RESTAURANT

Pound Lane, Burley, Nr. Ringwood, Hampshire BH24 4ED
Tel: 01425 402305

Jenny and Christopher Tabb changed direction two years ago when they said goodbye to careers in banking to take over the **Forest Tea House**. Opened in the 1940s, and serving the good people of Burley and the New Forest ever since, this tea house in the classic English tradition is open for breakfast, morning coffee, traditional lunches, all-day snacks and afternoon tea - open 7 days a week all year round.

Cane-backed chairs are set at neat round tables, and a conservatory at the back opens on to a very pleasant cottage garden complete with a gazebo - and sometimes cattle and ponies looking over the garden gate! Jenny is in charge of the cooking, and her home-made delights include scones and a selection of cakes, bread for the ploughman's platters and daily-changing hot lunchtime specials. The grilled panini - crispy on the outside, melting on the inside - are great favourites, as are the afternoon set teas.

Christopher runs two neighbouring enterprises in The Mall, about 100 yards from the tea house. The Burley Fudge Shop sells home-made fudges, Turkish Delight, natural candy, luxury chocolates, sucrose-free fudges, chocolates and Swiss chocolate gifts. Right next door, the Burley Gift Shop has a stock of some 5000 gift items, from Cardew teapots and Russian porcelain to crystal, jewellery and dolls house miniatures (Fudge Shop and Gift Shop Tel: 01425 403513).

RED SHOOT CAMPING PARK

Linwood, Nr. Ringwood, Hampshire BH24 3QT
Tel: 01425 473789 Fax: 01425 471558
e-mail: enquiries@redshoot-campingpark.com
website: www.redshoot-campingpark.com

The **Red Shoot Camping Park**, with space for touring caravans and electric hook-ups available, enjoys a fine setting with direct access to a beautiful part of the New Forest. The site, which is personally supervised by owner Sonya Foulds in partnership with her daughter Jackie and son-in-law Nick, includes a general store, toilet block, laundry room, safe play area and a friendly inn serving excellent real ales.

the Avon that was once a noted centre for smuggling. It also has, down the years, a strong association with witches, and though the last paid-up witch got on her broomstick and high-tailed it to America nearly 50 years ago the town still has some witchcraft shops. Burley is home to New Forest Cider, where cider is still made the old-fashioned way. A mile northwest of Burley is Castle Hill, where traces of an Iron Age fortress can be seen.

FORDINGBRIDGE
7 miles N of Ringwood on the A338

Mentioned in the Domesday Book, the town unsurprisingly takes its name from ford and bridge, and the medieval Great Bridge, upstream from the ford, is a major feature of the town with its seven elegant arches. The bohemian painter Augustus John (1878-1961) loved Fordingbridge and spent much of the last 30 years of his

Augustus John Statue, Fordingbridge

life at Fryern Court, an austere Georgian house just north of the town. Much of the painter's colourful life was the subject of scandal, often on a national scale, but the townspeople were proud of their most famous resident and erected a robust, rugged bronze statue of the painter by a recreation ground near the bridge. The Early English parish church has many fine features and should not be missed on a visit to Fordingbridge. Also well worth a visit is **Branksome China Works**, where visitors can see how the firm, established in 1945, makes its fine porcelain tableware and famous animal studies. They're a sociable crowd here, with an annual carnival and the Fordingbridge Show in July and a grand civic fireworks display on the Saturday nearest Guy Fawkes Day.

Two miles west of Fordingbridge off the B3078 - follow the signposts - is **Alderholt Mill**, a restored working water-powered corn mill standing on Ashford Water, a tributary of the Hampshire Avon. The site includes an arts and crafts shop and a place for the sale of refreshments and baking from the mill's own flour.

North of Fordingbridge on the A338 is the lovely and largely unspoilt 17th century village of **Breamore**, which has a very interesting little church with Saxon windows and other artefacts. Most notable, in the south porch, is a Saxon rood, or crucifixion scene. **Breamore House**, set above the village overlooking the Avon Valley, was built in 1583 and contains some fine paintings, including works of the 17th and 18th century Dutch School and a unique set of 14 Mexican ethnological paintings; superb period furniture in oak, walnut and mahogany; a very rare James 1 carpet and many other items of historical and family interest. The house has been the home of the Hulse family for well over 250 years, having been purchased in the early 18th century by Sir Edward Hulse, Physician in

WOODFALLS INN

The Ridge, Woodfalls, Hampshire SP5 2LN
Tel: 01725 513222 Fax: 01725 513220
e-mail: woodfallsi@aol.com
website: www.woodfallsinn.co.uk

Extrovert Australians Pamela and James Campbell promise 'good food, good friends and good times' at **Woodfalls Inn**, which has been dispensing hospitality since 1870. It started life as a cider house, where locals would come with their pots to have them filled with favourite brew. It became the Bat & Ball when the local cricket ground was relocated alongside in 1932, but reverted to its original name after top-to-bottom refurbishment and an extension of the accommodation.

The ten bedrooms are individually decorated in traditional English style, and each is named after a flower of the forest. All have en suite facilities, television and dial-out telephone, and two of the rooms offer the luxury of four-poster beds. In the public area, a comfortable bar serves a good range of drinks, and there's a delightful residents' lounge with an open fire. Copper and brass ornaments and prints and paintings of local scenes are attractive elements in the stylish decor. The inn fields darts and skittles teams, and live music sessions take place at the weekend. A traditional breakfast is served either in the bedroom or in the conservatory and lunch here or in the bar (a packed lunch can be provided for guests going out and about for the day).

In the evening the choice is alight supper in the bar or a leisurely dinner in the intimate Lover's Restaurant (the nearby village of Lover inspired the romantic name). A fresh, perky salad or a bowl of

mussels will satisfy small appetites, but the kitchen is also well up to preparing a first-class three-course meal. Typical choices on the table d'hote menu might be cauliflower and cumin soup, honey-roast beast of duck with raspberries and a red wine sauce, and roast pork tenderloin with mustard sauce and green beans. To finish, there's an excellent cheeseboard or some super home-made ice creams.

Special occasions are very much part of the service at Woodfalls, and the Forest Suite, with a skittle alley and its own bar, is a popular choice for a party, with plenty of room for 50 or more to have a good time. The inn enjoys an attractive village setting on the B3080, just off the A338 road that links Salisbury (7 miles) and Bournemouth (25 miles). Horse riding (the in has stabling facilities), trekking, cycling and orienteering are among the more vigorous pursuits available nearby, and the championship golf course at Breamore is only two miles away; the same lovely village has a grand manor house with two museums and a marvellous little Saxon church.

Breamore House

Ordinary at the Courts of Queen Anne, George l and George ll. In the grounds of the house, the **Countryside Museum** is a reconstructed Tudor village: a wealth of rural implements and machinery, replicas of a farm worker's cottage, smithy, dairy, brewery, saddler's shop, cobbler's shop, general store, laundry and school. Amenities for visitors include a tea shop and a children's adventure play area. The Museum's Millennium project was the restoration of an extremely rare Bavarian

four-train turret clock of the 16th century. On **Breamore Down** is one of those oddities whose origins and purpose remain something of a mystery: this is a mizmaze, a circular maze cut in the turf down as far as the chalk. Further north can be seen part of Grim's Ditch, built in late-Roman times as a defence against the Saxons.

A short distance east of Breamore, on the B3080, is the village of **Woodfalls**, situated on the border with Wiltshire.

ROCKBOURNE
3 miles NW of Fordingbridge off the B3078

One of the prettiest villages in the region, Rockbourne lies by a gentle stream at the bottom of a valley. An attraction that brings in visitors by the thousand is **Rockbourne Roman Villa**, where excavations of the site, which is set in idyllic countryside, have revealed the remains of the largest known Roman

THE ROSE & THISTLE

Rockbourne, Nr. Fordingbridge, Hampshire SP6 3NL
Tel: 01725 518236
website: www.roseandthistle.co.uk

Dating from the 16th century, the **Rose & Thistle** enjoys a picturesque setting in this downland village reached by taking the A3078 from Fordingbridge to Sandleheath, following the signs to the Rockbourne Roman Villa, then continuing to the other end of the village. The public house itself is as pretty as a picture, with its cob walls and immaculate thatched roof, and the scene within is

delightfully traditional, with flagstone floors, small-paned windows and low-beamed ceilings. Old coach lanterns, hunting horns, brass and copper ornaments and old coloured bottles share the wall space with old prints of village life and cartoons of sports personalities.

Exposed timbers separate the two parts of the restaurant, where the excellence of the cooking attracts a strong and loyal following. The finest quality ingredients, many of them locally sourced, are used as the basis for a range of dishes to suit any palate or purse. The lunchtime and evening menus

are supplemented by numerous daily specials, among which might be devilled kidneys on rice, chicken & mushroom pie and seasonal game. Fish dishes usually feature prominently and many of them are just that little bit different: cod fillet on bubble & squeak with a chive butter sauce; sea bass baked on fennel served with a red pepper sauce. With food this good, it's not surprising that reservations are recommended, especially at the weekend. The owner, Tim Norfolk, a cheerful host and keen-as-mustard sailor, welcomes one and all to his delightful pub, which in summer has the additional appeal of tables and chairs set out on the front lawn.

villa in the area, and visitors can see the superb mosaics, part of the amazing underfloor heating system and the outline of the great villa's 40 rooms (see panel below).

A mile or so beyond the Roman Villa, looking out on to the downs, is the little village of **Whitsbury**, a major centre for the breeding and training of racehorses.

The New Forest is a place of unique beauty, a place where man and nature have always been in harmony. This is the way it will continue if visitors adhere to the few simple rules issued by the authorities. These are based on common sense principles designed to protect the environment; to protect the animals from the humans and the humans from the animals; and to ensure that this remarkable corner of the English countryside remains the special place it was when singled out by William the Conqueror more than nine centuries ago.

ROCKBOURNE ROMAN VILLA

Rockbourne, Fordingbridge, Hampshire SP6 3PG
Tel: 01725 518541

Rockbourne Roman Villa, the largest of its kind in the region, was discovered in 1942 when oyster shells and tiles were found by a farmer in the course of digging out a ferret. A local chartered surveyor and noted antiquarian, the late AT Morley Hewitt, recognised the significance of the finds and devoted 30 years of his life to the villa. Excavations of the site, which is set in idyllic countryside, have revealed superb mosaics, part of the amazing underfloor heating system and the outline of the great villa's 40 rooms. Many of the hundreds of objects unearthed are on display in the site's museum, and souvenirs are for sale in the well-stocked museum shop.

THE CARTWHEEL INN

Whitsbury, Nr. Fordingbridge, Hampshire SP6 3PZ
Tel: 01725 518362 Fax: 01725 518886
e-mail: thecartwheelinn@lineone.net

In a tiny downland hamlet close to Rockbourne Roman Villa, The Cartwheel Inn is well worth seeking out for its food, its ale and its hospitality. Laura and Patrick Lewis own and run this delightful inn with the help of Kerry Bell. A handsome redbrick building, it has an interior of outstanding character, with old beams, rustic furniture, a copper-canopied hearth and assorted bric-a-brac, notably a cartwheel dividing two seating areas in the bar. The inn is open every lunchtime and evening, and real ale fans will find a choice of anything up to six varieties, including the local Ringwood brew. Once a year, on the second weekend in August, the inn holds a Beer Festival, when 30 or more real ales, spit-roasts, a barbecue and live bands create a party atmosphere for three fun-filled days. The

popularity of the Cartwheel as an eating pub is due largely to the fact that Laura and Kerry, who share the cooking, set great store by the freshest seasonal produce from local suppliers on a menu of home-cooked dishes that offers something for everyone. Food is served every session except Monday evening out of season. Tuesday night is fish night, when traditional fish 'n' chips is served between 6 and 9. Booking is strongly advised at the weekend. Families are welcome, and there's a children's play area in the garden. Whitsbury is noted for the breeding and training of racehorses, its most famous equine son being none other than Desert Orchid.

Bournemouth and East Dorset

Within a comparatively small area, East Dorset provides an extraordinary variety of attractions. It contains the county's two largest towns, Bournemouth and Poole (virtually one nowadays), where some of the best beaches in the country can be enjoyed by day and some of the best classical music concerts by night. Across Poole Harbour, the Isle of Purbeck is famous for the marble that has been quarried since Roman times. The Isle of Purbeck's 'capital', the delightful seaside resort of Swanage, is linked by the steam-hauled Swanage Railway to the magnificent ruins of Corfe Castle. Set high on a hill above the

Corfe Castle

charming village of the same name, this is one of the grandest sights in southwest England and should not be missed. Two other historic houses in the area also deserve special mention: Kingston Lacy, which boasts an incomparable collection of 17th century Old Masters, and Cloud's Hill, the austere cottage where the enigmatic World War I hero T E Lawrence (Lawrence of Arabia) spent his short retirement. And no visitor to this part of the county should leave without paying a visit to glorious Wimborne Minster, a triumph of medieval architecture. To the west of Swanage are two of the most spectacular features in the county, the enchanting Lulworth Cove and the soaring limestone arch carved by the sea and known as Durdle Door. Inland, a string of villages along the River Piddle (coyly changed to Puddle by the Victorians) culminates in Tolpuddle,

Bournemouth Beach

honoured in the history of the trades unions as the home of the Tolpuddle Martyrs. Woodland, heathland and valleys offer a beautiful range of scenery; ancient earthworks provide links with pre-history; country parks have been opened where the natural beauty of the land is conserved for public enjoyment; and, as in all the counties of Britain, the churches, some simple, almost cottagy, others among the finest in the land, including St Peter's and St Stephen's in Bournemouth and the wonderful Priory at Christchurch.

BOURNEMOUTH AND EAST DORSET

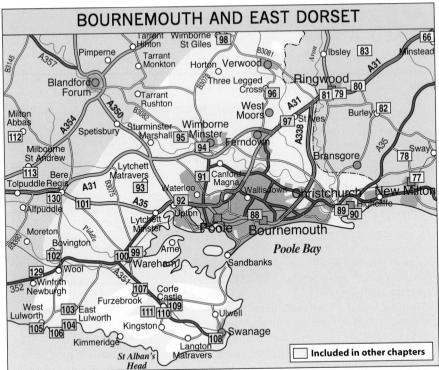

© MAPS IN MINUTES ™ (2000)

Included in other chapters

PLACES TO STAY, EAT, DRINK AND SHOP

BOURNEMOUTH

Tiny village to fully-fledged town and perhaps England's most exotic coastal resort. Two hundred years ago, the tiny village of Bourne was a mere satellite of Poole, a few separate miles to the west. The empty coastline was ideal for smugglers, and Revenue men were posted to patrol the area. One of them, Louis Tregonwell, was so taken by the setting at the head of three deep valleys that he and his wife bought some land, built a house and planted the valleys with the pine trees that today give the town its distinctive appearance. The fresh sea air, with its pine-scented ozone, was considered to be effective in the treatment of tuberculosis, and one of the many who sought relief was the writer Robert Louis Stevenson, who wrote *Kidnapped* while living in the town.

Throughout Victorian times, Bournemouth, as it had become known, grew steadily, and the prosperous new residents added to the beauty of their

Bournemouth Beach

town with wide boulevards, grand parks and handsome public buildings, creating a Garden City by the sea. Bournemouth has many lovely gardens and is a frequent winner of "Britain in Bloom" competitions. The suburb of Boscombe, on the Christchurch side of town, is particularly lucky in this respect, with the **Italian Gardens**, **Boscombe Cliff Gardens** and **Boscombe Chine**. Above the Cliff Gardens is **Shelley Park**, named after Sir Percy Florence Shelley, son of the poet Percy Bysshe Shelley and sometime lord of the manor. The townspeople also built a splendid pier in 1855 which was rebuilt in 1880 to extend to 900 feet with a theatre at the end. The town has several museums, including the **Russell-Cotes Art Gallery &**

Bournemouth Beach and Pier

Russell-Cotes Art Gallery & Museum

Museum, based on the collection of the globe-trotting Sir Merton Russell-Cotes (see panel below). Others include the **Rothesay Museum** with a mainly nautical theme, the **Teddy Bear Museum**; and the **Aviation Museum** at Bournemouth International Airport.

The **Casa Magni Shelley Museum** in Shelley House, where the poet Shelley's son lived for 40 years, is the only one in the world devoted entirely to the life and works of the poet. His heart, saved from his funeral pyre in Italy, is, it is claimed, buried, along with the body of his wife Mary, the author of *Frankenstein*, in a tomb in the marvellous **Church of St Peter**, where in 1898 the ailing former Prime Minister William Gladstone took his last communion. Also buried here is John Keble, founder of the Oxford

Movement. The church, started in 1854 and finished 25 years later, has a 200ft spire and a richly decorated interior by GE Street and the man who did his carving, Thomas Earp. **St Stephen's Church**, built as a memorial to a vicar of St Peter's, is in more restrained style, light and serene, and, as John Betjeman concluded, 'worth a long journey'.

The Thomas Hardy connection is strong throughout Dorset, and Bournemouth is no exception. As Sandbourne, the town is mentioned in *Tess of the d'Urbevilles* and *Jude the Obscure*, and is featured in the lesser-known *Hand of Ethelberta*.

AROUND BOURNEMOUTH

CHRISTCHURCH
5 miles E of Bournemouth on the A35

Like its near neighbour Bournemouth, Christchurch was until 1972 part of Hampshire. At the junction of the Avon and the Stour, it started life as a Saxon village and is today best known for the magnificent **Christchurch Priory**, begun

---

THE RUSSELL-COTES ART GALLERY & MUSEUM

East Cliff, Bournemouth, Dorset BH1 3AA
Tel: 01202 451800 Fax: 01202 451851

Named after the globe-trotting Sir Merton Russell-Cotes, this award-winning art gallery and museum has recently been restored with the help of a generous lottery grant. A wealth of visual treats awaits the visitor, from a world-famous Victorian art collection to Japanese art and artefacts, new displays and contemporary art exhibitions. A new children's gallery called 'Stories, Voices, Journeys' lets children enjoy drawing and exploring the 'feely box' and audio box situated on the walls; Scorch the Dragon has crayons, jigsaw puzzles and funny faces to make. The museum, which has a café, is open Tuesday to Sunday.

Christchurch Beach

harbour and the countryside. Beneath the tower can be seen a memorial to the poet Shelley. All that remains of the Norman castle, situated just to the north of the Priory, is a section of the massive walls of the keep.

The Priory is by no means the only reason for visiting Christchurch. Other places of great interest include the **Red House Museum**, with a rich variety of displays on a local theme (see panel below). Also not to be missed are a Saxon mill and quay and the **Museum of Electricity** (see panel on page 122).

in 1094 by Ranulf Flambard and in continuous use ever since as a place of prayer and worship. Reputedly the longest parish church in England (311ft), it contains many styles of architecture and many treasures. Not to be missed are the vast 14th century stone reredos with a Tree of Jesse in the Great Quire, where the monks would conduct their daily worship, and the beautiful Lady Chapel, with a marvellous stained-glass window depicting episodes in the life of the Blessed Virgin Mary. Above the Lady Chapel is St Michael's Loft Museum with a fascinating exhibition of the history of the Priory. At certain times visitors (but not children under 10) can climb the 176 steps of the 15th century belltower and enjoy splendid views of the town, the

The Guinness Book of Records notes that Christchurch boasts the most modern of all Scheduled Ancient Monuments, a World War II pillbox and anti-tank obstacles.

Along the coast on the eastern edge of town lies the village of **Mudeford**, former haunt of smugglers and scene of a famous battle between smugglers and excisemen in which victory went to the smugglers.

To the south of Christchurch are the ancient ditches called **Double Dykes**, an area which offers great walking and superb views. It was close to the ditches,

---

RED HOUSE MUSEUM & GARDENS

Quay Road, Christchurch, Dorset BH23 1BU
Tel: 01202 482860 Fax: 01202 481924

A charming Georgian building filled with a rich variety of displays and objects, all with a local theme. Topics covered include local and natural history, archaeology, costumes and regularly changing temporary exhibitions. Another attraction is a fine old English garden with herbaceous borders and old-fashioned roses, a gift shop and a coffee shop. Open Tuesday to Saturday, Sunday afternoons and Bank Holidays.

Brownsea Island

HIGHCLIFFE
7 miles W of Bournemouth
on the A337

The most easterly community in the county, with a fine beach and views of the eastern tip of the Isle of Wight. Best known for its castle, built in the first years of the 19th century.

POOLE
5 miles E of Bournemouth
on the A35

Now more or less a continuation westward of

but of course on level ground, that Britain's first air show took place in 1910, attended by the great names of early aviation, including Wilbur Wright, Blériot and the Hon Charles Rolls. The last-named, the Rolls of Rolls-Royce, was killed when his plane crashed at this event.

Bournemouth, just as Christchurch is to the east, Poole was once the largest settlement in Dorset and is a pleasant, bustling port. Its huge natural harbour, actually a drowned river valley, has a shoreline of some 50 miles (the longest after Sydney), and its history goes back

THE MUSEUM OF ELECTRICITY.
The Old Power Station, Bargates, Christchurch, Dorset BH23 1QE
Tel: 01202 480467 Fax: 01202 480468

Only five minutes walk from the centre of Christchurch, the Museum of Electricity is a must for all ages. Everything here is electric, from one of the old Bournemouth trams to a pair of boot warmers!

There really is something to interest everyone, and as far as possible the exhibits are hands-on and the demonstrations for children tie in with the national curriculum. Car parking is free on site and there are even picnic tables.

TARVEN
Corfe Lodge Road, Broadstone, Dorset BH18 9NF
Tel: 01202 694338

Marion Browning offers Bed & Breakfast accommodation, with the option of a splendid three-course dinner, in her large Tudor-style house set in beautiful grounds among woods. There are three letting bedrooms - a large family room and two singles, up to a maximum of 4 guests at any one time. They share a bathroom and a shower room, both with toilets. Meal times are arranged to suit guests, including an early breakfast for passengers catching the ferry at Poole. No smoking in the house.

beyond Roman times. A 33ft boat hollowed out from an oak tree and dating back to around 295BC, was discovered off **Brownsea Island**, largest of the several islands in the harbour. Reached by a ferry from the quay in Poole, the Island has quiet beaches with quiet bathing as well as scenic walks in 500 acres of heath and woodland that are one of the few refuges of the red squirrel. Here, in 1907, General Robert Baden-Powell carried out an experiment to test his idea of teaching boys from all social classes the scouting skills he himself had refined during the Boer Wars. The experiment, involving 20 boys, was a great success, and in 1908 Baden-Powell put his thoughts into words by writing *Scouting for Boys* and into deeds

Brownsea Island from Sandbanks

by founding the Boy Scout movement. Two years later he and his wife founded the Girl Guides. A stone at the western end of Brownsea commemorates this historic first camp. Two thousand years of local history are displayed in Poole's **Waterfront Museum**, set in an 18th century warehouse and the adjoining medieval town cellars on the Quay. Also on the Quay is the **Poole Aquarium & Serpentarium**, where major exhibits include sharks, piranhas and coral reefs, pythons and rattlesnakes, crocodiles and

alligators, tarantulas, toads and creepie-crawlies - and one of the largest OO gauge model railway layouts in the country with 3,000 feet of track. The third major attraction on the Quay is **Poole Pottery**, an expanding complex where the famous red tiles for the London Underground were made.

SANDBANKS
2 miles SE of Poole on the B3369

This is the spit of land which, with Studland reaching out opposite, almost cuts off the harbour from the sea. Close to the road that runs along to Sandbanks, by the steep chine of Canford Cliffs, is one of the finest gardens in Europe. **Compton Acres** is the realisation of the dream of Thomas William Simpson, who in 1920 spent the equivalent of £10 million in today's money in creating independent themed gardens separated by paths, steps, rock walls and terraces. The visitor will find delightful features and surprises at every turn, with quiet corners, waterfalls, lakes, streams, sculptures and original artefacts from around the world. There are ten gardens in one, ten different worlds, from Roman and Old English to Canadian, Indian, Japanese and Egyptian. The Garden of Memory, a quiet, secluded little corner of the ten acres, was created in memory of J S Beard, who was the leading figure in the restoration of Compton Acres from decline after World War II.

UPTON
3 miles W of Poole on the A35/A3049

Upton Country Park has formal gardens, picnic tables, bird-watching hides and a handsome early 19th century manor house (see panel on page 124).

UPTON HOUSE

Upton Country Park, Upton,
Poole, Dorset BH17 7BJ
Tel: 01202 262748 Fax: 01202 262749
e-mail: s.booth@poole.gov.uk
website: www.poole.gov.uk

On the south side of the A35/A3049 a short drive west of Poole, **Upton Country Park** consists of 100 acres of parkland, gardens and meadows on the northern shore of Poole Harbour.

Its focal point is the house, built in 1818 by Christopher Spurrier, son of a wealthy merchant from Poole. Notable features inside the Grade II listed building include fine art nouveau wallpapers, elaborate plaster ceiling work and, in the drawing room, a chimney piece of Italian statuary marble originally carved for a palace of the Emperor Napoleon I. The house is an ideal setting for conferences, meetings and exhibitions, and since 1998 has been a popular venue for wedding ceremonies. Public tours of the ground-floor rooms take place most Sunday afternoons.

The formal gardens present a very colourful picture throughout the year, and the Grove woodland features a trail that provides children with the opportunity to learn about the animals whose home is among the semi-natural beech, oak and ash woodland. Marking the boundary of the park, the shoreline

gives visitors the chance to spot little egrets, herons and gulls from the north-east shoreline, the bird hide or the bird screen. The shoreline trail introduces visitors to the plant and bird life at this Site of Special Scientific Interest (SSSI). To the south of the house are the walled garden, a garden centre and the Romano-British farmstead, the county's first reconstruction using basic techniques to give a particularly authentic insight into ancient agricultural methods.

The Countryside Heritage Centre, once the estate's stable block, was converted into an information point in 1987. Here, visitors can follow the history of the estate from Roman times and the Doomsday Book to the time it passed into the care of the Borough of Poole (1957) right up to the present day.

'Friends of Upton County Park' is a charitable body established in 1976 to assist in the running of the Park. Today they organise special events such as the Wessex Teddy Bear Fair and also run the garden centre and a refreshment kiosk. Various pedestrian and cycle paths cross the Park, and National Cycle Network route 25 is planned to be routed through the Park.

LYTCHETT MINSTER
4 miles W of Poole on the A35

A pretty village with a church with the unusual dedication of **St Peter ad Vincula**. In the churchyard is the grave of the great explorer Sir Francis Younghusband (1863-1942), the first European to cross the Gobi Desert and the first white man to see the northern slopes of the mountain now called K2, second in height only to Everest. He made several expeditions to Tibet, and his grave has a unique headstone with a relief carving of the Potala Palace in Lhasa.

LYTCHETT MATRAVERS
5 miles NW of Poole on the A350

The largest of the three Lytchetts (the third is Lytchett Heath), this one gained its name from a family of Norman lords. The interesting village church dates from the 16th century.

WIMBORNE

The A31 by-passes this fine old market town set among meadows beside the Rivers Stour and Allen. The glory of the town is **Wimborne Minster**, a distinctive building of multi-coloured stone boasting some of the finest Norman architecture in the county. The foundation goes back to about 705AD, when Cuthburga, sister of the king of the West Saxons, founded a nunnery which later was home to as many as 500 nuns. The nunnery was destroyed by the Danes in 1013, but a notable survivor from Saxon times is a marvellous oak chest, still to be seen in the Minster. Margaret Beaufort, mother of Henry VII, founded a school at the Minster in 1497, and one of the first lending libraries was established there in 1686. This library - the books are chained - includes some priceless gems, among them three Breeches Bibles and a book of

HOLLY HEDGE FARM

Bulbury Lane, Lytchett Matravers, Poole, Dorset BH16 6EP
Tel: 01929 459688

Ceri and Dave Davies' **Holly Hedge Farm** is a handsome redbrick house built in 1892 and set in 11 acres of woods and grassland with a lake. Bed & Breakfast accommodation, available all year round, comprises a single room, a twin and two double/family rooms, all centrally heated, with en suite shower, television, radio-alarm and tea/coffee makers. The house stands next to Bulbury Woods Golf Course and is a 15-minute drive from the Purbecks and the coast.

MOOR ALLERTON

Holtwood, Wimborne Minster, Dorset BH21 7DU
Tel/Fax: 01258 840845 e-mail: martinoliver@talk21.com

Tucked away down a quiet lane in glorious countryside, Martin and Ann Oliver's smart modern house, with distinctive red-tiled roof and dormer windows, is the perfect base for a touring holiday. Bed & Breakfast accommodation comprises a ground-floor double room with private bathroom and a twin room and large single upstairs that share a family bathroom. Rooms have TVs, tea-makers and lovely views. A mammoth breakfast will last most of the day!

advice to priests, *Regimen Animarum* or Direction of Souls, written on vellum in the 14th century. Other notable treasures here are the 14th century astronomical clock and the Quarter Jack, a life-size figure of a grenadier from the Napoleonic Wars who strikes his bells every quarter hour of the day and night. Close by the Minster, in the High Street, is the **Priest's House**, a 16th century town house with many original architectural features, restored rooms, a museum of East Dorset life and a gallery with hands-on activities. Behind the house is a charming walled garden. In King Street is **Wimborne Model Town and Gardens**, a tenth-scale model of the town as it was in the 1950s, accurate down to the miniature working railway and the goods in the windows of the little shops. Wimborne also has plenty of big shops, as well as the famous covered Grand Bazaar and Market: market days are Friday, Saturday morning, Sunday and Bank Holiday Monday.

KINGSTON LACY HOUSE

Wimborne, Dorset BH21 4EA
Tel: 01202 883402 Fax: 01202 882402
website: www.nationaltrust.org.uk

The 3,440 hectare Kingston Lacy estate was bequeathed in 1981 to the National Trust, along with 3,000 hectares on the Isle of Purbeck, in the will of Ralph Bankes. Much of the land has been declared inalienable, meaning that it can never be sold, developed or mortgaged. Kingston Lacy House, home of the Bankes family for over 300 years, is a beautiful 17th century building with an outstanding collection of Old Masters, Egyptian artefacts and the amazing Spanish room with gilded leather hanging on the walls. All four floors are

AROUND WIMBORNE

The area around Wimborne has much to interest the visitor. At **Hampreston**, a short distance to the east, are **Knoll's Garden & Nursery**, delightfully informal and essentially English gardens where planting began 30 years ago with a collection of rhododendrons and Australasian plants. The nursery predates the gardens and offers for sale to the public an ever-increasing variety of plants, including the national collections of Deciduous Ceanothus and Phygelius. A little further east are the 30 acres fascinating acres that make up **Stapehill**, a 19th century Cistercian nunnery that is now a craft centre, countryside museum and farm with beautiful gardens, woodland walks, coffee shop, adventure playground and much more.

A mile west of Wimborne is one of the county's most visited attractions, the

open to visitors, and the Edwardian laundry gives a fascinating insight into life below stairs 100 years ago. The garden has two formal areas, the parterre and the sunken garden. The Victorian Fernery supports over 25 types of fern, the Blindwalk contains flowering shrubs and groundcover plants, and the 18th century Lime Avenue leads to Nursery Wood, where specimen trees, rhododendrons, azaleas and camellias grow. The landscaped park covers 250 acres and is home to the North Devon herd of cattle. There are lovely walks through the woodland areas, some suitable for wheelchairs, and Coneygar Copse has three different areas of woodland play equipment.

Kingston Lacy

National Trust's **Kingston Lacy**, an estate with countryside rich in history and wildlife. Kingston Lacy House is a beautiful 17th century building designed by Roger Pratt for the Bankes family; it features an outstanding collection of paintings, Egyptian artefacts and the amazing Spanish Room, its walls hung with gilded leather (see panel opposite).

The estate surrounding Kingston Lacy is dominated by the Iron Age hill fort of **Badbury Rings**, three concentric rings of banks and ditches cut and raised by the Celtic tribe of Durotriges. A walk round the site passes ancient defences and burial mounds. The River Stour runs through the estate past the 18th century White Mill, and other places on the estate include the Beech Avenue planted by William John Bankes in 1835, Shapwick village and a number of waymarked walks, one of them accessible by visitors in wheelchairs. The estate villages of Cowgrove and Pamphill contain many thatched houses and cottages which have been preserved unspoilt down the years. One of the newer buildings is St Stephen's Church, designed in 1907 in a style influenced by the Arts and Crafts Movement.

HORTON
6 miles N of Wimborne off the B3078

Horton is the site of an important monastery built in the 10th century, some parts of which were later incorporated into the parish church. Just outside Horton stands a curiosity in the tall shape of **Horton Tower**, built in 1762 as a lookout tower for deer-hunters.

THREE LEGGED CROSS
6 miles NE of Wimborne off the B3072

A curiously named village just below Ringwood Forest, close to the border with Hampshire.

ST IVES
6 miles NE of Wimborne on the A31

Close to the village of St Ives lies the Avon

Kingston Lacy Church

WOOLSBRIDGE MANOR FARM CARAVAN PARK

Three Legged Cross, Wimborne Minster, Dorset BH21 6RA
Tel: 01202 826369 Fax: 01202 813172

In a small village with shops, a petrol station and two public houses, **Woolsbridge Manor Farm Caravan Park** is part of a 100-acre farm in a quiet, sheltered setting. Linda Johnson and her family offer all the expected modern facilities, including toilets with wheelchair access, a baby-changing area and a laundry room. Bread, milk, general goods and newspapers may be bought in the shop on site, and children can be left safely in a play area with slides, a sandpit, a tree house and various other things to climb or explore. Many of the pitches have electrical hook-up facilities - these should be booked well in advance in high season. Dogs are permitted as long as they are kept on leads.

Ringwood Forest and Moor Valley Country Park are both accessible without recourse to roads - ideal for cycling or walking - and private fishing and birdwatching are on hand next to the site. Within a short drive are the picturesque delights of the New Forest and the historic towns of Wimborne and Ringwood, and the amenities of a family seaside resort are less than 10 miles away, at Bournemouth.

AVON HEATH COUNTRY PARK

Birch Road, St Ives, Ringwood, Dorset BH24 2DA
Tel/Fax: 01425 478082

Dorset's largest country park offers a unique opportunity to explore some of the county's internationally important heathland and its rare wildlife. There are miles of tracks for walking and cycling, kids' fun trails, activities and playground; regular events are run throughout the year. Easy to find along the A31, North Park has all the facilities for visitors including the Visitor Centre (Tel: 01425 478470), gift shop, café, BBQ hire and toilets (all are wheelchair accessible). Visitors can join in the family fun or explore deeper and experience the tranquillity and wildness of the Park.

THE BULL INN

Wimborne St Giles, Dorset BH21 5NF
Tel: 01725 517284

Join the locals for a chat or perhaps a game of darts in this focal point of village life, which has been owned and run by Mr Sharp for 18 years. **The Bull Inn** has a quiet, pleasant atmosphere, with a log fire to ward off winter chills, and its menu proposes a good choice of home-cooked dishes, with fresh fish a speciality. The River Allen runs by the village, whose green is overlooked by almshouses and a church.

Heath Country Park, the largest in Dorset (see panel opposite).

VERWOOD
8 miles NE of Wimborne on the B3081

One of the county's most alluring family attractions is the **Dorset Heavy Horse & Animal Centre** just north of the village. Open daily from 10.00 to 17.00, it is home to Shires, Clydesdales, Percherons, Suffolks and Ardennes, along with miniature ponies and donkeys, llamas, pygmy goats and kune kune pigs. Also on the site are a working Arabian stud, a display of harness and traditional farm implements, trailer rides, pets corner, café and play area for children.

WIMBORNE ST GILES
10 miles N of Wimborne off the B3078

Wimborne St Giles is a pretty village on the River Allen, with a church that was rebuilt after a fire by the distinguished architect Sir Ninian Comper. The **Church of St Giles** contains stained glass by Comper and some marvellous monuments, notably to Sir Anthony Ashley and to the 7th Earl of Shaftesbury (who is even more memorably honoured by the statue of Eros in Piccadilly Circus).

GUSSAGE ST ANDREW
10 miles N of Wimborne off the B3078

The villages of the picturesque Gussage Valley include Gussage St Andrew, whose

12th century flint church has an exceedingly rare depiction of the hanging of Judas, Gussage St Michael and Gussage All Saints.

CRANBORNE
12 miles NE of Wimborne on the B3078

A picturesque village in a glorious setting, Cranborne sits on the banks of the River Crane, with a fine church and manor house creating a charming picture of a traditional English village. The large and imposing **Church of St Mary** is notable for its Norman doorway, 13th century nave and exquisite 14th century wall paintings. Cranborne Manor, home of the Cecil family, stands on the site of a royal hunting lodge built by King John for his excursions into Cranborne Chase.

WAREHAM

Situated between the Rivers Frome and Piddle, or Puddle, Wareham is an enchanting little town lying within the earthworks of a 10th century encircling wall. Standing close to an inlet of Poole Harbour, Wareham was an important port until the River Frome clogged its approaches with silt. Then, in 1726, a devastating fire destroyed the town's timber buildings, a disaster which produced the happy result of a rebuilt town centre rich in handsome Georgian

THE RAILWAY TAVERN
Northport, Wareham, Dorset BH20 4AT
Tel: 01929 552006

Next to the railway station, and ten minutes' walk from the town centre, the **Railway Tavern** has very welcoming leaseholders in Ian Littlecott and Tracy Best. Rail travellers drop in for a drink and something to eat, and the locals do the same; they also make sure that the pub plays a major role in the local sports leagues by fielding five teams for darts and two for pool. Sunday is quiz night. The tavern has a large beer garden for sipping in the summer.

stone houses. Wareham's history goes back much further than those days. It was Roman conquerors who laid out its street plan: a stern grid of roads which faithfully follows the points of the compass. Saxons and Normans helped build the **Church of St Mary**, medieval artists covered its walls with devotional paintings of remarkable quality. It was in the grounds surrounding the church that King Edward was buried in 879AD after his stepmother, Queen Elfrida, contrived his murder at Corfe Castle. Elfrida added insult to injury by having the late King buried outside the churchyard, in unhallowed ground. The town **museum** has a section devoted to T E Lawrence, and another period piece is the **Rex Cinema**, restored to its heyday in the golden age of the cinema. The building is Victorian, the auditorium gaslit, and the original antique carbon-arc projectors are still in use.

AROUND WAREHAM

ARNE
4 miles E of Wareham on minor road

At Arne, four miles east of Wareham on a peninsula jutting into Poole Harbour, is a fascinating attraction in the **Vintage End of Pier Amusement Machines and World of Toys**. Here is assembled a fine collection of tin toys, Victorian dolls, musical boxes, dolls houses, rocking horses - thousands of toys of all kinds dating from 1850 to 1970, plus some splendid old penny-in-the-slot, end-of-pier amusement machines, naturally including What the Butler Saw!

BOVINGTON
7 miles W of Bovington off the A352

Bovington Camp, where T E Lawrence served as a private in the Royal Tank Corps, is home to an impressive collection

THE ANGLEBURY HOUSE & RESTAURANT

15-17 North Street, Wareham, Dorset BH20 4AB
Tel: 01929 552988 Fax: 01929 554665

Tony and Jane Spencer, with many years experience in the catering and hospitality business, have a friendly, personal greeting for visitors to historic **Anglebury House**, which stands at the heart of the Saxon walled town of Wareham. The double-fronted building, with its distinctive small-paned windows, is one of the comparatively few that survived the disastrous fire of 1762, and the ambience and decor throughout - beamed ceilings, cosy nooks, old prints and photographs - are in keeping with its age. The seven letting bedrooms, all but one of them with en suite facilities, are quaint and comfortable, with TV and tea-makers. For daytime visitors, Anglebury House has a quintessential coffee shop serving teas, coffees, confections to make

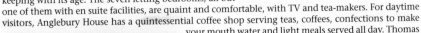

your mouth water and light meals served all day. Thomas Hardy and TE Lawrence (Lawrence of Arabia) were both regular patrons of the coffee shop, and the latter is remembered by a brass plate on the wall above his favourite corner seat. In the Tudor-style restaurant son Andrew offers a choice of à la carte and fixed-price menus featuring a fine variety of dishes to appeal to all tastes and appetites. The town of Wareham is a great place to explore and the Anglebury House is an ideal base for trips to the countryside, the coast and local attractions such as the Bovington Tank Museum, Monkey World and Corfe Castle.

of over 150 tanks and armoured vehicles from 26 countries, starting with Little Willie, Britain's first tank, built in 1915. Besides the static exhibits at the **Tank Museum** there are audio tours, tanks in action displays, armoured vehicle rides and a reconstruction of life under tank siege in the trenches (see panel on page 132).

The Lawrence connection is very strong in the area, notably at **Cloud's Hill**, a tiny redbrick and tiled cottage, austere and isolated, where Aircraftsman T E Shaw lived after retiring from the RAF in 1935. His retirement was brief, as he was killed while riding his motorcycle in a country lane near the cottage (now owned by the National Trust and open for visits in the summer). The life of Lawrence was memorably chronicled in the film *Lawrence of Arabia* starring a young, dashing Peter O'Toole (of whom one wag said that if he had been any prettier the film would have been called *Florence of Arabia*).

MORETON
10 miles W of Wareham off the A352

The funeral of T E Lawrence was held on 21 May 1935 in Moreton parish church and the list of distinguished attendees included the King of Iraq, Winston Churchill, Robert Graves and Siegfried Sassoon. The headstone on his grave was executed by his great friend Eric Kennington. The **Church of St Magnus**

and St Nicholas dates largely from the 1770s, when it was rebuilt by the leading local Frampton family. A German bomb caused considerable damage to the church in 1940, blowing out all the windows. In 1950, by which time the structural damage had been repaired, the artist Lawrence Whistler was commissioned to engrave new windows. His themes ranged from the two patron saints of the church to aerial combat, but the most controversial of the windows, showing the suicide of Judas Iscariot, has never been installed.

Close to the church are **Moreton Gardens**, a tranquil place of woodland, lawns, flower beds, streams and ponds. A plant centre in the gardens has a wide variety of plants for sale. The Gardens were originally the kitchen garden of Moreton House, the Frampton family home. This family had many illustrious members, including Tregonwell, founder of Newmarket racecourse; James, for whom the house was built in the 1740s and who founded the Dorset Yeomanry; and another James, who led the prosecution of the Tolpuddle Martyrs. A well-known landmark on a hill to the south of the village is an obelisk dedicated to James Frampton in 1784.

WOOL
6 miles W of Wareham on the A352

Dorset's Family Attraction of the

WOODLANDS

Hyde, Nr Wareham, Dorset BH20 7NT
Tel: 01929 471239

Mrs Constantinides offers a choice of self-catering accommodation at **Woodlands**, a large period country house about eight miles north of Wareham - take the minor road that leads to Bere Regis and you'll find Woodlands near the East Dorset Golf Club. The Cottage is a converted 400-year-old barn comprising lounge, diner, kitchen, three bedrooms, bathroom and two toilets. The Maisonette, with its own entrance in the north wing of the house itself, has a kitchen-diner, lounge, two bedrooms and a bathroom.

THE TANK MUSEUM

Bovington, Dorset BH20 6JG
Tel: 01929 405096 Fax: 01929 405360
e-mail: info@tankmuseum.co.uk
website: www.tankmuseum.co.uk

The **Tank Museum**, defined by the Government as a Designated Collection, houses the world's finest and most extensive indoor collection of armoured fighting vehicles. It tells the story of tanks and armoured warfare illustrated through scientific and technological developments, woven together with the stirring story of human endeavours on the battlefield.

In 1919 the tanks came back from France and hundreds of them, awaiting scrap, filled the fields around Bovington, where tank training had started in 1916. A few were rescued from the scrapman and fenced off from the rest. The plan was to provide young Tank Corps soldiers with an idea of their heritage and tank designers with historical references. When Rudyard Kipling visited Bovington in 1923 he suggested that a proper tank museum be established, and the museum, its stock much expanded after the Second World War, opened to the public in 1947.

The display of over 150 vehicles has continued to expand ever since, ranging from a unique collection of First World War tanks, starting with Little Willie from 1915 and the nimble Renaults; through to the awesome machines of the Second World War - the Tiger, the Sherman and the T34 - and modern-day battle tanks that saw action in the Gulf. These include the superb Centurion, which was developed over the years from the first version, which appeared in 1945. 'The Trench - Tanks on the Somme 1916' is one of many enthralling exhibitions ('Take a walk from the recruiting office, arrive on a railway platform in France then head straight for the trenches'), and the new TE

Lawrence exhibition is proving a great attraction. Lawrence was called Shaw while serving with the Tank Corps at Bovington in 1922-23. In addition to the 150 vehicles assembled from 26 countries the Museum has displays of medals, uniforms and personal articles.

The library and archive are available for research and there is an education service. A free audio-guided tour of the Museum is available in three languages, and there are regular Vehicle Rides, Tanks in Action displays and School Holiday special events. The Museum has a large model, book and gift shop, fully licensed restaurant, grass picnic area, outdoor play area and ample car and coach parking. Bovington still trains all branches of the Army in tracked vehicle driving and its tank repair workshops are one of the largest employers in the county.

Millennium is the 60-acre **Monkey World**, which lies on the minor road that runs from Wool to Bere Regis. Set up in 1987 to provide a permanent home for abused Spanish beach chimpanzees, the centre has rescued chimps from all over the world and rehabilitated them into social groups in large natural areas. Other primates in residence include orang-utans, gibbons, woolly monkeys, lemurs, macaques and marmosets. In the visitor centre is an education zone describing conservation and rehabilitation, and there are keeper talks throughout the park at set times. Children can test their skills on a 15-stage obstacle course or monkey around in the three outdoor play areas. The centre also has a nursery and adoption area, gift shop and cafeteria. Also between Bere Regis and Wool is **Winfrith Heath**, in the care of the Dorset Wildlife Trust. The 255 acres of heathland

support a large range of plants, animals and birds, including sand lizards, smooth snakes, nightjars and Dartford warblers.

WINFRITH NEWBURGH
7 miles W of Wareham off the A352

This charming little village stands on a minor road that leads to one of the country's best-known beauty spots, **Lulworth Cove**. An almost perfectly circular bay, the Cove is surrounded by towering 440ft cliffs. Over the centuries, the sea has eaten away at a weak point in the limestone, creating in its raging a breathtakingly beautiful scene. A couple of miles inland at East Lulworth, **Lulworth Castle** (English Heritage) looks enormously impressive from a distance, but, close up, the effects become clear of a disastrous fire that destroyed most of it in 1929 (see panel below). In the grounds is

LULWORTH CASTLE

East Lulworth, Wareham, Dorset BH20 5QS
Tel: 01929 400352 Fax: 01929 400563
website: www.lulworth.com

Lulworth Castle was built primarily as a hunting lodge in the first decades of the 17th century and down the years has played host to no fewer than seven monarchs. It was reduced to a virtual ruin by a devastating fire in 1929, but in the 1970s restoration work was begun with the help of English Heritage. The exterior is now exactly as it was before the fire, and visitors can climb the tower to enjoy some spectacular views. A video presentation brings the history of the castle to life,

and interior features including the Weld family, owners of the estate since 1641, a Victorian kitchen, dairy, laundry and wine cellar. There is also a children's activity room.

Lulworth Castle House, the modern home of the Weld family, contains 18th century sculptures as well as portraits and furniture rescued from the castle fire. In the grounds of the castle are a delightful walled garden and a curious circular building dating from 1786. This was the first Roman Catholic Church to be established in Britain since Henry VIII's defiance of the Pope in 1534. Permission to build it was given to Sir Thomas Weld by King George III; the King cautiously added the proviso that Sir Thomas' new place of worship should not offend Anglican sensibilities by looking like a church - so it doesn't! The beautifully restored chapel contains an exhibition of 18th and 19th century vestments, a collection of church silver and a wonderful Seede organ. A short walk from the Castle and Chapel are the animal farm, play area and woodland walk. The old castle stables house the licensed café serving morning coffee, light lunches and cream teas, and the courtyard shop offers a wide range of gift ideas. Special events, including horse trials, country fairs and jousting shows, are held regularly throughout the season. Lulworth Castle Park is open all year Sunday to Friday, Lulworth Castle House on Wednesday afternoons in summer.

THE MILL HOUSE HOTEL

Main Road, Lulworth Cove, West Lulworth,
Dorset BH20 5RQ
Tel: 01929 400404 Fax: 01929 400508
e-mail: dukepayne@hotmail.com
website: http://millhousehotel.tripod.com

The setting, opposite the duck pond and 150 yards from the shore of Lulworth Cove, is one of the many attractive features of Jenny and Julian Payne's friendly, family-run hotel. Originally built as a thatched cottage in the 18th Century, and once owned by Sir Alfred Fripp (surgeon to King GeorgeV) **The Mill House** has been considerably extended over the years, and now offers comfortable bed and breakfast accommodation (evening meals by arrangement) in nine en-suite bedrooms; furnished in a country-house style.

All bedrooms (six double, one twin, and two family rooms) have telephone, television, radio, hospitality trays and well appointed bathrooms. The superior bedroom (regularly used by guests celebrating honeymoons, birthdays and anniversaries) offers private sun balcony and splendid sea views. Four of the double rooms afford views over the duck-pond and the rolling hills which lead to Stair Hole.The residents lounge offers comfortable sofas, big-screen T.V., video, writing material and

magnificent views over the cove and surrounding countryside. The cosy bar leads out on to the garden; a popular spot for a cream tea, or relaxing with a drink on a warm Summer's evening.

Jenny Hen's Tea Room, with indoor seating for up to 50, and garden seating for approximately 40 persons, is open every day for breakfast, morning coffee, light lunches and afternoon teas. The menu includes a variety of home-made cakes including Dorset Apple Cake, home-made soups, crumbles etc. Various local specialities are offered: dressed crab salad platters, crab sandwiches, three types of pasty, smoked trout, hot-smoked mackerel and Dorset Blue Vinney Ploughmans' being just a few. Hot meals are available and vegetarians are well catered for. Customers eating a knife and fork meal can enjoy a glass of wine or beer (many local bottled beers are available). Why not try a delicious Dorset Cream Tea or take home some Dorset Honey. Children under ten are catered for with their very own "Little Chicks" Menu. The Duck Pond Take Away is also open daily in season, offering a wide selection of hot and cold foods, drinks and New Forest Ice-Creams.

WEST DOWN FARM

West Lulworth, Wareham,
Dorset BH20 5RY
Tel/Fax: 01929 400308

In a beautiful, peaceful location down a secluded drive, **West Down Farm** is an ideal base for walking, touring the lovely coast and countryside or simply enjoying a well-earned rest. Sarah Weld has two rooms to let for Bed & Breakfast accommodation, and guests have their own lounge. There are stables in the grounds, so visitors who want to bring a horse can do so!

Lulworth Cove

drawings, when he was working with the architect John Hicks in Dorchester, and during later restoration work. (Thomas Hardy, the son of a master stonemason, was apprenticed to Hicks at the age of 16, and, after a spell in London, he returned to Dorset, where he made money as an architect in Weymouth while looking for publishers for his books; his interest in architecture stayed with him for the rest of his life.)

a curious circular building dating from 1786, the first Roman Catholic church to be established in Britain since Henry VIII's defiance of the Pope in 1534.

A hundred yards south of the Castle a permanent exhibition of Thomas Hardy's life and works is on display in St Andrew's Church. The writer was closely connected with the church, both with the original

About a mile west of Lulworth Cove stands another remarkable feature which has been sculpted by the sea. **Durdle Door** is a magnificent archway carved from the coastal limestone. There's no road to the coast at this point, but it can be easily reached by following the South West Coast Path from Lulworth Cove. Along the way is another strange

DURDLE DOOR HOLIDAY PARK

Lulworth Cove, Wareham,
Dorset BH20 5PU
Tel: 01929 400200

Durdle Door Holiday Park enjoys the best of sea and land that this magnificent part of the county has to offer: beautiful rolling hills and farmland, and the glorious Purbeck coastline. The Park, which is situated on gently sloping land interspersed with woodland areas, gives the visitor a choice of sites when they bring their tents or arrive by touring caravan, and also has available a number of comprehensively equipped modern caravan holiday homes that are the last word in luxury.

All the expected up-to-the-minute amenities are on site, and more besides, including a fish and chip shop, a licensed bar, an adventure trail and mountain bike hire. The countryside around the Park is a paradise for walkers, cyclists and riders (there's an equestrian centre close by) and motorists have ready access to many great family days out. Durdle Door itself is a remarkable natural feature sculpted by the sea into a stunning archway of coastal limestone. A mile or so to the east, Lulworth Cove is one of the country's most famous beauty spots, and among the many other attractions on the 12,000-acre Lulworth Estate are Lulworth Castle and the Children's Farm. The Holiday Park is open from 1st March to 31st October.

Durdle Door

sight, a forest of tree stumps which have become fossilised over the centuries.

FURZEBROOK
3 miles S of Wareham off the A351

An oasis of peace and calm, **Barbrook Blue Pool** has been attracting visitors for 65 years (see panel below).

SWANAGE

A seaside town, complete with fully restored Victorian pier whose early fortune was based on Purbeck stone. The man who really put it on the map was a native of the town, John Mowlem, who trained as a quarryman and started his own company; he built the town's first proper roads and developed the industry with the aid of his nephew and partner George Burt. They built several civic buildings and gave the town piped water. The Town Hall has a fine frontage that was designed by Christopher Wren - but not for Swanage. It was originally part of Mercers Hall in Cheapside, London, and when that building was demolished the front was rescued and rebuilt in Swanage. Purbeck House, where George Burt lived, and some other Swanage buildings have parts salvaged from London buildings; John Mowlem's house has a turret on the roof from which he could observe the night sky. **Swanage Heritage Centre**, built a century ago as a market hall, has been restored to tell the story of the town, with special features on the Jurassic coast, Purbeck stone, the War years and the two men who transformed the town - Mowlem and Burt. One attraction that certainly should not be missed (literally!) is the Swanage Railway, which uses old Southern Region and BR Standard steam locomotives to haul trains on the scenic six-mile route to Norden, just north of Corfe Castle. The line starts at Swanage and calls at Herston Halt (request stop only), Herman's Cross, Corfe

BARBROOK BLUE POOL

The Blue Pool Tea House, Furzebrook, Nr. Wareham, Dorset BH20 5AT
Tel: 01929 551408 Fax: 01929 551404

Tea house, shops and museum - an oasis of peace which has been attracting visitors since 1935. The Blue Pool itself, once a clay pit, retains particles of clay which cause a kaleidoscope of colour changes, and the 25 acres that surround it offer calm and gentle exercise among the heather, gorse and pine trees. Rare flora and fauna can be glimpsed, and after their stroll visitors can enjoy excellent home baking in the tea house.

Swanage Beach

Park, where George Burt built a castle in 1887 and also a 40-ton Portland stone globe, 10 feet high, picking out in relief the continents and major features. The Globe is surrounded by stones and tablets carved with information concerning the solar system and quotations from the classical poets. The park is well known for its varied wildlife and is a Site of Special Scientific Interest (SSSI). Rare flowers and butterflies abound, and the park is home to a large colony of guillemots. Bottlenose dolphins are a regular sight at play off the cliffs, and the park runs a dolphin adoption programme. The coastal path offers marvellous walks and great sights and scenery all the way to Devon; the first of these, close to the great

Castle and Norden. Ancillary delights include driving tuition courses and dining on the Wessex Belle.

To the north of Swanage is **Studland**, whose well-preserved Norman church is well worth a visit. To the south lie Durlston Head and **Durlston Country**

THE CROWS NEST INN

11 Ulwell Road, Swanage,
Dorset BH19 ILE
Tel: 01929 422651

A period private house with ornate brickwork and large bay windows has been converted into a cheerful, welcoming inn where Ian and Paula Dowdeswell are the most delightful hosts. Ideally situated only 200 yards from the sea, the **Crows Nest Inn** is a great place for all the family and a very popular choice for parties and other jolly occasions. A morning or afternoon spent sightseeing or sporting on the beach is guaranteed to build up a thirst and an appetite, and the Crows Nest Inn copes admirably with both.

It stocks a fine selection of ales and wines, and there's plenty of choice on the menus, both in the bar and in the non-smoking restaurant. Value for money is excellent, with good deals such as two steaks for £10. Sunday lunches are a speciality, and the 25 seats in the restaurant fill up quickly, so booking is advisable. A log fire keeps things cosy in chilly weather, while when the sun shines the large enclosed garden with a children's play area is where the action is.

Guests staying overnight at the inn have two en suite bedrooms at their disposal, one of them suitable for families. An unusual feature of the town, whose fortune was built originally on Purbeck stone, is the number of buildings, or parts of buildings, 'imported' from London. These include the Town Hall, whose facade was designed by Sir Christopher Wren and originally adorned the Mercers Hall in Cheapside. The Crows Nest could not be more handily placed for combining sightseeing with a traditional seaside holiday.

CORFE CASTLE MODEL VILLAGE & GARDENS

The Square, Corfe Castle, Dorset BH20 5EZ
Tel: 01929 481234 Fax: 01929 481200

Corfe Castle is an attraction that draws many thousands of visitors to this delightful part of Dorset each year, but almost literally in the shadow of the magnificent ruins is equally fascinating sight for tourists. Liz and Tony Agnew own and run what they rightly describe as '3 Great Venues in One': **Corfe Castle Model Village**, Traditional Dorset Gardens and The Courtyard Café. The real castle was destroyed by Cromwell's troops in 1646, but the Model Village faithfully restores both the castle and the village. Visitors can therefore make the intriguing comparison between the heritage castle laid out at their feet and the imposing ruin that towers above, dominating the landscape even in its ruined state.

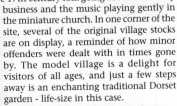

Liz's family have lived in the (real!) village for several generations, owning many properties, and it was her father, Eddie Holland, who built the model, which took two years to complete and was opened to the public for the first time in 1966. The detail in the 1/20th scale model, built with Purbeck stone, is extraordinary, right down to the miniature 17th century folk going about their daily business and the music playing gently in the miniature church. In one corner of the site, several of the original village stocks are on display, a reminder of how minor offenders were dealt with in times gone by. The model village is a delight for visitors of all ages, and just a few steps away is an enchanting traditional Dorset garden - life-size in this case.

The gardens have recently been restored and landscaped anew by a professional gardener who is also a horticultural lecturer. Many rare trees and shrubs have been planted, which along with the glorious borders provide a variety of wonderful colours and scents throughout the season.

After exploring the village and gardens, visitors can relax in the Courtyard Café over a cup of tea or coffee, or tuck into a filled jacket potato, home made soup, a well-filled sandwich or a full Dorset cream tea. All three venues - the model village, the gardens and the café - are open daily from April to the end of October: high season 10-6, mid-season 11-5. The model village is without doubt one of the most fascinating attractions of its kind in the whole country, and no visit to the area would be complete without spending a few hours peeping back into history.

Durlston Head

of the stone-quarrying industry, with a splendid Norman church. A notable occupant of the churchyard is a man called Benjamin Jesty, a farmer who, it is claimed, developed inoculation against smallpox years before Jenner. The walls of the Church of St Nicholas are thick and sturdy, but not so thick and sturdy as those of the extraordinary **Church of St Aldhelm** in a wild clifftop location south of the village. The story goes that on a stormy day in 1140 a local man was watching his daughter and son-in-law setting out in a boat for their new married home along the coast when the boat was overwhelmed by a sudden gust and all on board were lost. The grief-stricken father built the church in their memory and little has changed to this day. The building is square and squat, its walls buttressed, with a sloping stone roof surmounted by a much more modern cross; inside is simple and unadorned, a suitably bleak sight for the often hostile surroundings of this far corner of Purbeck.

globe, is **Tilly Whim Caves**, named after the owner Mr Tilly, who used a whim, or wooden derrick, to load stone into barges for transporting to Swanage. The caves are no longer accessible to the public, on safety grounds. On bleak, rugged Round Down stands the Anvil Lighthouse, built in the 1880s, with a light that can be seen for 24 miles out to sea. Also here is an old telegraph station, one of a series built against the threat of a French invasion.

AROUND SWANAGE

LANGTON MATRAVERS
2 miles W of Swanage on the B3069

A stone-built village in the heart of Purbeck stone country. The **Coach House Museum** provides a picture of the quarrying and uses of the stone and includes displays of apprentice pieces, a gift shop and an audio-visual presentation. The museum is located behind the parish church of St George in St George's Close.

WORTH MATRAVERS
3 miles W of Swanage off the B3069

Worth Matravers is another former centre

CORFE CASTLE
6 miles NW of Swanage on the A351

One of the grandest sights in the whole country is the impressive ruin of **Corfe Castle**, standing high on a hill and dominating the greystone village that grew up around the castle and took its name. Once the most impregnable fortresses in the land - it even had its own well - Corfe dates back to the days of William the Conqueror, with later additions in the reigns of King John and King Edward I. On one occasion King John threw 22 French knights into the dungeons from the hole in the ceiling and left them there to starve to death. Later, Edward II was imprisoned here before

Farriers Lodge

36 East Street, Corfe Castle, Dorset BH20 5EQ
Tel/Fax: 01929 480386

Farriers Lodge, a 17th century thatched cottage close to the village centre, has been converted in stunning style to provide exceptional self-catering accommodation. Impeccable style and taste are evident throughout, and the whole place is in immaculate condition after recent top-to-tail refurbishment.

On the ground floor are a fully equipped kitchen/diner with oak-beamed ceiling and gas-fired stove in an inglenook fireplace; a lounge with tv, video, and log burning gas open fire; and a bathroom with shower and toilet. A dual-purpose garden room has stowaway twin beds. The lounge and garden room both have access through French windows to the delightful secluded garden. No smoking or pets. Stairs lead up from the kitchen to the main bedroom, which has a king-size double bed, plenty of drawer and cupboard space, TV and an adjoining shower room and toilet.

The contact point for bookings is next door at no.38, the Old Forge, which, like Farriers lodge, is run with meticulous care by a delightful couple Eileen and Lucas van Lelyveld. The Old Forge is also home to the Blacksmith's Shop with the sign of the anvil over the door. The past comes alive in this 15th century building, where wrought iron, metal craftwork, genuine horseshoes and country life cards fill the space and provide unusual gifts. As Eileen and Lucas put it, 'this is not just any old iron'. So strike while the iron is hot!

Woodland Camping & Caravan Park

Glebe Farm, Bucknowle, Wareham, Dorset BH20 5PQ
Tel: 01929 480315/480280

Family farmers and noted bell-ringers Rodney and Hazel Parker recently bought **Woodlands Camping & Caravan Park** as a successful going concern with many visitors returning year after year. Woodland Park is a five-acre site in a wooded setting that provides peace and seclusion for its users, with space for 25 caravans and 40 tents. Tents and touring caravans are only permitted round the perimeter and in clearings in the trees, so the green is kept free as an area for recreation and for admiring the peace and beauty of the setting. A separate play area has climbing frames, swings and other equipment to keep the children happy for hours. The site includes toilets, showers, laundry and washing-up sinks, and camping and calor gas, milk and bread are available from the little shop at reception. It's a pleasant walk of less than a mile, with only one minor road to cross, to Corfe village, where there are plenty of shops and public houses. The possibilities are endless for walkers and cyclists, and among the many local attractions are the Purbeck Hills, the beautiful coastline, the magnificent ruins of Corfe Castle, the animal sanctuary at Church Knowle and the steam-hauled Swanage Railway, whose western terminus is at nearby Norden.

Corfe Castle

being sent to Berkeley Castle and his horrible death. The Castle remained important right up to the time of the Civil War, when it withstood two sieges before falling through an act of treachery. The Castle Museum has a collection of domestic and agricultural implements and a set of dinosaur footprints - this is fossil country. The Castle now stands in ruins, but visitors can see a smaller, intact version at the **Model Village** in West Street. This superbly accurate replica, of the whole village, is built from the same Purbeck stone as the real thing and the details of the streets, the buildings and the medieval folk going about their business are wonderful (see panel on page 138).

KIMMERIDGE
8 miles W of Swanage off the A351

Kimmeridge Bay, a mile from the village, is a popular spot with lovers of both the sea and the countryside. The Dorset Wildlife Trust runs an information hut by the beach with a small tank of marine creatures. Close to the village stands **Smedmore House**, a handsome mid-18th century Portland stone mansion with fine period furniture, an original kitchen and a small museum.

Corfe Castle

7 North Dorset

Mainly agricultural, North Dorset represents rural England at its most appealing. It's a peaceful, largely unspoilt area embracing half a dozen small market towns and a large number of picturesque villages. The most glorious building in the region is Sherborne Abbey, where the superb fan vaulting in the nave is among the oldest in existence. The most recent feature is John Hayward's Great West Window, which was dedicated in 1998 by the Queen and the Duke of Edinburgh. In the same small town are Sir Walter Raleigh's New Castle as well as many other striking medieval houses. In the market place Giles Winterborne stood with his apple trees in Hardy's *The Woodlanders*, and in the Abbey he talked with Grace Melbury

Ashmore Village Pond

about their future. Blandford Forum, the administrative base of the district, is mostly Georgian, and its handsome appearance is the result of a fire that destroyed the greater part of the town in 1731. Blandford has a strong military connection, mostly nowadays through the Royal Corps of Signals, whose depot is at Blandford Camp. In the Great War it was a training base for the Royal Naval Division, and one of those who passed through was the poet Rupert Brooke. In Shaftesbury, Gold Hill became one of the most familiar streets in the county as a result of being featured in the classic TV commercial for Hovis bread. Shaftesbury is the county's only hill town, and the views from Castle Hill were among those singled out by Hardy when he was asked by the editor of the *Saturday Review* in 1898 to describe 'The Best Scenery I Know'. Running along the northwest border of the region, Blackmore Vale is still much as Hardy described it in *Tess of the d'Urbervilles*. The landscape here is on an intimate scale, with tiny fields bordered by the ancient hedgerows which were such a charming feature of the English countryside but which in some parts have all but disappeared. This part of the world has its fair share of hill forts, the strongholds that were built in the often turbulent times between about 1000BC and 50AD to defend the precious land around them. The most notable examples in this chapter are Hambledon Hill and Hod Hill.

NORTH DORSET

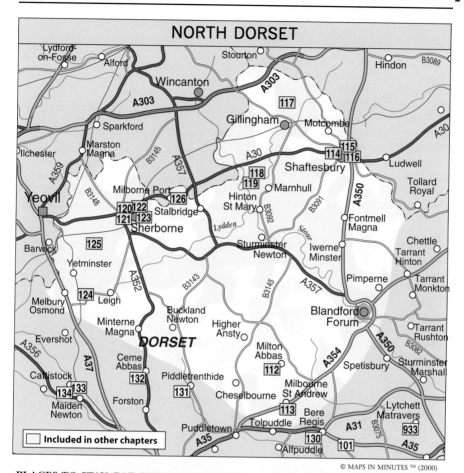

© MAPS IN MINUTES ™ (2000)

PLACES TO STAY, EAT, DRINK AND SHOP

BLANDFORD FORUM

Blandford Forum is the administrative centre of North Dorset, beautifully situated along the wooded valley of the River Stour. Granted a market charter in 1605, the town prospered as the market centre for the Stour Valley and was also known for the production of lace and buttons. It's a handsome town, due mainly to the effects of a great fire in 1731 that destroyed most of the old town. The gracious Georgian buildings that replaced the old were mostly designed by two talented architect-builders, the brothers John and William Bastard, pupils of Sir Christopher Wren. Three important buildings escaped the fire: the Ryves Almshouses of 1682, the Corn Exchange and the splendid 15th century Old House in the Close, which was built in Bohemian style to house Protestant refugees from Bohemia. The rebuilding of the town ended in 1760 with the erection of a classically-styled monument to the fire, which stands in front of the **Church of St Peter and St Paul**. This is the town's best-known landmark, topped with a cupola which the brothers had intended to be temporary while funds for a spire were sought. There are some interesting features inside the church, too, including box pews, a pulpit from a long-gone Wren church in London, an organ presented by George III and a memorial tablet listing all the buildings of the Bastard brothers, whose tomb is in the churchyard. Lime Tree House, close to the market place, contains the unique **Cavalcade of Costume**, the inspiration of Mrs Betty Penny. This remarkable lady, a tireless worker for charity, set up a collection which traces 250 years of costume history. Over 500 items are on display, gathered from countless sources by Mrs Penny over a period of 35 years. The house, which

like most of the 'new' town was designed by the Bastard brothers, has a garden, a shop and a tea room. Another fascinating place to visit is the **Royal Signals Museum** at Blandford Camp, with interactive displays based on Communication, Science and Technology, and features on the SAS and the Long-Range Desert Group, Animals at War, and Codes and Codebreakers, including the Enigma machine. Back in the centre of town, opposite the church, **Blandford Forum Museum** depicts the history, culture and industries of Blandford, with special displays on the great fire. **Stour House**, on East Street, has a beautiful town garden that is occasionally open for visits. Part of the garden is a romantic island in the River Stour which the owner has planted with some lovely trees.

AROUND BLANDFORD FORUM

MILTON ABBAS
5 miles SW of Blandford off the A354

The site of important ecclesiastical buildings since 935, when King Athelstan founded an abbey for 40 monks. **The Abbey Church**, though never actually completed, is an impressive building with some wonderful Pugin glass and some very fine monuments. One of these, designed by Robert Adam, is the tomb of Joseph Damer, the Earl of Dorchester, who bought the abbey estate and for a while lived in a house converted from monastic use. In 1771 he decided that he needed somewhere larger to live, so he demolished the monastic buildings and built a new house on the site, with grounds designed by Capability Brown. The view of the town of Milton, which had grown to a considerable size around the Abbey, clearly did not please the Earl, so he organised the demolition of the houses and built a new village a mile away, to which he moved the old town's inhabitants.

A country road leads north from Milton to one of the highest points in the county, **Bulbarrow Hill**, which takes its name from the prehistoric burial mound not far from the summit 'Homely Bulbarrow' is mentioned in Hardy's *Wessex Heights*.

Milton Abbas

MILBORNE ST ANDREW
8 miles SW of Blandford Forum on the A354

An attractive village in the valley of a tributary of the River Piddle, straddling the main road (A354) that runs from Salisbury through Blandford, round Dorchester and on to Weymouth. In the church are several monuments to the leading local Morton family. One of them gave his name to the expression 'Morton's Fork'. This was John Morton, born in 1420, who became Archbishop of

PRIMROSE COTTAGE

29 Milton Abbas, Blandford Forum, Dorset DT11 0BL
The contact address for reservations is:
　　Tony Garvey, 1 Long Street, Cerne Abbas,
　　Dorchester, Dorset DT2 7JF.
　　Tel/Fax: 01300 341352
　　e-mail: tgarvey@ragtime99.freeserve.co.uk

Mr & Mrs Garvey's **Primrose Cottage** is part of the unique 'model village' of Milton Abbas in a beautiful setting between Dorchester and Blandford Forum. The 'model village', considered by many to be the prettiest in England, was the creation of a local man, Joseph Damer, who married the daughter of the Duke of Dorset and became Lord Milton, later the Earl of Dorchester. In the 1770s this man ordered old monastic buildings to be demolished in order to construct his own grand stately home and various other buildings. The landscaping he entrusted to none other than Capability Brown.

　　Part of this development, Primrose Cottage is a Grade ll listed cob and thatch house with an abundance of period charm. A wood-burning stove in an inglenook fireplace keeps things cosy in the beamed sitting room, and the low doors are typical of the period. But the accommodation is thoroughly up to date, with everything in the two bedrooms and the kitchen designed to guarantee a comfortable self-catering holiday for up to six people. Young families are very welcome and will find all they need for babies and toddlers. A walk through Capability Brown's parkland, with a lake at its heart, leads to the older part of the village and the massive Abbey Church.

Canterbury (1484) and Lord Chancellor (1487) to Henry VII. He devised a system of parting the rich (and the not so rich) from their money that would have been the envy of many a later Chancellor. His system was simple: if a man was living in grand style he clearly had money to spare; if he lived frugally, he obviously kept his wealth hidden away. That was Morton's Fork, and many a citizen was caught on its vicious prongs. The system delighted and enriched the King, who made John Morton a Cardinal in 1493.

The area to the east of the main road (A350) that links Blandford and Shaftesbury contains the chalk downland of **Cranborne Chase**, the royal hunting ground that later became a hiding place for smugglers and their loot (see also Chapter 6). A short distance from Blandford, the road passes close to two impressive Iron Age hill forts, **Hod Hill** and **Hambledon Hill**, the former covered in cowslips in spring and early summer, the latter a nature reserve famous for its rare flowers and very rare butterflies.

THE TARRANTS
East of Blandford Forum

On the east side of Blandford lie no fewer than eight charming villages bearing the name Tarrant, after the river that runs through or near them. The most northerly in this beautiful, sparsely populated valley is **Tarrant Gunville**, where the river runs

in a gulley by the road and the houses are reached by little brick arches. The **Church of St Mary**, dating from the 12th century, rebuilt in the 16th and restored in the 19th after falling into neglect, has a marble memorial to Thomas Wedgwood, FRS, pioneer photographer and third son of the famous potter Josiah. To the east of the village stands Eastbury House, a grand mansion designed by Sir John Vanbrugh for one of the first governors of the Bank of England and modelled on Vanbrugh's Blenheim Palace. It was for a time the home of Josiah Wedgwood's widow and her son Thomas.

Following the river and the minor road south, the next villages are **Tarrant Hinton** (at the junction of the valley road and the busy A354; scene of the annual Great Dorset Steam Fair), **Tarrant Launceston** and **Tarrant Monkton**, which has a lovely old packhorse bridge and ford. In Tarrant Monkton's **All Saints Church** is a huge wooden bell-wheel which was used for swinging the tenor bell. The churchyard contains the graves of four German POWs who died while interned at Blandford Camp.

The road continues south to **Tarrant Rawston** and **Tarrant Rushton**, whose lovely 12th century church contains some interesting features, including squint holes, a leper squint and two huge pitchers built into the chancel whose purpose was to improve the acoustics.

ORCHARD COTTAGE

Deverel Farm, Milborne St Andrew, Blandford, Dorset DT11 0HX
Tel: 01258 837195 Fax: 01258 837227

Charlotte and John Martin's **Orchard Cottage** is situated on a working farm near the A354 Blandford-Dorchester road. Built in 1968, the cottage sleeps up to six guests in three bedrooms; a comfortable lounge-dining room adjoins the kitchen, which has everything needed for a self-catering holiday. The Martins have small children of their own, and families are very welcome; but no pets, please.

Next comes **Tarrant Keyneston**, where the valley road meets the B3082, and finally the most southerly of the eight, **Tarrant Crawford**. This was the site of one of the largest Cistercian nunneries in the whole country, founded in the 13th century by Bishop Richard Poore. Nothing of the nunnery buildings survives except for several massive buttresses incorporated into an ancient barn, but the **Church of St Mary** on the same site is notable for a series of 14th century wall paintings depicting, among other subjects, episodes in the life of St Mary of Antioch.

CHETTLE
6 miles NE of Blandford Forum on the A354

The best-known building in the lovely village of Chettle is its Queen Anne manor house, designed by Thomas Archer (1668-1743) in English Baroque style and built by our friends the Bastard brothers, who completed the job in 1720. Archer's work was marked by lavish curves, inverted scrolls and grand scale, and owed much to the Italian architects Bernini and Borromini. His other designs include the north front of Chatsworth and the Church of St John, in Smith Square, Westminster. The beautifully laid-out grounds of **Chettle House** include splendid herbaceous borders, a vineyard a new rose garden and a croquet lawn, which visitors can use by arrangement (mallets and balls supplied) The house was owned by several generations of the Chafin family, whose portraits hang in the house and whose monuments are to be found in the village church, which is situated in the grounds of the house.

The A357 running northwest from Blandford passes through a number of attractive villages, including **Shillingstone**, which once boasted the country's tallest maypole, and **Fiddleford**, whose 14th century manor house has been fully restored by English Heritage.

STURMINSTER NEWTON
8 miles NW of Blandford Forum on the A357/B3091/B3092

The chief town of the lovely rich agricultural area of Blackmore Vale. An unspoilt market town (Hardy's Stourcastle) on the River Stour, Sturminster Newton was where Hardy and his wife Emma had their first real home together, from 1876 to 1878, in 'a pretty cottage overlooking the Dorset Stour, called Riverside Villa'. Here he wrote *The Return of the Native* and he often referred to 'our happiest time' in his poems. The house is not open to the public but can be seen from a footpath by the river. Two other writers were residents of Sturminster: William Barnes, the 19th century poet who wrote about Dorset in dialect, and his friend and fellow dialect poet Robert Young, who died at the age of 97 at Riverside, the villa his family had rented to the Hardys. Until Elizabethan times Sturminster and Newton were separate communities on opposite sides of the Stour.

Shortly after the graceful Town Bridge was built to link the two, a mill was built a little way upstream. Fully restored, and powered by a 1904 turbine, **Newton Mill** offers guided tours explaining the milling process. On the old bridge, a metal plaque carries the dire warning: 'Any person wilfully injuring any part of this county bridge will be guilty of felony and upon conviction liable to be transported for life by the court'. The town was granted a market charter 700 years ago and still holds a market every Monday. Features of **St Mary's Church**, rebuilt in 1486 and enlarged in the 19th century, include some fine stained glass and a 15th century 'wagon' roof.

LA FLEUR DE LYS

25 Salisbury Street, Shaftesbury, Dorset SP7 8EL
Tel/Fax: 01747 853717
e-mail: lafleurdelys@fsbdial.co.uk

Shaftesbury is a town full of charm and character, a very pleasant place to explore on foot. And after a stroll around the streets and the sights there's no better plan than to relax over a meal in the first floor dining room of the delightful **La Fleur de Lys** restaurant. Owned and run by the talented threesome of David Shepherd, Mary Griffin and Marc Preston, the 40-cover restaurant attracts a discerning clientele with its quiet, civilised ambience and classically-based country-style cooking of a very high order (recommended by Michelin and the Good Food Guide). The lunch menu proposes eight or nine dishes for each course, with the starters additionally available as main courses. Smoked chicken salad or poachdating bed eggs soubise with smoked salmon could be followed by herb-crusted collops of monkfish, tenderloin of pork with a spicy mango chutney or pancakes with asparagus, spinach, samphire and courgettes. Thoughts of a light lunch will probably disappear when the dessert list arrives - should it be Dorset apple cake with clotted cream, a selection of home-made ice creams and sorbets, or perhaps a plate of fine cheeses with oatmeal biscuits and walnut bread? Candlelit evenings bring an even more enticing choice on à la carte and set menus, and the top-quality food is complemented by a wide-ranging, fairly priced wine list. Closed Sunday evening and Monday lunch. No smoking in the evening before 10 o'clock.

THE RETREAT

47 Bell Street, Shaftesbury, Dorset SP7 8AE
Tel/Fax: 01747 850372
e-mail: at.retreat@virgin.net www: the-retreat.org.uk

Home-from-home comforts are very much to the fore in **The Retreat**, a delightful town house in a quiet side street in the centre of Shaftesbury. Behind the distinguished Georgian frontage, urbane owners Sheena and Bernard Skam offer very comfortable Bed and Breakfast accommodation in large, airy bedrooms with high ceilings and ornate friezes. Carpets, fittings and furnishings are all of the highest standard, and all the bedrooms have en suite facilities, tv and refreshment tray. A full English or Continental breakfast is served in the warmly inviting dining room, and with notice special dietary needs can be catered for - a typical thoughtful touch.

Guests are therefore well set up for exploring the hilltop town of Shaftesbury, many of whose sights are but a brisk walk away. A modicum of energy is required for the climb up Gold Hill, but the reward for reaching the top is stunning views across the lovely Vale of Blackmore. Further-flung attractions such as Stonehenge and the New Forest are easily accessible by car, making The Retreat a perfect base for either total rest and relaxation or serious sightseeing. Parking is available behind the house, while arrangements can be made to meet guests arriving by train at Gillingham station. The Retreat is suitable for disabled guests, with easy wheelchair access.

HINTON ST MARY
10 miles NW of Blandford Forum on the B3092

A mile north of Sturminster Newton lies the village of Hinton St Mary, which has a well-preserved 17th century manor house. In 1960 a large Roman mosaic pavement was discovered nearby, which is now in the British Museum.

IWERNE MINSTER
5 miles N of Blandford Forum on the A350

The A350 running from Blandford to Shaftesbury passes through the villages of Iwerne Courtney and Iwerne Minster, where motorists should pause to look at the church with its medieval spire and the lovely Victorian Lady Chapel, the work of JL Pearson. Six miles south of Shaftesbury are 730 acres of ancient chalk downland in the care of the National Trust. The downs include **Fontmell Down**, **Melbury Down** and **Melbury Beacon**, and the first in particular, currently leased to the Dorset Trust for Nature Conservation, affords superb views over Blackmore Vale and Cranborne Chase. The downs are home to many rare grasses and flowers, to 50 species of bird and to a variety of butterflies, among which the National Trust Countryside Handbook notes chalkhill and adonis blues, silver-spotted skippers, Duke of Burgundy and dark-green fritillary.

SHAFTESBURY

Set on a hill 700 feet high, Shaftesbury was officially founded in 880AD by King Alfred, who fortified the place and founded a Benedictine abbey for women where he installed his daughter as the first Prioress. A hundred years later, the King Edward who was murdered by his stepmother at Corfe Castle was buried here and **Shaftesbury Abbey** became an important place of pilgrimage. The excavated remains of the Abbey lie in a quiet garden, and a nearby museum tells the story of the Abbey and the people who lived in it (see panel below).

The town has other royal connections, too: King Canute is said by some to have died in the Abbey; Elizabeth, wife of Robert the Bruce, was imprisoned here for two years; and Catherine of Aragon, first wife of Henry VIII, stayed here on her way to London to marry Prince Arthur, Henry's brother.

Shaftesbury is a pleasant town to explore on foot, and indeed you have to walk to see its most famous sight. **Gold Hill**, a precipitous cobbled street, stepped in places and with a handrail to assist the ascent (or descent), is lined with delightful 18th century cottages. Already well known for its picturesque setting and the splendid views of Blackmore Vale, it became even more famous when it was

SHAFTESBURY ABBEY MUSEUM & GARDEN
Park Walk, Shaftesbury, Dorset SP7 8RJ
Tel/Fax: 01747 852910
e-mail: anna@shaftesburyabbey.fsnet.co.uk

Visitors can explore the site of Saxon England's foremost Benedictine nunnery, founded by King Alfred, who installed his daughter as the first prioress. The excavated remains of the original abbey church lie in a peaceful walled garden, and a nearby state-of-the-art museum, decorated in dramatic medieval colours chosen to reflect the original colours of the church, houses a fascinating collection of carved stonework, medieval floor tiles and other excavated objects. There's also an interactive touch-screen exhibition and a gift shop.

Gold Hill, Shaftesbury

and some of the products can be seen in the museum; they include the decorative Dorset knobs, which share their name with a famous biscuit, also locally made. Stones from the Abbey, which quickly fell into disrepair after Henry VIII's Dissolution order, were used to build some of the cottages on Gold Hill.

featured in the classic television advertisement for Hovis bread. **Shaftesbury Museum** is housed in a cottage at the top of the hill; each of its little rooms is filled with objects of local interest, and outside is a cottage-style garden. Button-making was once an important cottage industry in the town,

The 17th century **Ox House**, which is referred to in Hardy's *Jude the Obscure*, is one of many interesting buildings in the town, others including the **Church of St Peter** near the top of Gold Hill and the Tudor-style **Town Hall** built in the 1820s. Shaftesbury was an important stop on the coaching route in the 17th and 18th centuries. Its

WHISTLEY WATERS

Milton-on-Stour, Gillingham, Dorset SP8 5PT
Tel/Fax: 01747 840666
e-mail: campbell.whistleywaters@virginnet.co.uk

Walkers, anglers and seekers after and peace and tranquillity make tracks for **Whistley Waters**, where Chris and Cleo Campbell have established a secluded self-catering retreat in a lovely woodland setting. The main accommodation is in two A-framed, timber-built lodges facing south, overlooking lakes and surrounded by lawns and tree-shaded areas. Lakes Lodge and Mallard Lodge can both sleep up to six in a twin and two single beds open-plan with WC and basin upstairs, and a double bedroom, bathroom and WC downstairs, along with a lounge with kitchenette and dining area and a sundeck with a barbecue and a picnic table and chairs. Both lodges are double-glazed. 'Up to two countrywise dogs' are welcome by arrangement in the lodges, but not in the no-smoking annexe. This adjunct to the owners' house has a lounge-diner, kitchen, bathroom and double bedroom with an additional folding bed. Amenities on site include two trout lakes and two carp and tench ponds, which can be fished for a small charge - rowing dinghies are also available. Walking is another favourite pastime hereabouts, and within a short drive are the shops and attractions of Gillingham (three miles), plenty of good public houses and a number of stately homes, National Trust properties, gardens and museums. Whistley Waters is situated close to the village of Milton-on-Stour about two miles from the A303.

Martinmas Market Charter was granted in 1603, and, ever since, the town has always had its share of lively market days, carnivals and fairs; one of the most popular is the Gold Hill Fair in July, when the town is closed to traffic.

AROUND SHAFTESBURY

The area around Shaftesbury is good for walking (the Wessex Ridgeway starts at Ashmore, a local village at the top of Cranborne Chase); and for cycling - the Dorset and Wiltshire Cycle Ways converge nearby.

MOTCOMBE
3 miles NW of Shaftesbury on a minor road

Close by, the **Dorset Rare Breeds Centre** is home to the county's largest collection of rare and endangered farm animals. They range from knee-high Soay sheep to mighty Suffolk Punches.

GILLINGHAM
5 miles NW of Shaftesnury on the B3092

A spread-out community that was once an important centre for the milling of silk and the manufacture of bricks. The parish church has a 14th chancel but is mostly much more recent, like much of the town. A **museum** at Chantry Fields charts the history of the town and its surroundings.

MARNHULL
7 miles SW of Shaftesbury off the B3092

Marnhull was Thomas Hardy's Marlott, where Tess (of the d'Urbervilles) had her home. The village pub, The Crown is the Pure Drop Inn in the novel. The scattered village of Marnhull claims to be the largest parish in England, spread over a very substantial area, and with a circumference of 23 miles. The village itself is well worth exploring for its part-Norman **Church of St Gregory** with a 15th century tower.

TOPSTALL FACTORY FARM

Fifehead Magdalen, Gillingham, Dorset SP8 5RS
Tel/Fax: 01258 820022

A short drive south from the A30 between Shaftesbury and Sherborne brings visitors to **Topstall Factory Farm**, a most unusual and appealing base for a self-catering holiday. Set in the beautiful Blackmore Vale, with the River Stour forming one of its boundaries, Topstall's accommodation is a converted cow stall adjoining the farmhouse, an 18th century former woollen and stocking factory founded and run in its early days by a Frenchman called A'Court; it is now the centre of a 270-acre working farm. David and Kathy Jeanes welcome families 'and well-behaved dogs' to Topstall, which comprises a lounge-diner with a fully equipped kitchen, three bedrooms with built-in wardrobes and vanity units and a shower room and WC. The whole place is suitable for assisted wheelchair users, with a ramp at the entrance and plenty of room to manoeuvre. It's an ideal base for exploring the beautiful local countryside and villages; among the latter is Marnhull, which claims to be the largest parish in England and which appears in Thomas Hardy's *Tess of the Durbervilles* as Marlott, the birthplace of his heroine. There's also plenty to see and do on the farm itself: guests can fish on the River Stour, watch the cows being milked, feed the calves, collect eggs from the hens or say hello to the five bottle-fed Peto lambs. There's excellent walking in the adjoining woodland, which includes Fifehead Wood, the oldest in the county. In the garden, for guests' use, are a barbecue, garden furniture and a small selection of games.

MIDDLE FARM

Fifehead Magdalen, Gillingham, Dorset SP8 5RR
Tel: 01258 820220

Jo and Roger Trevor's **Middle Farm** stands in the hamlet of Fifehead Magdalen, a short drive south of the A30 six miles west of Shaftesbury. Three of the Dorset stone barns, built about 200 years ago, have

been turned into self-catering cottages that offer guests a real taste of country living - but with the modern comfort and amenities that a town-dweller would expect! The most recent of the three conversions is the superb Stable Cottage, which comprises three double bedrooms, separate bath and shower room, spacious sitting room with a wood-burning fireplace, exposed beams and comfortable sofas and armchairs, and a fully-equipped kitchen with stripped oak floor, set as a diner. Each cottage is self-contained, situated some distance from its neighbours in the courtyard of the farm. Children and pets are welcome, and ground-floor bedrooms provide easy access for the less able. The cottages are available throughout the year for short or long breaks.

The farm itself covers some 300 acres of arable land, and also has 50 young heifers. There are some lovely woodland and riverbank walks within the perimeter, and coarse fishing can be arranged on the River Stour. The nearest village of any size is two miles away, with a selection of shops and pubs, and

there is almost no end to the places of interest to visit in the area. Many of the towns and villages are associated with Thomas Hardy: Shaftesbury itself, known as Shaston in the novels; Marnhull, a scattered village that appears as Marlott, birthplace of Tess, in *Tess of the d'Urbervilles*, and where the present Crown Inn appears in the novel as the Pure Drop Inn; and, a short drive down the B3092, Sturminster Newton, where the writer and his wife Emma had a home and where he wrote *The Return of the Native*. Other places well worth a visit include Fiddleford Manor, a 14th century house with a splendid Great Hall, and the thatched village of Okeford Fitzpaine. Further afield, Sherborne, Salisbury and Bath are all an easy drive away, and the coast can be reached in an hour.

Back in Fifehead Magdalen, the Old Orchard has a garden full of interesting shrubs and perennials; the owners hold an open day each year and private visits can be arranged at certain other times. After exploring the locality, the farm beckons with its uninterrupted peace, where a wander in the woods, sinking into a sofa or pottering round the patio are among the pleasures of life.

STALBRIDGE

10 miles W of Shaftesbury on the A357

The 15th century parish church has a striking 19th century tower which provides a landmark throughout the Vale of Blackmore. Perhaps even more impressive is the town's market cross, standing 30ft high and richly carved with scenes of the Crucifixion and Resurrection.

SHERBORNE

One of the most beautiful towns in England, Sherborne beguiles the visitor with its serene atmosphere of a Cathedral City; but it is not a city, and the lovely Abbey has not enjoyed the status of cathedral since 1075. But in 705AD, when it was founded by St Aldhelm, **Sherborne Abbey** was the Mother Cathedral for the whole of southwest England. Of that original Saxon church only minimal traces remain, and most of the present building dates from the mid-15th century. The wonderfully executed fan vaulting is among the earliest and certainly among the finest in the land, but the Abbey has many other treasures to enchant the visitor. These include 15th century misericords under the Victorian choir stalls with subjects ranging from the sublime (Christ sitting in majesty on a rainbow) to the everyday (an old man selling cherries) and the scandalous (a wife beating her husband, a schoolmaster beating his monkey-faced pupil). Among the magnificent tombs are a lofty six-poster from Tudor times, a baroque 17th century memorial to the 3rd Earl of Bristol, and , in the Wykeham Chapel, a monument to Sir John Horsey, who bought the Abbey after the Dissolution and then sold it to the town as their parish church. In the north aisle are two

THE WHITE HART

2 Cheap Street, Sherborne, Dorset DT9 3PX
Tel: 01935 814903

A row of private dwellings, built some 300 years ago, was combined to form what is now the **White Hart**, a convivial public house at the top end of town. With its long history and many fine old buildings, the beautiful little town of Sherborne (population around 8,500) is an ideal stopping point adjacent to the A30 for travellers to and from the West Country and a destination in its own right. After a walk round the abbey and the castle and the school thoughts are likely to turn to a spot of refreshment, and a natural place to head for is the White Hart, to enjoy the hospitality and good cheer on offer. The bars. lounge and dining room are very traditional (open fires, brass and copper ornaments, old bottles, a cross-looking locally-caught pike in a glass display case) and pool is among the classic pub games played in the separate games room. Ploughman's platters, salads and filled jacket potatoes provide excellent light meals, while in the 20-cover non-smoking restaurant more substantial dishes such as steaks, curries or steak & kidney pie are served. Sue and Steve Loader, both in their early 40s, managed other pubs before taking over the tenancy here a couple of years ago. The pub enjoys a strong local following, particularly among the more mature citizens, and the Over-50s Club has a thriving membership who enjoy special offers and discounts.

SHERBORNE ART & ANTIQUE DEALERS ASSOCIATION

6 Cheap Street, Sherborne, Dorset DT9 3PY
Tel: 01935 816816
website: www.sherbornetown.co.uk

Sherborne is one of the most beautiful towns in England, and the Abbey Church, the Castle and the School attract thousands of visitors each year. But there are plenty of other reasons to visit the town, including a large number of outlets dealing in art and antiques. Twenty five or so dealers have combined to form the **Sherborne Art & Antique Dealers Association** (S.A.A.D.A.), which consists of dealers,

restorers, art gallery owners and fair organisers, all of them working in or around Sherborne. The aim of the Association is the promotion of all aspects of their trade in the area, offering the widest possible variety of furniture, both antique and contemporary, objects and paintings, as well as fairs, exhibitions and other special events.

The Association's members are spread throughout the town, some in stand-alone premises, others in antiques centres that allow visitors to look at the wares and services of many dealers under one roof. These include the Sherborne World of Antiques & Fine Art in long Street, where visitors can get valuable advice on the buying and selling of antiques, on the sale and valuation of fine oils, drawings and sculpture, and on conserving, restoring and framing. Cheap Street is the home of many

of the dealers, among them Wessex Antiques, whose wares include 18th and 19th century English and Continental furniture and furnishings; Staffordshire figures; early English drinking glasses; and Oriental rugs. Other dealers trade in British watercolours and oil paintings; antique maps and prints; and antique and collectable silver from the 16th century onwards.

Cheap Street runs down into South Street, where the Alpha Gallery has, in the ten years since its opening, gained an international reputation for contemporary paintings, sculptures and ceramics. Its exhibitions offer West End quality at country prices. Another outlet, Bedouin, is a specialist in authentic furnishings from the Middle East and Asia including Persian rugs, runners, carpets and kilims. In Hound Street, next to the Library, Sherborne Antiques & Collectors Fair is a high-quality fair with 35-40 stalls set up in Digby Hall. Operating from 8am to 4pm on one Saturday a month, it offers a great opportunity for browsing and perhaps picking up a bargain, with the added attractions of free parking and delicious home-made refreshments. Plenty of time should be allowed for exploring all Sherborne's antique shops and galleries, which are nearly all within easy walking distance of each other and which no one interested in art and antiques should miss - not one but dozens of Aladdin's Caves in a town that is filled with many other delights. The marketing manager of S.A.A.D.A is Mrs Frances Bryant.

Sherborne Abbey

Lawrence Whistler and John Hayward's Great West Window, which was dedicated by the Queen and the Duke of Edinburgh in 1998.

Those elder brothers, and perhaps Alfred as well, were among the earliest pupils at **Sherborne School**, where in more recent times the Poet Laureate Cecil Day-Lewis and the writer David Cornwell (John Le Carré) were educated. The school has been the setting for three major films, *The Guinea Pig* (1948), *Goodbye Mr Chips* (1969) and *The Browning Version* (1994).

The best-known resident of Sherborne is undoubtedly Sir Walter Raleigh, who in 1592, at a time when he was a favourite of Queen Elizabeth I, asked for and was

enormous stone coffins which according to legend contain the remains of two Saxon kings, Ethelbald and Ethelbert (Ethel is Old English for 'noble'). These two were the elder brothers of Ethelred (not the Unready) and Alfred the Great. There are more modern treasures, too, notably an engraved glass reredos by

THE MERMAID

Bristol Road, Sherborne, Dorset DT9 4JD
Tel: 01935 812229

Norman and Jo Bawden, a happy South African couple with three sons and several grandchildren, have recently taken over the reins at this 1930s redbrick pub on the B3124 Wincanton road on the western edge of town. Hanging baskets and a tub garden are attractive features at the front of the pub, while at the rear a patio with barbecue area and ornamental fish pond overlooks a park and, beyond it, the rolling Dorset countryside.

Tables and chairs are set out under parasols in summer, making it a delightful spot for taking alfresco refreshment.

Inside, the ground floor includes a large bar with a 16-cover dining room and a pool area, while upstairs is a function room with its own bar. The food is mainly traditional English, and the bar offers the usual range of beers and spirits as well as some interesting drinks from South Africa and weekly-changing cocktail specials. This is a friendly, convivial pub and a sporting one, too - the skittle alley is a popular place, and the pub

fields three skittles teams and also teams for pool and darts. Music is another important feature, with live performers every Friday evening and a jazz band adding to the cheerful atmosphere at lunchtime on the last Sunday of the month.

SHERBORNE CASTLE

Sherborne, Dorset DT9 3PY
Tel: 01935 813182
e-mail: enquiries@sherbornecastle.com
website: www.sherbornecastle.com

As soon as Sir Walter Raleigh was given the Old Castle and its estates by Queen Elizabeth I, he realised that the stark, comfortless castle was not his ideal residence, and instead of restoring it he built a new castle alongside the old one. He called it Sherborne Lodge to distinguish it from the Old Castle, and this unusual rectangular, six-turreted building became his home.

Upon Sir Walter Raleigh's death on the block his estates were forfeited to the Crown, but in 1617 King James I allowed Sir John Digby to purchase the new castle and this gentleman added four wings in a similar style to the old building. During the Civil War, the Old Castle was reduced to a ruin by Cromwell's Parliamentary forces - the siege in 1645 lasted 16 days and prompted Cromwell to talk of this 'malicious and mischievous castle'. The name Sherborne Castle came to be applied to the new building, where today splendid collections of Old Masters, porcelain and furniture are on display.

Other attractions at the castle, which is still in the care of the Digby family, include the library, a Tudor kitchen and an exhibition of finds from the Old Castle. Lancelot 'Capability' Brown was called in to create the lake in 1753 and gave Sherborne the very latest in landscape gardening. The Castle, which was a Red Cross Hospital for wounded soldiers in the First World War and the HQ for D-Day Commandos in the Second, was opened to the public in 1969 and hosts a variety of events in the summer season. The gardens, tea room and shop are open every day except Wednesday; the Castle on Tuesday, Thursday, Saturday, Sunday and Bank Holiday Mondays.

CHETNOLE INN

Chetnole, Nr Sherborne, Dorset DT9 6NU
Tel: 01935 872337

Very much the heart and soul of the village, the **Chetnole Inn** has a large and loyal band of regulars. They come for the warm, friendly atmosphere generated by owners David Lowe and Jane Taylor-Wilby and their families; they come for an evening's jollity in the public bar or the skittle alley; they come for a quiet chat and a drink in the music-free lounge bar; and, perhaps most important of all, they come for the top-quality real ales - several small local breweries are represented - and for the outstanding food that embraces everything from bar snacks to gourmet dinners. The surroundings are very much part of the appeal of any pub, and the Chetnole Inn holds its own with the best in terms of character and ambience. Converted from 19th century farm cottages,

it has a cosy lounge bar, a spacious restaurant and a warm, friendly public bar with darts, pool and shove ha'penny. Log fires are always lit in the cooler months, while in summer the beer garden is a big attraction with its aviary, fishpond, barbecue and garden lights. The locals aren't the only ones in the know about this terrific inn, which has long been a favourite stopping place for walkers, cyclists and tourists. The owners' passion for good beer, good food and good company puts the Chetnole Inn firmly at the top of the hospitality tree.

given the house and estate of **Sherborne Old Castle**, which had been built on a grand scale in the 12th century by the Norman Bishop Roger of Salisbury. Raleigh soon realised that the stark, comfortless castle was not the ideal residence for a man of his sophistication and ambition, and instead of restoring it he built a new castle alongside the old one. **Sherborne New Castle**, originally called Sherborne Lodge, is a strange rectangular, six-turreted structure which was enlarged shortly after Raleigh's execution by Sir John Digby, a member of the family who have owned the castle since 1617. Huge windows let the light into gracious rooms with elaborately-patterned ceilings and superb collections of porcelain, furniture and paintings (Van Dyck, Gainsborough, Reynolds, Lely, Kneller and the famous portrayal by Robert Peake of Queen Elizabeth I on procession being carried on a litter and

surrounded by a sumptuously dressed retinue). Other attractions include the library, a Tudor kitchen and an exhibition of finds from the Old Castle (see panel opposite).

Located in the old walled garden, **Castle Gardens Plant Centre** offers a huge selection of plants and garden products, and wine produced by the Sherborne **Castle Estate Vineyard** can be purchased in the shop at the castle.

The Abbey and the Castles are by no means the only attractions in this most appealing little town. The **Almshouse of St John the Baptist and St John the Evangelist**, near the Abbey, was founded in 1437 to house 12 men and four women, and considerably extended in the mid-19th century, still fulfils its original role. The almshouse chapel houses one of the town's greatest treasures, a 15th century Flemish altar triptych.

TRILL COTTAGES

Trill House, Thornford, Sherborne, Dorset DT9 6HF
Tel: 01935 872305

Jane Warr and her husband greet visitors of all ages to **Trill Cottages**, set among acres of grassland in beautiful countryside. The centrally heated cottages stand back to back in a redbrick building dating from the early 1900s, and the self-catering accommodation consists of three bedrooms (one double bed and four singles), shower and toilet room, lounge with tv and open fire, dining room and well-equipped kitchen. A cot and high chair will be made available on request - children are very welcome, but no pets.

The cottages are situated at the western edge of picturesque Blackmoor Vale mile from the villages of Thornford and Yetminster and five miles from both Sherborne and Yeovil. The cottages and their

grounds are ideal for enjoying a complete rest in the most peaceful of surroundings, but there is plenty of interest in the nearby villages, and the beautiful town of Sherborne is rich in history. Bradford Abbas has a really fine church with a splendid tower, and Yetminster, on the River Wriggle, has some delightful 17th century buildings, including a school founded by Sir Robert Boyle, who gave us Boyle's Law. Jane is very much a mine of information on this most attractive and pleasant part of the world.

Close by, the **Conduit House** is an attractive, small hexagonal building from the early 1500s that was originally used as a washroom, or lavatorium, by the monks. It was moved to its present spot after the Reformation and has been used variously as a public fountain and a police telephone box. Conduit House is mentioned specifically in Hardy's *The Woodlanders* as the place where Giles Winterborne, seeking work, stood in the market place 'as he always did at this season of the year, with his specimen apple tree'.

Another striking building is the former Abbey Gatehouse, where **Sherborne Museum** has exhibits on pre-historic Sherborne, artefacts from the Civil War, a 1480 wall painting, rural implements, displays of silk manufacturing, a scale model of the Old Castle, a famous dolls house and a superb collection of photographs - definitely a museum not to be missed.

In the south of the town, down by the railway station, are **Pageant Gardens**, funded by the great pageant of 1905 which marked the 1,200th anniversary of the founding of the town, the bishopric and the school. This historical pageant was devised and arranged by Louis N Parker, one-time music master at the school. The pageant was a great success and inspired many other towns to mark special events with grand occasions.

AROUND SHERBORNE

YETMINSTER
6 miles SW of Sherborne off the A352

Fine 17th century buildings in the centre of the village by the River Wriggle include a school that was founded by Sir Robert Boyle, well-known by students of science as the creator of "Boyles Law".

MILBORNE PORT
3 miles NE of Sherborne on the A30

A sizeable village that straddles the busy A30. Very close to Milborne Port is the pretty village of **Purse Caundle**, which has a fine 15th century manor house with an imposing Great Hall .

THE TIPPLING PHILOSOPHER

High Street, Milborne Port, Nr Sherborne, Dorset DT9 5AQ
Tel: 01963 250289

Tenants Scott and Lillian Rigler bring years of experience in the catering and business management spheres to the **Tippling Philosopher**, which stands on the main street of Milborne Port (A30). Good company, good food, good value is their admirable philosophy, and in the traditional surroundings of the bars and dining area - wooden floors, open fires, beams, original memorabilia - all are to be found in abundance. The food is traditional English fare served in generous helpings, with particularly scrumptious home-made puddings. In the winter, party games, mulled wine and chestnuts roasting on an open fire guarantee a festive spirit, while in summer the scene shifts to the beautiful 'hidden' garden with a play area and pet rabbits. Other assets of this splendid hostelry include a large car park, a skittle alley and a function room. For guests staying overnight there are three letting bedrooms. Children, dogs and walkers are all welcome.

8 Central Dorset

Taking centre stage in this fascinating part of Dorset is its county town, Dorchester, whose known history goes back to 74AD, when the Romans established a settlement called Durnovaria a little way from the River Frome. The name perhaps derived from the tribe they had conquered, the Durotriges. The area covered in this chapter is at the heart of the land beloved of the poet and novelist Thomas Hardy 1840-1928), whose main inspiration came from the county of Dorset, part of the place he called Wessex after the ancient kingdom of central, southern and western England. Most of his stories are centred on South Wessex, or Dorset, though his Wessex extended into Oxfordshire, Hampshire, Somerset and Devon. Born and educated near or in Dorchester, Hardy was apprenticed to an architect in the town, and after a spell in London returned to Weymouth, where he both wrote and pursued his first career. In 1885 he moved to the outskirts of Dorchester to Max Gate, a house where he was to live for more than 40 years

Poxwell Village

until his death in 1928. From here he wrote his last novel, *Jude the Obscure*, in 1895, after which he turned to poetry. He was accorded a state funeral at which the pallbearers included JM Barrie, George Bernard Shaw, John Galsworthy, Rudyard Kipling, AE Housman, Stanley Baldwin and Ramsay MacDonald. His ashes were interred in Poets Corner in Westminster Abbey, but his heart is buried in the churchyard at Stinsford, in the grave of his wife. Hardy's works are among the best known in the English language, and the novels set in Dorset show an unsurpassed insight into the nature, the seasons and the lives of the agricultural folk who inhabited his favourite county. World-famous sights bring visitors in their thousands to this part of Dorset. Some of the sights are natural, like the extraordinary Chesil Beach, bane of seafarers in the days of sail, a pebble ridge that joins the Isle of Portland to the mainland. Others are man-made, notably the ancient hill forts (but nature has largely taken them over) and the intriguing pagan image of virility, the Cerne Abbas Giant.

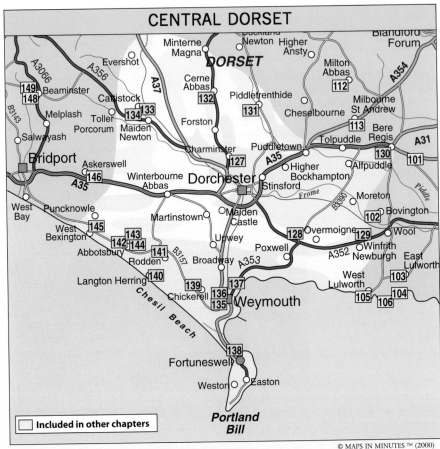

CENTRAL DORSET

Minterne Magna · Newton Higher Ansty · Blandford Forum

DORSET

Evershot

Cerne Abbas

Beaminster

Cattistock

Piddletrenthide

Milton Abbas [112]

Milbourne St Andrew

Melplash

Toller Porcorum

Maiden Newton

Forston

Cheselbourne

[113] Bere Regis

Salwayash

Charminster

Puddletown

Tolpuddle

[130] [101]

Bridport

Askerswell

Winterbourne Abbas

Dorchester

[127]

Higher Bockhampton

Alfpuddle

[146]

Stinsford

Frome

Moreton

West Bay

Puncknowle

Martinstown

Maiden Castle

[102] Bovington

West Bexington [145]

[143] [142][144]

Upwey

Overmoigne [128] [129] Wool

Abbotsbury

[141]

Poxwell

Winfrith Newburgh East Lulworth

Rodden

Broadway

West Lulworth [103]

Langton Herring [140]

[139] [136] [137]

Chickerell [135] **Weymouth**

[105] [106] [104]

Chesil Beach

[138]

Fortuneswell

Weston · Easton

☐ **Included in other chapters**

Portland Bill

© MAPS IN MINUTES ™ (2000)

PLACES TO STAY, EAT, DRINK AND SHOP

DORCHESTER

The Roman origins of one of England's most appealing towns are clearly displayed in its street plan, in the beautiful tree-lined avenues known as the Walks which follow the course of the old Roman walls and at Maumbury Rings, an ancient stone circle which the Romans converted into an amphitheatre and which was later used as a gun emplacement during the Civil War. As Hardy himself put it, Dorchester "announced old Rome in every street, alley and precinct. It looked Roman, bespoke the art of Rome, concealed dead men of Rome". Hardy was in fact describing Casterbridge in his novel *The Mayor of Casterbridge* but his fictional town is immediately recognisable as Dorchester. One place he describes in great detail is Mayor Trenchard's House, which is now Barclays Bank in South Street. **Max Gate**, which Hardy designed and where he passed the second half of his life, is a sturdy, suburban villa which his brother built at a cost of £450. The house took its name from Mack's Tollgate, which stood previously on the site. At Max Gate he would entertain a rollcall of great names, including Robert Louis Stevenson, George Bernard Shaw, Walter de la Mare, Rudyard Kipling and HG Wells. TE Lawrence (Lawrence of Arabia) visited as often as he could. But Hardy was never completely at ease, even though he spent more than half his life here: "The house is bleak and cold, built so new for me". Hardy and his wife Emma, and later his second wife Florence, had no children but lots of pets, many of whom are buried in a pets' graveyard which can still be seen among the trees.

From Max Gate a walk across the fields and paths would bring Hardy to **Winterborne Came**, where his friend, the dialect poet and philologist William Barnes was rector. Barnes, whose best known work is *Linden Lea*, is buried in the churchyard. A reconstruction of Hardy's Max Gate study, along with many of his possessions, is one of the highlights of the excellent **Dorset County Museum** in High Street West. Also honoured in the Writers Gallery is William Barnes, who was the first secretary of the Dorset Natural History and Archaeological Society. The museum, which features cast ironwork inspired by the Great Exhibition of 1851 at the Crystal Palace, contains a wealth of exhibits spanning the centuries, from fossil trees and a Roman sword to a 19th century cheese press, from skeletons of Iron Age warriors to a stuffed great bustard, a large bird often seen in Dorset until becoming extinct in Britain in 1810. Outside the museum is a statue of William Barnes and, nearby, a statue of Thomas Hardy that was sculpted by Eric Kennington and erected in 1931.

Dorchester

THE THREE COMPASSES INN

The Square, Charminster,
Dorset DT2 9QT
Tel: 01305 263618

The Three Compasses is a fine village pub with two priceless assets in its owners, mine host Terry Dixon and his wife Margaret. They generate a particularly friendly, convivial atmosphere, and at least once a week the place enjoys the extra buzz of live music. Good home-cooked food is served in the bar from a short but select list that includes excellent lasagne and some really great omelettes.

For guests staying overnight the pub offers comfortable accommodation in a three-bed family room en suite, a double en suite and a twin and single that share a bathroom. The inn is a good base for exploring a fascinating part of the country with excellent walking and a wealth of tourist attractions. And right on the doorstep the sizeable village of Charminster itself has a lot to offer; the most interesting building is undoubtedly the church with its magnificent tower and the numerous memorials to the Trenchards, a leading local family. A little way south of the village is Wolfeton House, a Graded Listed medieval and Elizabethan house lying in water meadows close to the point where the River Cerne meets the River Frome. This house was the home of Lady Penelope in a lesser known work of Thomas Hardy, *A Group of Noble Dames*. Back from the walking and the sightseeing, the handsome redbrick Three Compasses beckons with its ever cheerful welcome and its friendly owners... and perhaps one of those terrific omelettes!

WARMWELL COUNTRY TOURING PARK

Warmwell, Dorchester, Dorset DT2 8JD
Tel: 01305 852313 Fax: 01305 851842
e-mail: touring@warmwell.fsbusiness.co.uk
website: www.welcome.to/warmwell

The resident manager Peter Bond runs a first-class caravan park in an area of outstanding natural beauty in the heart of Thomas Hardy country of Dorset. **Warmwell Country Touring Park** extends over 15 acres, offering a choice of pitches to settle your caravan or tent - either in secluded natural arbours among trees, or individual landscaped plots bounded by flowering shrubs. The site has mains electricity, heated toilet blocks with showers, disabled facility laundry, and children's play area. The shop will provide for most of your immediate needs while the clubhouse enables you to relax with glass of your favourite tipple with an assortment of games for the our younger members.

With the friendly support offered by the manager the options of things to do and see are almost endless with many hidden places to explore, from gentle country walks to the superb beaches of Weymouth. Visit the many pretty villages, historic towns, stately homes and museums within the surrounding area.

The park is located on the B3390, which links the A35 between Bere Regis and Tolpuddle, the A353 to Weymouth and the A352 Dorchester-Wareham road. It is open throughout the year, and in mid- and low-season a special deal offers seven nights for the price of six. Colour brochure's are available on request.

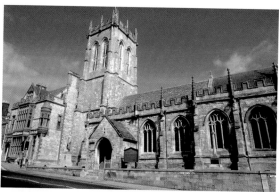

Dorchester

Dorchester has many other attractions which visitors should not miss: the **Keep Military Museum**, which tells the story of the men and women who fought and served in the County Regiments of Dorset and Devon; the **Old Crown Court and Cells**, where visitors can get a feel of the trials and gruesome punishments of four centuries; the **Tutankhamun Exhibition**, an impressive reconstruction of the young Pharaoh's tomb and treasures, including his golden mask, located in what was the **Church of Our Lady, Queen of Martyrs & St Michael** (a very successful exhibition now in its 15th year and open every day of the year); **Teddy Bear House**, where life-size teddy bears live their daily life and 'manufacture' smaller bears; and the **Dinosaur Museum**, where actual fossils and skeletons and life-size reconstructions combine with audio-visual and hands-on displays to entertain and instruct. Dorchester's medieval Church of St Peter was restored in the mid-19th century by the architect John Hicks and his assistant Thomas Hardy.

On the northern outskirts of Dorchester lies the village of **Charminster**, on the River Cerne. The 12th century church with its fine 16th century tower and Trenchard family memorials is the most important building in Charminster, while just outside the village is **Wolfeton House**, home of Sir Thomas Trenchard, the man who sponsored the tower of the church. This fine Grade I listed medieval and Elizabethan house lies in water meadows near the confluence of the Cerne and Frome rivers; its major features include fine carved oak panelling, splendid plaster ceilings, a superb stone great staircase and a cider house, with cider for sale.

A mile or so northeast of the town, **Kingston Maurward Gardens** comprise 35 acres of classic 18th century parkland and lawns sweeping down to a lake from a stately Georgian house that was built for George Pitt, a cousin of William Pitt the Elder. The Edwardian Gardens include a croquet lawn, rose garden, herbaceous borders and a large display of tender perennials, including the national collections of Penstemons and Salvias. Also in the grounds are an animal park and a nature trail.

AROUND DORCHESTER

OVERMOIGNE
6 miles SE of Dorchester on the A352

Just north of the village, on the way up to the B3390, is a dual attraction in the shape of the **Mill House Cider Museum** and **A Dorset Collection of Clocks**. The former has displays of antique cider-related equipment in full working order and videos of the cider-making process, while the latter is a collection of clocks both grand and humble including Dorset long case clocks.

Thomas Hardy Memorial Window

STINSFORD
2 miles E of Dorchester off the A35/A354

Stinsford is Melstock in Hardy's *Under the Greenwood Tree*. It was in **St Michael's Church** at Stinsford that Thomas Hardy was christened and where he attended services for a large part of his life. He sang hymns to the accompaniment of the village band (among whom were several of his relatives), which played from a gallery at the back of the church. The gallery was demolished in Hardy's lifetime, but many years later he drew a sketch from memory which showed the position of each player and the name of his instrument. A copy of this drawing is on display in the church, alongside a tablet commemorating the Hardys who took part. In the graveyard is the tomb of Hardy's first wife Emma and the heart of Hardy himself. The Poet Laureate Cecil Day Lewis is also buried here.

Thomas Hardy Gravestone

THE COUNTRYMAN INN

Blacknoll Lane, East Knighton, Nr Dorchester, Dorset DT2 8LL
Tel: 01305 852666 Fax: 01305 854125

Nina and Jeremy Evans offer true country hospitality at their splendid old inn situated in the heart of Hardy country just off the A352. There's a cosy, rustic atmosphere in the bars, where a good choice of beers and lagers is served, and in the large, airy restaurant a varied selection of home-cooked food is complemented by well-chosen wines. All appetites are catered for on a menu that runs from sandwiches and filled rolls to jacket potatoes, omelettes, fish dishes, classic grills and pan-fried chicken breast. Vegetarians have a choice of half-a-dozen main courses, and home-made sweets round off an excellent meal.

The inn also offers overnight accommodation, in six very comfortable bedrooms, all with en suite bathrooms. This is very much an inn for all ages, with much thought given to young visitors: a family room is supplied with toys and games, there's a safe play area and a spacious garden, and children even have their own special menu. With Lulworth Cove and historic Wareham just five miles away, the Countryman (spot him with whiskers and clay pipe on the inn sign) is the ideal base for exploring a beautiful part of the country.

HIGHER BOCKHAMPTON
3 miles NE of Dorchester on a minor road off the A35

In the woods above the village, reached by a series of narrow lanes and a ten-minute walk, is a major shrine for devotees of Thomas Hardy. **Hardy's Cottage** is surrounded by the trees of Puddletown Forest, a setting he evoked so magically in *Under the Greenwood Tree*. The delightful thatched cottage and gardens have been owned by the National Trust since 1947 and the rooms are furnished much as they would have been when the novelist was born here in 1840. Visitors can see the very room in which his mother gave birth, only to hear her child proclaimed stillborn. But an observant nurse noticed that the infant was in fact breathing, and the world of literature became a richer place thanks to

her awareness. The house was built by Thomas Hardy's grandfather in 1801.

PUDDLETOWN
5 miles NE of Dorchester on the A35

Birthplace of Hardy's grandfather and great grandfather, this was formerly

Athelhampton Gardens

Piddletown until changed by Victorian sensibilities ('piddle' is the Saxon word for 'clear water'). Nearby **Athelhampton** is one of the finest 15th century houses in England, with many magnificently furnished rooms including the Great Hall, Great Chamber and State Bedroom with an early Charles I tester bed. The house has a fine collection of art by Pugin, much of it relating to the Palace of Westminster. The glorious grounds feature world-famous topiary pyramids, fountains, the Octagonal Garden designed by Sir

Hardy's Cottage, Higher Bockhampton

THE ROYAL OAK

West Street, Bere Regis, Nr Wareham,
Dorset BH20 7HQ
Tel: 01929 471203 Fax: 01929 472636
e-mail: info@theroyaloakhotel.co.uk

Mike and Laura Jones, a young, go-ahead couple, invite visitors to the **Royal Oak** to enjoy the relaxed atmosphere, hassle-free service, comfortable accommodation and good food. On the edge of town, just off the main A31 and A35 roads, the building dates from the 17th century, and in the open-plan bar area beams and knick-knacks present a delightfully traditional picture; the fine collection of vintage water

jugs is reason enough for a visit in itself.

Skittles is a favourite pastime in West Country hostelries, and the skittle alley at the Royal Oak does extra duty as a big-screen TV room and a function room. The locals also like a game of pool or darts. Outside, the secure walled beer garden is a perfect spot for children and dogs to let off steam. The Royal Oak has a strong golfing connection: a golfing society is run from the hotel, and a history of the golf ball is contained in a special display case in the bar.

The hotel has won a great reputation for its food, and in the spacious dining room the home-cooked choice runs from traditional English fare - steak & Guinness pie is perennially popular - to pasta, curries and vegetarian dishes. The wine list is short but well chosen, and there's a selection of real ales; the coffee is great, too.

Overnight accommodation is provided in five newly renovated bedrooms, all furnished to a very high standard, with en suite facilities, TV, radio and hairdryer. Each room is named after a town from a Hardy novel. Families are warmly welcomed, and cots or additional beds are available on request. Breakfast, served from 8.30, is as simple or as hearty as each guest wants.

Dining Room

The village of Bere Regis is a must-visit for all Thomas Hardy enthusiasts, appearing as Kingsbere-sub-Greenhill in *Tess of the d'Urbervilles*. The family vault of the Turbervilles, whose name Hardy adapted for his novel, lies beneath the south aisle of the church. Many aspects of the church attract visitors, and elsewhere in the vicinity the Bovington Tank Museum, Corfe Castle and Lulworth Cove are all essential stops on the tourist trail. The whole area is a scenic delight, and, for shopping and family entertainment, the A35 provides a direct route to Bournemouth and Poole, each only half an hour away. The Royal Oak offers reduced rates for mid-week and out-of-season breaks.

Athelhampton Gardens

a new life first in Essex and later in Canada. The story of the Martyrs is told in the **Tolpuddle Martyrs Museum** housed in memorial cottages built in 1934 by the TUC.

Other places of pilgrimage in the village include the Martyrs Shelter and Tree, Thomas Standfield's cottage and the grave of James Hammett, who worked as a builder, lived to a great age and was buried in Tolpuddle churchyard.

Robert Cooke in 1971, a magnificent 15th century dovecote and a 19th century tollhouse.

TOLPUDDLE
6 miles NE of Dorchester on the A35

The village of the **Tolpuddle Martyrs**, six villagers who in 1833 attempted to escape from grinding poverty and harsh employers by forming a union and taking an oath of mutual support. Their leader was George Loveless, a Wesleyan Methodist preacher, and the others were his brother James Loveless, James Brine, James Hammett, John Standfield and his father Thomas Standfield, in whose cottage the union, the Friendly Society of Agricultural Labourers, was formed and the oath sworn. The landowners, fearing a spreading uprising, acted quickly, and, invoking the Mutiny Act of 1797, the court found the six guilty (swearing the oath was the crime, not the forming of a union, which had been made legal in 1824) and sentenced them to transportation for seven years to Australia. The public outcry at the harsh sentence was led by Dorchester's MP and resulted in the granting of a free pardon. Only one of the six, James Hammett, returned to Tolpuddle, the others seeking

BERE REGIS
10 miles E of Dorchester on the A35

Many visitors to the church at Bere Regis (Regis because it was a favoured stopping place of kings on their way to the West Country) are attracted by its associations with Hardy's *Tess of the d'Urbervilles*. They come to see the crumbling tombs of the once-powerful Turberville family whose name Hardy adapted for his novel.

But the **church** is well worth a visit in its own right, for the magnificent carved and painted roof, the figures of the Apostles in Tudor dress and the many humorous carvings showing characters suffering various forms of discomfort. There's also a carving of Cardinal Morton (of Fork fame), who had the roof installed in 1497 and was a native of Bere.

The history of the church goes back much further than that. In Saxon times Queen Elfrida came here to spend the rest of her days in penitence for her part in the murder of young King Edward at Corfe Castle in 979, and there's more evidence of the church's great age in the fact that around 1190 King John paid for the pillars of the nave to be restored. In the porch are some old fire hooks, which would have been used for pulling burning

FERN COTTAGE

Main Road, Piddletrenthide, Dorset DT2 7QF
Tel/Fax: 01300 348277

Comfortable, characterful Bed & Breakfast accommodation in a charming village setting, with the beautiful and historic Dorset countryside all around. **Fern Cottage**, built in about 1780, offers three double rooms and one single, all en suite, with central heating, tv and tea-makers. There's plenty of car parking space in the extensive grounds. The cottage is run by Caroline Gossage, a former tennis player for Zambia and Malawi, and her husband Steven, and is a perfect base for a walking holiday.

Dorset Roamers, based at the cottage, proposes a flexible variety of walking possibilities, and all-in walking holidays include Bed & Breakfast, a packed lunch and guided walking, with the additional option of an evening meal (otherwise, there are several excellent pubs nearby). The amount of walking depends entirely on the individual: for example, the Cerne Abbas Circle, a walk of about eight miles, starts directly opposite the cottage and takes in the village of Cerne Abbas, the giant carved in the hillside and the Piddle Valley. Other walks include the Abbotsbury Amble, the Durdle Door Doddle and the Hardy Hike - the last is a 19-mile hike spread over two days. The guide is Pete Senior, a Scouser who fell in love with the Dorset countryside 20 years ago - and stayed! If the weather (or energy levels) are against walking, there are plenty of interesting places within an easy drive, including the historic town of Dorchester, six miles away.

THE ROYAL OAK

23 Long Street,
Cerne Abbas,
Dorset DT2 7JG
Tel: 01300 341797

Visitors come from near and far to pass a pleasant few hours at the **Royal Oak**, a marvellous country pub in the most charming village setting. Behind an exterior that is almost hidden behind an impressively luxuriant covering of creepers and climbing plants, the pub is full of character, with flagstone floors, old wooden beams in abundance and a gleaming assortment of brasses and horseshoes. Owners David and Janice Birch and their staff make visitors very welcome, and the bar is a great place to enjoy a glass of real ale (choice of five brews).

But the Royal Oak's real trump card is the superb food, all prepared and cooked on the premises by an experienced team in the kitchen. Light bites run from the day's soup served with a Dorset cobber to chicken and pork liver paté made to a local recipe, deep-fried calamari and the ever-popular prawn cocktail. But this is a place to settle down to a full meal, and the main-course choice could be anything from grilled plaice or poached salmon to one of the wonderful speciality pies - perhaps steak & stilton or the exceptional game pie with local venison, pheasant, rabbit, pigeon and wild boar. There's always a good choice for vegetarians, along with some very tempting desserts.

thatch off roofs to halt the spread of fire - Bere suffered severe fire damage in 1633, 1717 and 1788.

PIDDLETRENTHIDE
7 miles NE of Dorchester on the B3143

A beautiful village in a lovely location, thought to be the home of Alfred the Great's brother Ethelred. The 12th and 15th century **Church of All Saints** is famous for its amazing animal gargoyles.

CERNE ABBAS
7 miles N of Dorchester on the A352

This pretty village beside the River Cerne takes the second part of its name from the **Abbey**, formerly a major Benedictine monastery of which an imposing 15th century gatehouse and a tithe barn of the same period survive, along with the holy well of St Augustine, who is said to have visited the place during his travels around the country. The Abbey was the centre of village life and with its decline the village declined, though it enjoyed a period of prosperity in the 19th century as a centre of malting and leathermaking. Well worth visiting, too, are the village church with its gargoyles, medieval statues and rare stone chancel screen, and **Abbey Farm**, a supreme example of an English manor house.

And, of course, there's the **Cerne Abbas Giant**, a colossal figure cut into the chalk hillside. He stands brandishing a club, naked, uncensored and full-frontal, a powerful pagan image of virility carved we know not why or when. As with most of these chalk figures, this one is best viewed from a distance, in this case from a lay-by on the A352 (though an ancient

tradition asserts that a couple wishing to have children must copulate on the phallus).

It was rumoured in Hardy's *The Dynasts* that Napoleon Bonaparte lived on human flesh and 'ate rashers o'baby for breakfast, for all the world like the Cerne Giant in old ancient times'. First mentioned in 1742, the Giant has always been well looked after, otherwise he would soon disappear into the hillside. At 182 feet, he is indeed a giant, but there's one even bigger - the Wilmington Long Man in Sussex, who measures a mighty 230 feet.

MINTERNE MAGNA
8 miles N of Dorchester on the A352

A couple of miles north of the Cerne Abbas Giant, Minterne Magna is notable for its **parish church**, filled with memorials to the Churchills, the Digbys and the Napiers, the families who once owned the great house here, as well as most of the Minterne Valley. The house itself, rebuilt in the style of the Arts &

Cerne Abbas Giant

Crafts Movement around 1900, is not open to the public, but its splendid **Minterne Gardens** are. The gardens are laid out in a horseshoe shape below the house and landscaped in the 18th century style of Capability Brown. They contain an important collection of Himalayan rhododendrons and azaleas, along with maples, cherries and many other fine and rare trees.

MAIDEN NEWTON
5 miles NW of Dorchester on the A356

Maiden Newton is a large chalk stream village straddling the River Frome. A walk through the village takes in an ancient stone cross, the 12th century Church of St Francis, the old water meadows and St Mary's Church with a Norman door still hanging on its original hinges.

THE FOX & HOUNDS INN

Cattistock, Dorchester,
Dorset DT2 0JH
Tel: 01300 320444

A totally unspoilt and authentically original village pub that delivers everything promised by the long, low exterior - part ancient exposed stonework and bricks, part smart white paint over the bricks. Log fires, beamed ceilings, classic pub furniture and an old bread oven create a time warp in the bar, and the main dining room, with its flagstone floor, also has a real feel of its 16th century origins.

All the food is prepared and cooked on the premises and is served every day except Monday and lunchtime Tuesday. The fine food is complemented by a good and expanding selection of wines, and the pub, where Jim Ovenden has recently taken over as manager, also stocks a number of real ales. Smoking is not permitted in the dining areas but is allowed in the roomy bar. Guests who want to stay overnight in this most agreeable environment have a choice of three bedrooms, two doubles and a twin. **The Fox & Hounds** is a good place to pause on a journey or to have as a base for exploring the many places of interest in the vicinity, starting perhaps with the historic town of Dorchester.

UPSHALLS

Cattistock, Dorchester, Dorset DT2 0JH Tel: 01300 320550

Close to the centre of a village within the Dorset Area of Outstanding Natural Beauty, **Upshalls** is the perfect base for a quiet, relaxing self-catering holiday in the country. Built as a forge in the 19th century - the original trade signs of horses painted on the front of the cottage are still maintained - it has three bedrooms with none of them being next door to the others. Owners John and Marie Walmsley can lend guests maps for walking and cycling trips, and they are very knowledgable about the area if you need to ask their advice.Their brochure sums up their approach "that you have a relaxing and happy time in a lovely part of West Dorset". No pets, no smoking. English Tourism Council 3 Stars.

CATTISTOCK
6 miles NW of Dorchester off the A356

Well worth a visit here is the mainly Victorian **church** built by the George Gilbert Scotts, père et fils containing a mural of St George and the Dragon, a vast Gothic font cover from 1904 and glass by Morris and Burne-Jones.

North of Dorchester, on the old Roman road (now the A37) that runs up to Yeovil, is **Melbury Osmond**, where Hardy's mother was born and where she was married.

MARTINSTOWN
3 miles SW of Dorchester on the B3159

For centuries this village was known as Winterborne St Martin, after the river that flows through the village and the village church. On the Black Downs southwest of Martinstown stands **Hardy's Monument**, which commemorates not Thomas Hardy the writer but Sir Thomas Masterson Hardy the flag captain of *HMS Victory* at Trafalgar to whom the mortally wounded Lord Nelson spoke the immortal words 'Kiss me, Hardy' (or perhaps 'Kismet, Hardy'). This Hardy was born in Portesham, a village just below the monument, and was, like the other Thomas, descended from the Hardys of Jersey. He escorted the body of Nelson home from Trafalgar and soon afterwards was made a baronet and eventually First Sea Lord. In retirement from active service he took over the running of Greenwich Hospital, where he died in 1839. The Hardy Monument is not a thing of beauty - variously described as a 'huge candlestick', a 'peppermill' and a 'factory chimney wearing a crinoline' - but if you stand with your back to it, there are grand views over Weymouth Bay. The area near the monument is rich in pre-historic remains, including long barrows, sarsens and the Kingston Russell stone circle.

MAIDEN CASTLE
2 miles SW of Dorchester off the A35

Even closer to Dorchester is Maiden Castle, one of the most impressive prehistoric sights in the country, a vast and spectacular fortification covering nearly 50 acres and dating back some 4,000 years to Neolithic times. Its steep earth ramparts, between 60 and 90 feet high, are nearly two miles round and together with the inner walls make a total of five miles of defences. The settlement flourished for 2,000 years until 44AD, when the occupying community was defeated by a Roman force under Vespasian. This was the army of the 2nd Augustan Legion, which with this conquering sweep overcame two tribes, 20 towns and the Isle of Wight. The Romans had really arrived; they briefly occupied the site of Maiden Castle before moving closer to the River Frome and founding Durnovaria (Dorchester). Apart from a brief spell as home to a small pagan group, Maiden Castle was never again settled, but the earthworks remain a most impressive sight.

WEYMOUTH

Two towns on opposite sides of the River Wey, Weymouth and Melcombe Regis, later amalgamated, and Melcombe is now the heart of the combined town. Early prosperity for the ports came from wool trading, but as elsewhere the Black Death caused a rapid, if temporary decline. Business picked up again, and the town received a boost when Henry VIII built **Sandsfoot Castle** (of which only the keep survives) here as part of the south-coast defences. Two and a half centuries later, like so many coastal communities, Weymouth began to be recognised for its health-giving properties. Royal patronage followed, and the good citizens of the town had good reason to erect a statue of George III to mark the 50th year of his reign in 1810. The King had brought great kudos and renewed prosperity to their little town by coming here to bathe in the sea water. George had been advised that sea bathing would help to cure his 'nervous disorder' so between 1789 and 1805 he and his royal retinue spent a total of 14 holidays in Weymouth. Fashionable society naturally followed in his wake. Close to his statue, which is unusual in being painted, his granddaughter Victoria's own 50th year as monarch is commemorated by a colourful Jubilee Clock erected in 1887. Nearby, the picturesque harbour is always busy with a profusion of boats, from little yachts and fishing boats to catamarans plying the routes to the Channel Islands and France, and even the occasional Tall Ship. One of

BREWERS QUAY

Hope Square, Weymouth,
Dorset D14 8TR
Tel: 01305 777622
Fax: 01305 761680

Brewers Quay is an imaginatively converted Victorian brewery in the heart of the picturesque Old Harbour. Amid the paved courtyards and cobbled alleys is a unique under-cover shopping village with over 20 specialist shops and attractions.

The Timewalk tells the fascinating story of the town as seen through the eyes of the brewery cat and her family, and in the Brewery Days attraction Hope Square's unique brewing heritage is brought to life with an interactive family gallery, audio-visual show and Victorian-style Tastings Bar.

Weymouth Museum contains an important record of local and social history; its latest exhibition is called Marine Archaeology and Associated Finds from the Sea. The Discovery Hands-on Science Centre has over 60 interactive exhibits, and this entertaining complex also has a bowling alley, gift shops, a traditional pub and a self-service restaurant.

DEEP SEA ADVENTURE & SHARKY'S PLAY ZONE

9 Custom House Quay, Old Harbour, Weymouth, Dorset DT4 8BG
Tel/Fax: 01305 760690
e-mail: deepsea_adventure@hotmail.co.uk
website: www.deepsea-adventure.co.uk

Deep Sea Adventure, opened in 1988 by HRH The Princess Royal, is a family attraction that tells the story of underwater exploration and marine exploits down the centuries.

Located in an imposing Victorian grain warehouse, it features a Titanic exhibition and an all-weather kids' adventure play zone called Sharky's. Open daily throughout the year, the complex has a gift shop and a licensed cafeteria.

Weymouth

town's brewing heritage from 1821 to the present day, while the Timewalk invites visitors to travel back through 600 years of Weymouth's history and to see, hear and smell the past.

From Brewers Quay, a path leads through Nothe Gardens to **Nothe Fort**, built between 1860 and 1872 as part of the defences of the new naval base being established on Portland. Ten huge guns face out to sea, while two smaller ones are directed inland. The fort continued in active service until 1956, when the British Army gave up its coastal artillery function. The fort's 30 rooms on three levels now house the **Museum of Coastal Defence** whose many interesting

the town's most popular tourist venues is **Brewers Quay** (see panel opposite), an imaginatively converted Victorian brewery with establishments ranging from craft shops to restaurants and a ten-pin bowling alley. Brewery Days explores the

MODEL WORLD

Lodmoor Country Park,
Preston Road,
Weymouth, Dorset DT4 7SX
Tel: 01305 781797

Model World is quite a unique attraction, which has been entertaining young and the not so young alike over the past 28 years. It is set in nearly three quarters of an acre of landscaped gardens with many interesting shrubs, trees and water features. All the models on display are hand made and are built to a true scale of 1:32 making a complete world in miniature.

An "0" gauge garden railway runs daily (subject to weather) together with a working quarry railway and branch railway which at a touch of a button YOU make work.

All the models depict an idyllic setting sometimes of a bygone era or you are brought right up to date with the space centre with its own monorail to transport the astronauts to the space launcher. Most of the models have there own special sound effects and many are activated by YOU to make them work. In addition some of the models replicate actual local buildings of special interest such as Thomas Hardy's cottage, Hardys Monument, Portland Bill and lots more for you to see.

Weymouth Harbour

Another statue of King George III is carved into the chalk hills above **Osmington**, a short distance east of Weymouth. This is one of many **White Horses** carved in chalk hills around the country, but this one, besides being one of the largest (354 feet by 279 feet) is the only one with a rider. The town fathers of Weymouth decided to show their gratitude at the King's patronage by paying the local militia to scrape this loyal but unrecognisable tribute in the hillside. An excellent walk hereabouts takes in Osmington village, where John Constable spent his honeymoon at the vicarage, and the coastal path to Osmington Mills.

displays illustrate past service life in the fort, history as seen from the Nothe headland, and the part played by the people of Weymouth in World War II. The gardens lead down to the shore and a small pebble beach at Newton's Cove. **Deep Sea Adventure**, on Custom House Quay, is a family attraction that tells the story of underwater exploration and marine exploits down the centuries. Housed in an imposing Victorian grain warehouse, it also includes Sharky's, an all-weather adventure play area for children of all ages (see panel on page 172).

AROUND WEYMOUTH

ISLE OF PORTLAND
3 miles S of Weymouth on the A354

Not an island at all, but a 4½ X 1½ mile peninsula joined to the mainland by the amazing Chesil Beach. A place of fortresses and maritime history, well known to devotees of the BBC's shipping forecast but most famous for the Portland stone that has been quarried for centuries. Buildings using the stone include St Paul's Cathedral, Buckingham Palace, Inigo Jones's Banqueting Hall in Whitehall and the UN building in New York. The best known building on the 'island' itself is **Portland Castle**, one of the finest of

Osmington White Horse

Henry VIII's coastal fortresses, whose active role lasted for 500 years up to World War II, when it was a D-Day embarkation point for British and American forces. Oliver Cromwell used it as a prison (the regular ones were probably all full) and in Victorian times it was the residence of Portland's governors. Visitors can try on armour, 'meet' Henry VIII in the Great Hall and enjoy the specials events that are held regularly throughout the year. The battlements provide superb views of Portland Harbour, whose breakwaters were constructed by convict labour to create the second largest man-made harbour in the world.

Close by is the **Verne Fortress**, built on the highest point on the island as a base for troops defending Portland and Weymouth and as a fortress with artillery to repel an enemy. The fortress became a prison in 1950. The oldest surviving building on Portland is the semi-ruined **St Andrew's Church** above Church Ope

Cove; this was Portland's parish church until 1756, when it was partially dismantled and much of the stone used to build the new parish church of St George at Reforne, built in grand style and on a grand scale by local architect Thomas Gilbert high up looking across to the west. This church was in turn replaced as the parish church by **All Saints at Easton**, which has an unusual feature in a sanctuary ceiling adorned with the signs of the zodiac.

Yet another church is **St Andrew's Avalanche Church** at Southwell, built in 1879 mainly as a memorial to those who perished when the clipper *Avalanche* sank off the Portland coast at the start of a passage to New Zealand. Not accessible, but clearly visible from the old St Andrew's, are the ruins of Rufus Castle (also known as Bow & Arrow Castle) built by Richard Duke of York in the mid-15th century.

ROYAL BREAKWATER HOTEL

Castle Road, Castletown, Portland, Dorset DT5 1BD
Tel: 01305 820476 Fax: 01305 826217
website: www.royalbreakwaterhotel.com

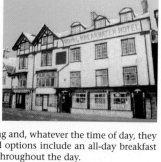

Robert Smail and his family run the **Royal Breakwater Hotel**, which is located in a terrace close to the harbour. The overnight

accommodation consists of 19 bedrooms, some with en suite facilities, all with television and tea/coffee-makers. Guests can be sure of a friendly greeting and, whatever the time of day, they will never go hungry: food options include an all-day breakfast and bar meals also served throughout the day.

No visit to Portland would be complete without spending some time looking round the Castle, the best preserved and one of the greatest of Henry VIII's chain of South Coast fortresses. That and the many other local attractions - the museum, the lighthouse, the extraordinary Chesil Beach - will take care of a large part of the day, while at night the divers take to the local waters.

They surface with healthy appetites, and find that the Royal Breakwater's late menu fits the bill admirably. The hotel is a particularly sociable place that can cater for parties and other events in its function room - and the celebrations can continue in the roomy, well-stocked bar.

Portland Museum, by **Church Ope Cove**, is a charming pair of thatched cottages where the island's fascinating history is told. The museum was founded by the birth control pioneer Marie Stopes in 1930. The tip of the island is **Portland Bill**, where the first lighthouse, long since decommissioned, is now a base for bird-watchers. A feature here is the tall, upright Pulpit Rock, an isolated rock which can be climbed and close to which are caves to explore.

The quarries on Portland still provide the renowned stone and are also used as study centres, for on-site sculpting and as nature reserves. Hardy called Portland the Isle of Slingers and said of its inhabitants: 'They are a curious and well nigh distinct people, cherishing strange beliefs and singular customs'. An observation which was probably wide of the mark at the time, and is certainly even wider now, when Portland has opened its doors to welcome visitors by the thousand every year.

EAST FLEET FARM

Fleet Lane, Chickerell,
Weymouth, Dorset DT3 4DW
Tel: 01305 785768
website: www.eastfleet.co.uk

In an Area of Outstanding Natural Beauty on the Dorset Heritage Coastal Path, **East Fleet Farm Touring Park** is the perfect base for enjoying the best of the sea and the countryside. The family-run 300-acre dairy and arable farm park, open from mid-March to mid-January, welcomes touring vans, tents and motor vans, providing all the necessary amenities for a short or long stay: mains electric hook-up, toilet and shower block, launderette, shop/off licence. Families are particularly welcome, and a games room, children's play area and licensed family bar with meals keeps everyone happy. There are separate toilet/shower facilities for families and disabled visitors, and a bathroom available to hire. Dogs are welcome, too, but they must be kept on a lead when on site.

The camping and caravanning area is mainly flat, sloping very gently down to the coastal path and the shores of the Fleet, a sheltered lagoon overlooking Chesil Bank and the sea that is known for its varied birdlife. A stay here can be as restful or as energetic as the visitor wants, from gentle walks in the country or by the sea to fishing, sailing, swimming or windsurfing. Weymouth is three miles away, and it's an easy drive to the Swannery and sub-tropical gardens of Abbotsbury. The park is located off the B3157 west of Weymouth.

CHARACTER FARM COTTAGES

Lower Farmhouse, Langton Herring, Weymouth,
Dorset DT3 4JB Tel: 01305 871187/871347
e-mail: jane@mayo.fsbusiness.co.uk

A number of delightful cottages (4 star Tourist Board rating), in the glorious Dorset countryside provide self-catering accommodation of immense charm and character. Four of the cottages are located in the attractive, unspoilt village of Langton Herring, overlooking Chesil Beach and Lyme Bay, the fifth in the hamlet of Rodden on the picturesque route to Abbotsbury Swannery. The Brambles, a stone bungalow, is the smallest of the cottages, with a double bedroom, while the largest, with three bedrooms, is Chelsea Cottage at Rodden.

Portland is connected to the mainland by the extraordinary **Chesil Beach**, a vast bank of pebbles worn smooth by the sea that stretches some 18 miles to the west. The effect of the tides is such that the pebbles are graded in size from west to east, and fishermen (and previously also smugglers) reckon that they can judge where they are landing on the beach by the size of the pebbles. In the west they are as small as peas and usually creamy in colour, while at Portland they are more often grey and are sometimes the size of large apples. The Beach has long been the bane of sailors, and many a ship has been grounded on the pebbles, sometimes even tossed bodily over them.

CHICKERELL
2 miles W of Weymouth on the B3157

Chickerell is the first community west of Weymouth, a pretty place of thatched cottages and an interesting church with a Norman font and Jacobean pulpit.

LANGTON HERRING
5 miles NW of Weymouth off the B3157

Langton Herring and Chickerell stand close to an inlet of the eight-mile stretch of shallow water between Chesil Beach and the land, known as **The Fleet** (after the village of the same name). The Fleet is a nature reserve and home to a wide variety of fish, fowl and plants. Trips along the Fleet in glass-bottomed boats allow visitors a close-up view of life just below the surface.

RODDEN
5 miles NW of Weymouth off the B3157

A village about 1 mile inland from the Fleet and Chesil Beach on a minor road that leads to Langton Herring in one direction and Abbotsbury in the other. The Dorset Coastal Path runs a little way inland to pass through the village.

DANSEL GALLERY

Rodden Row, Abbotsbury,
Nr Weymouth, Dorset DT3 4JL
Tel: 01305 871515
Fax: 01305 871518

Set in a delightful thatched converted stable block near the centre of the village, **Dansel Gallery** is Britain's leading showcase for contemporary craftwork in wood and one of the Craft Council's Selected Shops. The Gallery, which truly is a Mecca for woodworkers, houses a superb collection of

high quality hand-made items from the cream of British designer craftsmen; everything on display is carefully selected for its good design and quality of finish.

The story of the Gallery begins in 1979, when Danielle and Selwyn Holmes set up a workshop and showroom, initially dedicated to their own work, but soon welcoming other artists in wood. A generation later, more than 200 British woodworkers are represented in the Gallery, probably the largest concentration of its kind in the country. The range is also impressive, running from individually designed pieces of furniture through elegant jewellery boxes to toys, puzzles and three-dimensional jigsaws to one-off decorative pieces that highlight the inventiveness and versatility of the woodworker.

The Gallery continues to win the highest praise from leading experts in the field of craftsmanship in wood, and its products are certain to be in demand by enthusiasts and collectors for generations to come.

ABBOTSBURY

Abbotsbury Tourism Ltd, West Yard Barn, West Street, Abbotsbury, Dorset DT3 4JT
Tel: 01305 871130 Fax: 01305 871092
e-mail: info@abbotsbury-tourism.co.uk
website: www.abbotsbury-tourism.co.uk

Surrounded by hills, with the sea close at hand, **Abbotsbury** is one of the county's most popular tourist spots and by any standards one of the loveliest villages in England. Very little remains of the Benedictine Abbey that gives the village its name, but what has survived is the magnificent Great Abbey Barn, a tithe barn almost 250ft long that was built in the 14th century to house the Abbey's tithes of wool, grain and other produce.

The village's three main attractions, which bring the crowds flocking in their thousands to this lovely part of the world, are the **Swannery**, the **Sub-Tropical Gardens** and the **Tithe Barn Children's Farm**. The most famous of all is Abbotsbury Swannery, which was established many centuries ago, originally to provide food for the monks in the Abbey. For at least 600 years the swannery has been a sanctuary for a huge colony of mute swans. The season for visitors begins in earnest in March, when the swans vie for the best nesting sites. From May to the end of June cygnets hatch by the hundred

and from then until October the fluffy chicks grow and gradually gain their wings. Cygnets who have become orphaned are protected in special pens until strong enough to fend for themselves. By the end of October many of the swans move off the site for the winter, while other wildfowl move in. An audio-visual show is run hourly in the old swanherd's cottage, and a few lucky visitors are selected to help out at the spectacular twice-daily feeding sessions. The swans' feed includes eelgrass from the River Fleet. In May of this year the Swanherd, who has looked after the colony for 40 years, Dick Dalley, retired. When he first started the birds were still being raised for the table, but today, the 159 breeding pairs - including 2 black swans - are protected by law. Also on site are a shire horse and cart service, a gift shop and a café housed in a delightful building that was converted from Georgian kennels.

At the western end of the village, Abbotsbury Sub-Tropical Gardens, established by the first Countess of Ilchester as a kitchen garden for her nearby castle, occupy a 20-acre site close to Chesil Beach that's largely protected from the elements by a ring of oak trees. In this micro-climate a huge variety of rare and exotic plants and trees flourish, and the camellia groves and the collections of rhododendrons and hydrangeas are known the world over.

There's a woodland trail, a children's play area, visitor centre, plant nursery, gift shop and restaurant with a veranda overlooking the sunken garden. Most of the younger children will make a beeline for the Tithe Barn Children's Farm, where they can cuddle the rabbits, bottle feed the lambs, race toy tractors, feed the doves and meet the donkeys and horses. The Farm's latest attraction is the Smugglers Barn, where the little ones can learn and play at the same time.

The Lake, Abbotsbury

ABBOTSBURY
8 miles NW of Weymouth on the B3157

Surrounded by hills, picturesque Abbotsbury is one of the county's most popular tourist spots and by any standards one of the loveliest villages in England.

Virtually nothing remains of the Benedictine Abbey that gives the village its name, but what has survived is the magnificent **Great Abbey Barn**, a tithe barn almost 250ft long that was built in the 14th century to store the Abbey's tithes of wool, grain and other produce. With its thatched roof and stone walls, it is a glorious sight and one of the largest and best-preserved barns in the country. It is surrounded by a children's farm where youngsters can feed the animals and drive little tractors

Its most striking feature on the approach is **St Catherine's Chapel**, perched high on a hill. Measuring only

THE OLD COASTGUARDS

Abbotsbury, Dorset DT3 4LB
Tel: 01305 871335 Fax: 01305 871766 website: www.oldcoastguards.com

A long, low building dating from the 1820s - once frequented by the Bloomsbury set and visited by Thomas Hardy - was converted in 1973 into four roomy self-catering cottages in one of the most beautiful parts of the Dorset Heritage Coast. The setting for **The Old Coastguards** is really stunning, with views of Chesil Beach and Lyme Bay ahead and the farmland and hills inland. The four cottages - Matthew, Mark, Luke and John - are equipped with all the essentials for an independent, go-as-you-please holiday. Matthew and John each have three bedrooms, while Mark and Luke have two; bed linen is provided, and a cot and high chair are available for families with small children; dogs are welcome by arrangement.

The friendly owners Cheryl and John Varley are regularly on hand with a welcome and advice.

Shops and pubs and restaurants are mainly a drive away - 2 miles to Abbotsbury, 9 to Bridport - but the opportunities around the cottages are almost endless: relaxing and soaking up the views from the terrace, lazing on the beach, a spot of fishing, studying the local wildlife; and for the more energetic a swim, a bracing walk along the beach track or over the hills to Abbotsbury Castle.

THE ILCHESTER ARMS

9 Market Street, Abbotsbury, Nr. Weymouth,
Dorset DT3 4JR
Tel: 01305 871243 Fax: 01305 871225
e-mail: enqs@ilchesterarms.co.uk
website: www.ilchesterarms.co.uk

The Ilchester Arms is a friendly country inn situated in a part of Dorset designated an Area of Outstanding Natural Beauty. The seascapes and landscapes hereabouts are equally breathtaking, and the National Heritage village of Abbotsbury has a full quota of interesting things to see and do.

The inn, which is managed by go-ahead local girl Sarah Williams, is very much at the heart of village life, and is also a popular stopping place for some of the thousands of visitors who come to Abbotsbury every year. Originally a coaching inn on the coast road west from Weymouth, it has been expanded and renovated down the years without losing all its period feel. A fine selection of wines and beers is served in the comfortable bar area, where a history in pictures of the village and the locality is an interesting feature.

Outside are a pleasant patio, a beer garden and a car park with space for 30 cars.

The chefs do a great job in the kitchen, preparing a 'lite bite' menu at lunchtime and a more formal evening menu to be enjoyed at leisure in the conservatory restaurant. Typifying the lunchtime choice are jacket potatoes with interesting fillings (prawn and lemon mayonnaise, creamy peppered mushrooms, five-bean chilli and cheese), chicken caesar salad and wild boar, leek and ginger sausages served with bubble & squeak on a red wine sauce. In the evening, chicken liver parfait or coriander mussels could precede a simply grilled sole, swordfish with Cajun butter, lamb cutlets on parmesan mash or steak, kidney and barley wine pie.

This is a part of the world that demands plenty of time to explore and admire, and the Ilchester Arms makes an excellent base for doing it. The ten en suite bedrooms - singles, doubles and twins - all have modem-compatible telephones, hospitality tray, trouser press and hairdryer, and three rooms boast four-poster beds.

The great Abbey Barn, the famous swannery with its 600 swans and the sub-tropical gardens are unique local attractions, and the village itself, one of the loveliest in England, is overlooked from its hilltop perch by the solidly built little St Catherine's Chapel. There are good cliff walks with grand views of the extraordinary Chesil Bank, which extends eastwards from Abbotsbury to the Isle of Portland. After a day in the bracing Dorset air, the time is right to return to the Ilchester Arms for refreshment and a good meal, and perhaps a game of darts or pool settling down for a good night's sleep.

45ft by 15ft, the 15th century chapel is solidly built to withstand the battering it receives from the elements, and its walls are more than 4 ft thick.

St Catherine was believed to be particularly helpful in finding husbands for unmarried women and in medieval times spinsters would climb the hill to her chapel chanting a dialect ditty:

St Catherine, St Catherine, lend me thine aid
And grant that I may never die an old maid.
A husband, St Catherine
A good one, St Catherine
But arn-a-one better than
Narn-a-one, St Catherine.

The most famous attraction of all is **Abbotsbury Swannery** where for at least 600 years the swannery has been a sanctuary to a huge colony of mute swans. At the western end of the village is yet another attraction, the **Abbotsbury Sub-Tropical Gardens**, a 20-acre site close

to Chesil Beach and largely protected from the elements by a ring of oak trees. In this micro-climate a huge variety of rare and exotic plants and trees flourish, and also on site are a woodland trail, a children's play area, visitor centre, shop and restaurant (see panel on page 179).

WEST BEXINGTON
11 miles W of Weymouth on the B3157

The pleasant village of West Bexington is home to sea-anglers and walkers and is generally taken to be the western limit of Chesil Beach.

PUNCKNOWLE
12 miles W of Weymouth off the B3157

It rhymes with tunnel. Puncknowle's best-known son was Henry Shrapnel 1761-1842), an English artillery officer who invented the bomb that was first used in the Crimean War. On which explosive note we head for the western reaches of Dorset.

TAMARISK FARM COTTAGES

(English Tourist Council rated 3-4 stars category 1)

Tamarisk Farm, West Bexington, Dorchester, Dorset DT2 9DF
Tel/Fax: 01308 897784
e-mail: tamarisk@eurolink.ltd.net website: tamariskfarm.co.uk

An organic farm by Chesil Beach is the setting for a self-catering holiday with a difference in the most serene and picturesque surroundings. **Tamarisk Farm**, owned and run by Josephine and Arthur Pearse, is a 500-acre farm with sheep, Devon Ruby Red cattle, Shires and Welsh ponies; and a six-acre organic market garden whose produce is readily available from the farmhouse. The guest accommodation comprises six characterful, well-equipped cottages sleeping from four to six guests. Each has its own individual appeal: 'Two Wings', built in the 1930s, enjoys breathtaking views of the coastline from its position at the top of the village; its large garden is completely enclosed and secure, making it good for families with young children and dogs. 'The Moat' is in the centre of Bexington by the tiny village green, with gardens front and rear, also fully fenced.

'Mimosa' is very special, designed specifically to cater for holidaymakers with disabilities; it has been awarded the Category 1 Wheelchair Accessible Status - the highest - by the English Tourism Council. The doorways and paths are extra wide, the switches all conveniently placed, and the kitchen is equipped with height adjustable hob and sink units. The floors are tiled with under floor heating,

and the duvets, pillows and cushions are filled with Hollofill rather than down to help allergy sufferers. There are two smaller holiday cottages, "Whispering Pines" and "The Fossil and the Cross", (purpose built), up the slope from "Mimosa" and in the same fully fenced garden. Nearly every village in the neighbourhood has a pub serving good food. The area for miles around is designated an Area of Outstanding Beauty and is part of the Dorset Heritage Coast.

9 West Dorset

The fascination of the sea, the beauty of the land, the historic buildings and, of course, Thomas Hardy, are all to the fore in this far corner of Dorset, which reaches west to the border with Devon and north to the border with Somerset. 'The Pearl of Dorset' is a frequent description of Lyme Regis, a delightful resort town in an area of outstanding natural beauty where the rolling countryside plunges down to the sea. The cliffs around Lyme Regis are fossil territory, and a window in Lyme's Church of St Michael commemorates Mary Anning, the daughter of a local shopkeeper, who was the first person to dig seriously for fossils in the blue lias cliffs. At the tender age of 12 her efforts were rewarded when she uncovered the remains of an ichthyosaurus. Later, as one of the first professional fossil collectors, she made many other important fossil discoveries, including a plesiosaur and a pterodactyl. The ichthyosaurus was sold to the British Museum, but many local fossil finds are on display in Dinosaurland in Lyme. The eight-mile stretch of coast between Bridport and Charmouth includes the highest cliff on the south coast, at 618 feet. **Golden Cap** takes its name from the cap of golden sandstone visible on the face. The 2,000 acre National Trust estate on which it stands contains a number of gorse-covered hills and valleys, several historical sites and many miles

Uploders

of footpaths. The cliffs themselves are rich in fossils but fraught with danger as the sea keeps up its constant bombardment. West Dorset is also famous for its Iron Age forts, which provide not only intriguing glimpses into the lives of the ancient British tribes but also the most stupendous views. The Hardy connection extends as far as this edge of the county, with Tess undertaking a long, fruitless walk to Beaminster (Hardy's Emminster) and Bridport (Port Bredy) being the setting for his story *Fellow-Townsmen*.

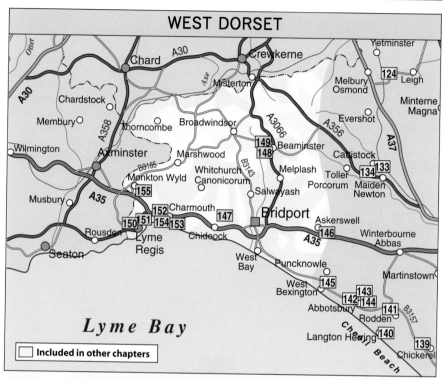

WEST DORSET

Yetminster

Chard — A30 — Crewkerne

Otter

Misterton

Melbury Osmond — 124 Leigh

A30

Chardstock

Minterne Magna

Membury — A358 — Thorncombe — Broadwindsor

A3066

Evershot

A356

Wilmington

Axminster — Marshwood

149 Beaminster
148

Cattistock

A37

B3165

Whitchurch Canonicorum — Melplash — Toller — 134 133

Monkton Wyld

Porcorum — Maiden Newton

Musbury — A35 — 155

Salwayash

152 Charmouth

Bridport

150 51 154 153 — 147

Askerswell

Rousden — Lyme Regis — Chideock

Winterbourne Abbas
146

A35

Seaton

West Bay — Puncknowle

West Bexington — 145

Martinstown

142 143 144

Lyme Bay

Abbotsbury — 141

Rodden

Langton Herring — 140

139

Chesil Beach

Chickerel

☐ **Included in other chapters**

© MAPS IN MINUTES ™ (2000)

PLACES TO STAY, EAT, DRINK AND SHOP

BRIDPORT

Bridport is an appealing little town with a fair number of handsome 17th and 18th century buildings, and a few from earlier times. Most notable among these are the medieval Prior's House, the stately Georgian Town Hall with its clock-tower and cupola, and Palmers Brewery (guided tours available in the summer). **Bridport Museum**, in a Tudor building in South Street, tells the story of the town and the history of the area.

Two distinguished visitors are among the many people 'encountered' in the Museum. One was Joan of Navarre, who landed at Bridport on her way to marry King Henry IV; the other was Charles II, who arrived in the town after his defeat at the Battle of Worcester. He was fleeing to France in the guise of the groom in a runaway marriage. As he attended to his horses in the yard of the George Inn, an ostler approached him saying 'Surely I know you, friend?'. The quick-thinking future monarch asked where the ostler had been working before. 'Exeter', came the reply, and Charles said 'Ay, that's where we must have met' and hurried away. If the ostler's memory for faces had been sharper he could have claimed the £1,000 reward for the capture of Charles, and history might have been very different.

The museum, and a small offshoot at nearby Loders, cover what was once the mainstay of the town, rope-making. Hemp grew in the area around Bridport 2,000 years ago, and the town's ropeworks were for centuries the basis of its prosperity, producing cables and hawsers for the Royal Navy, nets for fishermen and hangman's nooses - these last were known blackly as Bridport Daggers. Production was severely curtailed when the Navy

WEST HEMBURY ORGANIC FARM

Askerswell, Dorchester, Dorset DT2 9EN
Tel: 01308 485289 Fax: 01308 485041
e-mail: hunt@westhembury.com website: www.westhembury.com

Holiday accommodation 'for people who care about the countryside' on an organic farm among the beautiful Dorset hills. Dr and Mrs Hunt, who live on the farm in a thatched Grade ll listed farmhouse, offer two cottages converted from18th century stone barns for self-catering holidays throughout the year. Badgers is a single-storey cottage with a twin bedroom and a shower room, while Barn Owls is on two floors, with three bedrooms (one en suite) and a separate bathroom. Both are fitted to a high standard, with full central heating , comfortable living rooms, fully equipped kitchens and private gardens.

The holiday accommodation is just one aspect of the farm, whose objectives include the production of safe, high-quality food with real taste, and the conservation of rare breed farm animals. They produce to Soil Association organic standards, beef from their herd of White Park cattle, lamb from their flock of Southdown sheep and cereals. The owners also keep Sussex chickens, and the grassland and woodland of the farm estate support many rare flowers and an abundance of bird life. No pets are allowed (and no smoking, except in the garden), but stabling can be provided for guests who want to bring their own horses.

decided to build its own rope-works, but the industry is still in existence on a much smaller scale - the nets for the tennis courts at Wimbledon are produced here.

Fishing at West Bay

Some of the town's pavements and alleys are unusually wide, a legacy of the rope-making days, when the ropes would be laid out along the sides of the streets for twisting and drying. This industry, along with some of the major buildings, appears in Hardy's story *Fellow-Townsmen*, which is set in his Port Bredy. Bridport has long been known for its thriving street market, which still takes place on the three main streets every Wednesday and Saturday. The town has been closely linked down the years with the nonconformists, and among the most interesting of its chapels are the extremely well-appointed Unitarian Chapel in East Street, dating from 1794, and the former Methodist chapel of 1838 in South Street.

A little way east of town, at **Mangerton**, is a working 17th century **water mill** and **museum of bygones** set in a quiet valley on the River Manger.

AROUND BRIDPORT

WEST BAY
1 mile S of Bridport on a minor road off the A35

When Bridport's own harbour silted up in the early 1700s, the townspeople built a new one at the mouth of the River Britt and called it West Bay. During the 19th century hundreds of ships docked here every year, though it could never accommodate the largest, and it even had its own shipbuilding industry. It never became a fashionable holiday resort, but it has a pleasant beach backed by 100ft sandstone cliffs and a nice little harbour. It is also the place where the drama series "Harbour Lights" starring Nick Barry was filmed. The story of the harbour is told in the **Harbour Life Exhibition**, which includes short films of West Bay shot in the 1930s. Guided tours of the exhibition and the harbour are available by arrangement.

ASKERSWELL
4 miles E of Bridport off the A35

Askerwell is an attractive, largely unspoilt village at the head of the Asker Valley, beneath the Iron Age hill fort on top of **Eggardon Hill**, from where there are lovely views over Marshwood Vale and across Lyme Bay.

TOLLER PORCORUM
7 miles NE of Bridport off the A3066

Good walking in and around this village nestling in the valley of the River Hooke. Its name derives from the pigs for which the area was once famous. The village trail takes in the site of the dismantled station of the Bridport branch line (it was removed and rebuilt on the Dart Valley

HELL BARN COTTAGES

Hell Farmhouse, Hell Lane, North Chideock, Bridport,
Dorset DT6 6LA Tel: 01297 489589
website: www.hellbarn.co.uk

Two miles inland from Seatown beach, tucked away in a quiet hollow by Winniford Stream in North Chideock, is this picturesque complex of four self-catering holiday cottages. Surrounded by rolling farmland, the garden is a peaceful haven in which to sit, stroll or play; yet the main A35 road is only a mile away, making this an ideal base from which to explore the area with its attractions for all ages and interests. Owned and run by Diana and Shigeaki Takezoe, **Hell Barn Cottages** are all in converted stone barns, each with two bedrooms, spacious living rooms and fully equipped kitchens and bathrooms. The extensive garden has an outdoor wooden

play area, patio with tables and chairs, and a large games room with equipment for toddlers through to adults. For an even more relaxed holiday, guests can choose from a selection of ready-made, home-cooked, frozen meals; or take the unique opportunity of enjoying a Japanese meal, cooked and served in the cottage or the farmhouse. Hell Farm was once an important part of the Chideock Manor Estate, and views differ as to the origin of its name; but whether it commemorates a Christian massacre or a famous Greek (Hellas), one thing is certain - it is a heavenly place to stay!

BEAM COTTAGE

16 North Street, Beaminster,
Dorset DT8 3DZ
Tel: 01308 863639

In the centre of the charming town of Beaminster, **Beam Cottage** is a very attractive Grade ll listed cottage which has been sympathetically altered and enlarged over the years. Margie Standeven's cottage is a sheer delight, but the real surprise is the large secluded garden at the back that makes a stay here almost like being in the country - a genuine case of enjoying the best of both worlds.

The accommodation thoroughly deserves its Tourist Board 4 Diamond rating: in the main building are three bedrooms - a double with its own sitting room, a twin and a family room. It's a lovely quiet place, but for complete peace and seclusion the choice would have to be the garden cottage, which has a twin-bedded room, bathroom, sitting room and kitchen - everything provided for a real escape to a delightful retreat. All the rooms are centrally heated and equipped with tvs. The little town of Beaminster has retained most of the old-world charm that Thomas Hardy's Tess found when she arrived here (Emminster in the novel *Tess of the Durbevilles*). The small rural crafts and industries may have largely disappeared, but the most notable buildings still stand: the stone-roofed market cross in the square; the 17th century almshouses; and the splendid church with its gold-tinted yellow limestone tower.

railway in Devon); some very attractive woodland; and the neighbouring larger hamlet of **Toller Fratrum**, where the Brethren of the Order of St John of Jerusalem (the Knights Hospitalers) founded a monastery in the 11th century. The village Church of St Basil contains some very interesting pieces, including an elaborately carved Norman font and a carving of Mary Magdalene wiping Christ's feet.

Parnham House, Beaminster

CHIDEOCK
3 miles W of Bridport on the A35

The village of Chideock (pronounced Chiddick) takes its name from Sir John Chideock, who built a castle nearby. Nothing remains of the castle, but a black marble effigy in the church is believed to represent Sir John.

BEAMINSTER
6 miles N of Bridport on the A3066

Set among rolling hills, with the River Britt running beside the main street, Beaminster (call it Bemminster or Bemster) is a delightful little market town described admirably by the dialect poet William Barnes:

'Sweet Be'mi'ster that bist a-bound
By green and woody hills all round.'

Many of its medieval buildings were destroyed by fires, the first a deliberate act by the occupying Royalist forces, and as a result the centre of the town has a handsome collection of 18th and 19th century properties. The stone-roofed market cross is the central feature of the market square, which in its heyday traded the produce of the town's many cottage industries, including ropes, shoes, embroidered buttons, shoes, wrought ironwork and clocks. Some older buildings survived the fires, including the 16th century Pickwick's Inn (originally the King's Head), the 17th century almshouses and the imposing 15th century **Church of St Mary** with its splendid multi-pinnacled 100ft tower from which, it is said, a number of citizens were hanged during the Bloody Assizes. Inside the church are impressive, larger-than-life sculptures and wall memorials to the Strode family, local gentry who lived at Parnham House (see below). Beaminster has a fairly grand second church, Holy Trinity, built in 1850. **Beaminster Museum**, housed in the former Congregational chapel of 1749, displays objects relating to the life of the town from medieval to modern times, as well as the archaeology and architecture of the area, an exhibition of the village of Mosterton and a working turret clock from the parish church at Burstock. Here, too, are the stories of the leading local families, including the Daniels, one of whom fought with Monmouth, the Hines (later to found the cognac dynasty) and the Strodes.

The Strodes had their family home at **Parnham House**, a gem of Elizabethan architecture on the A3066 about a mile south of town that was later enlarged and then refurbished by John Nash at the beginning of the 19th century. The current residents John and Jennie Makepeace have transformed the house by a 'spirit of adventure in craft and design', enhancing the Plantagenet splendour with contemporary design and putting superb examples of modern furniture into a heritage context. The pieces are made on site in the **John Makepeace Furniture Workshop**, where visitors can see John and his students at work. The house is set in grand and beautiful gardens, laid out by Jennie, which include unusual plants, a lake rich in wildlife, a play area for children and a tree trail showing how the different trees

Mapperton Gardens

are utilised to create tomorrow's antiques. The studio shop, situated in the old library, stocks a wide variety of gifts in wood, ceramics and textiles, and home cooking is on offer in the Oak Café. A mile or so to the south of Parnham is **Loscombe House**, whose four-acre garden offers a sample of the real rural Dorset, with woodland, an attractive stream and winding grass paths among the shrubs and flowers. The B3163 leads from Beaminster to another garden attraction. **Mapperton Gardens** surround a fine Jacobean manor house with stable blocks, a dovecote and its own Church of All Saints (see panel opposite). Praise for this lovely peaceful location comes from many sources, including Pevsner's Dorset Guide ('There can hardly be anywhere a more enchanting manorial group than Mapperton') and Candida Lycett Green ('From the house and down the first slopes there stretches a magical garden worth travelling a hundred miles to see').

This part of the county is made for garden-lovers and plantspeople, and on the other side of Beaminster is yet another lovely garden. **Horn Park Gardens**, set around a house built in 1910 by a pupil of Sir Edwin Lutyens, are full of unusual shrubs and trees, with terraced lawns, lovely herbaceous and rose borders, water

Furniture Warehouse, Parnham House

MAPPERTON GARDENS

Beaminster, Dorset DT8 3NR
Tel: 01308 862645 Fax: 01308 863348
e-mail: office@mapperton.com website: www.mapperton.com

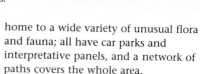

Two miles from Beaminster, five miles from Bridport, Mapperton Gardens surround a fine Jacobean manor house with stable blocks, a dovecote and its own Church of All Saints. The grounds, which run down a gradually steepening valley, include an orangery and an Italianate formal garden, a 17th century summer house and a wild garden planted in the 1960s. The gardens, which are open to the public from March to October, are a natural choice for film location work, with *Emma* and *Tom Jones* among their credits.

gardens, ponds, woods and a natural wildflower meadow with more than 160 different wild flowers and grasses. Many of the garden's unusual and interesting plants are for sale in the garden shop. The location, which enjoys splendid views to the east and south, is immediately before Beaminster road tunnel, which, when built in 1831-2, was a forerunner of the great railway tunnels that were soon to follow.

BROADWINDSOR
9 miles N of Bridport on the B3163

A terraced village with a handsome church and a plaque commemorating a visit in 1651 by Charles II. Three miles south of the village is trio of hill forts, for which the county is renowned. **Pilsden Pen** (the highest point in Dorset at over 900 feet), **Lambert's Castle** and **Coney's Castle** all offer a real feeling of history and wonderful views over Marshwood Vale to the sea. The poet William Wordsworth once took a house on Pilsden Pen and declared that there was no finer view in England. The three are

home to a wide variety of unusual flora and fauna; all have car parks and interpretative panels, and a network of paths covers the whole area.

THORNCOMBE
12 miles NW of Bridport off the B3165

The village church contains some remarkable brasses commemorating 15th century members of the Brook family.

A short distance from Thorncombe, right up on the border with Somerset, is **Forde Abbey**, founded in the 12th century by Cistercian monks after they had made an unsuccessful attempt to found an abbey in Devon. Over the years it became one of the richest and most

Forde Abbey

learned monasteries in the country, but had already declined greatly by the time of the Dissolution of the Monasteries in 1539. It then lay empty for more than 100 years, until in 1649, partly demolished, it was sold to Edmund Prideaux, Attorney-General to Oliver Cromwell. The remains of the abbey were incorporated into the grand private house of the Prideaux family, including the old chapter house, which became a family chapel, the monks' dining and sleeping quarters and the Great Hall, which had not even been completed at the time of the Dissolution. The later additions include magnificent 17th century plaster ceilings and the renowned Mortlake Tapestries. Based on cartoons by Raphael made for Pope Leo X, they were made by weavers brought over from Brussels by Charles I to teach the English the art of tapestry work, and were a gift from Queen Anne to Sir Francis Gwyn, who owned the house at the time of the donation in 1702. Among the

Biblical scenes depicted in the tapestries is Saints Peter and John healing the lame man at the gate of the temple. 'One of the ten best places in England' is the verdict of Candida Lycett Green, and Alan Titchmarsh sums up the glorious gardens as 'one of the greatest gardens in the West Country'. The elegant grounds include wide sloping lawns, ponds and fountains, statuary, arboretum, working kitchen garden, bog garden, shrubbery, rock garden and a nursery selling rare and unusual plants. The garden is open daily throughout the year, the nursery daily from April to end-October and the house Tuesday to Thursday, Sunday and Bank Holidays from April to end-October.

LYME REGIS

The 'Pearl of Dorset' enjoys a setting unrivalled in the county in an area of outstanding natural beauty as it sweeps

KENT HOUSE HOTEL

Silver Street, Lyme Regis,
Dorset DT7 3HT   AA 3 Diamonds
Tel: 01297 443442 Fax: 01297 444626
e-mail: thekenthouse@talk21.com
www: kenthousehotel.co.uk

Since taking over **Kent House Hotel** in September 1999, Theresa and John Robertson have lavished a great deal of time and care in renovations and refurbishment. A large Victorian house which has been a hotel since 1945, it has nine letting bedrooms, six of them with en suite facilities; some enjoy views out to sea, while others look over Lyme Valley.

The main rooms are large and airy, and two second-floor twin-bedded rooms that share a shower room make an ideal suite for a family or a group of friends. A fully licensed bar is located in the dining room, which leads to a terrace that overlooks the garden and the valley. Breakfast is served from 8 till 9, dinner from 6 to 9.30 and Sunday lunch from 12 to 2.30. The hotel, the town and the area around invites visitors to do as little or as much as they please: relax in the guest lounge or out in the garden with a good book, visit the numerous local historic houses and sites, explore the rock pools and hunt for fossils, or take some serious exercise enjoying a swim or a spot of windsurfing. There's plenty of parking space at the hotel, which is a non-smoking establishment.

The Cobb, Lyme Regis

In 1588 Sir Francis Drake's fleet fought a small battle with the Spanish Armada in Lyme Bay, and almost a century later, in 1685, the Duke of Monmouth, chose Lyme as his landing place to start the unsuccessful rebellion that would lead to the Bloody Assizes of Judge Jeffreys. James, Duke of Monmouth, Duke of Buccleuch, Earl of Doncaster, Baron Tyndale, was born in Rotterdam in 1649, the illegitimate son of Charles II and Lucy Walter. When Charles died and his brother succeeded to the throne as James II, the Duke of Monmouth, a committed Protestant, began to conceive a plot to oust the new Roman Catholic King. He landed in Lyme Regis Bay with a small band of about 80 supporters; these numbers had grown to about 3,500 when they were routed at the Battle of Sedgemoor and the rebellion was quelled. Monmouth was captured at Hopton, taken to London and beheaded, not very competently, by the state executioner Jack Ketch. Ketch was notorious for his barbaric incompetence, and allegedly took eight strokes of his axe to behead Monmouth.

The end of the rebellion heralded the beginning of the infamous Bloody Assizes, the trials of the supporters and sympathisers of Monmouth presided over by Judge Jeffreys, later 1st Baron Jeffreys of Wem, and four others. The trials were held throughout the West Country, starting at Winchester and moving on to Salisbury before really getting under way at Dorchester. They resulted in some 300 men being hanged, 800 transported to Barbados and hundreds of others fined, flogged or imprisoned. Judge Jeffreys made sure that every town learned a

down to the sea. The town itself, described by Daniel Defoe as 'a town of good figure', is a maze of narrow streets with many charming Georgian and Regency houses, and the picturesque harbour will be familiar to anyone who has seen the film *The French Lieutenant's Woman* based on the novel by Lyme resident John Fowles (he also wrote another famously filmed novel *The Collector*).

The scene of a lone woman standing on the wave-lashed Cobb is one of the cinema's most enduring images. **The Cobb**, which protects the harbour and the sandy beach from the south-westerly storms that frequently hit this part of the coast, is made of rows of tree trunks driven into the sea and the spaces filled with rocks and stones.

It was first recorded in 1294 but the town itself goes back at least another 500 years to Saxon times when there was a salt works there. A charter granted by Edward I allowed Lyme to add 'Regis' to its name, but during the Civil War the town was staunchly anti-Royalist, routing the forces of Prince Maurice and killing more than 2,000 of them. History has touched the town at various other times down the centuries.

of London, where he died soon afterwards.

Happier days arrived in the 18th century when Lyme Regis became a fashionable seaside resort famed for its fresh, clean air. Jane Austen and her family visited in 1803 and part of her novel *Persuasion* is set in the town; the **Jane Austen Garden** on Marine Parade commemorates her visit. The Jurassic rocks in and around Lyme have been famous for fossils ever since Mary Anning's first discoveries, and some fine specimens can be found in the multi-award-winning **Lyme Regis Philpot Museum**, along with the town's history and displays on the sea, The Cobb, smuggling, the local railway, World War II and literary Lyme. Sir David Attenborough described the museum as ' a delightful and remarkable museum, a jewel'.

Lyme Regis Harbour

lesson by being made to witness the hanging of some of Monmouth's supporters, and 12 men were hanged in Lyme Regis. The Judge, although a Protestant, went on to become the man in charge of implementing the unpopular religious policies of the Catholic King James II. He tried to escape disguised as a sailor when James was overthrown in 1688 by the Protestant William of Orange (later William III) who landed at Torbay, but he was arrested and put in the Tower

Dinosaurland (see panel below), housed in a grand mid-18th century building, also features Jurassic fossils, and of course dinosaurs, and it has a fossil clinic where visitors can bring their own fossil finds for expert analysis, a Time Gallery chronicling the history of the

DINOSAURLAND & FOSSIL MUSEUM

Coombe Street, Lyme Regis, Dorset DT7 3PY
Tel: 01297 443541
e-mail: steve@dinosaurland.co.uk
website: www.dinosaurland.co.uk

Dinosaurland is housed in an 18th century building that was previously a church where the renowned fossil hunter Mary Anning worshipped. It features a collection of local Jurassic fossils large and small, a Time Gallery chronicling the history of the Earth from earliest times and an animal room where animals and skeletons show how present-day life evolved and hoe dinosaur fit into the jigsaw. It also has a shop and a clinic where visitors can bring their own fossil finds for expert analysis. Regular fossil hunts are arranged by the Museum.

Earth from earliest times, a fossil shop and a natural history room with a collection of live animals. Just around the corner from Dinosaurland, in Mill Lane, is one of the most interesting buildings in the town.

It was in January 1991 that a group of Lyme Regis residents got together in an effort to save the old **Town Mill** from destruction. There has been a mill on the River Lym in the centre of town for many centuries, but most of the present buildings date back to the mid-17th century when the mill was rebuilt after being burned down during the Civil War. Today, the restored Town Mill is one of Lyme's major attractions, housing two art galleries which stage a regular exhibitions, concerts, poetry readings and other live performances. There is also a stable building which houses craft workshops.

For its size, Lyme Regis has an extraordinary range of activities on offer, including the week-long **Regatta** and **Carnival** held in August. Bands play on the Marine Parade, there are displays by Morris Men and folk dancers, and an annual **Town Criers Open Championship** is held. Lyme has maintained a town crier for over 1,000 years without a break and the present incumbent, in his colourful 18th century costume, can be seen and heard throughout the town during the summer months.

The **Church of St Michael**, east of The Cobb, has a handsome Jacobean pulpit and a window commemorating the fossil hunter Mary Anning (see introduction to this chapter). Also in Lyme, though no longer in religious use, is one of the earliest nonconformist chapels to survive in Dorset. The original building was a congregational chapel dating from 1662, but its replacement, in classical style, was completed in Coombe Street in 1756.

The **Dorset Coastal Path** runs from Sandbanks in the east to Lyme Regis, where it joins the South Devon Coastal Path. It provides great walking along the whole of the Dorset coast apart from moving inland near Abbotsbury to avoid Chesil Beach.

AROUND LYME REGIS

CHARMOUTH
2 miles NE of Lyme Regis off the A35

What better recommendation could there be for 'The Heritage Coast Village' than the fact that it was Jane Austen's favourite resort? 'Sweet and retired', she called it, and to quote Arthur Mee, 'She loved the splendid sweep of country all round it, the downs, the valleys, the hills like Golden Cap, and the pageantry of the walk to Lyme Regis'.

Charmouth remains an attractive little place with a wide main street and a quiet stretch of sandy beach that gradually merges into shingle. The beach, foreshore and cliffs, owned by the Parish, extend from Evans Cliff to the Spittles, being divided by the River Char as it enters the sea. In 1925 a section of the river mouth was exposed to reveal various fossils, including the vertebrae, skull and antlers of a red deer, which are now all housed in the British Museum.

Charmouth Beach has been designated as a Site of Special Scientific Interest (SSSI); fossil hunters should restrict themselves to the beach, as the cliffs - which have suffered major collapses in recent years - are dangerous, or to marked paths. The beaches face south and there's safe bathing; beach huts can be hired by the day, week or season. The **Charmouth Heritage Coast Centre**, in an old cement works on the foreshore immediately west

QUEENS ARMES HOTEL

The Street, Charmouth,
Dorset DT6 6QF
Tel/Fax: 01297 560339

Easy to find on Charmouth's main street, the **Queens Armes** is one of the oldest buildings in the village, dating from about 1480 and reputedly built as a manor house for nearby Forde Abbey. The new owners are Phillip and Carole Mapstone, who previously farmed in the area. Guests have the choice of 11 characterful bedrooms, all but one with en suite bath or shower room; the other has its own bathroom not en suite.

Each room has individual appeal, and top of the range is the four-poster room that was part of the old upper hall. Two rooms on the ground floor - one with its own sitting room - are popular with guests who find stairs difficult, while the room in the roof is for the nimbler visitor: the staircase is quite steep and the doorway quite narrow, but the room itself is quite spacious.

In the dining room, part of the main hall of the medieval manor house, breakfast is served between 8.30 and 9.15 and dinner from 6.30 to 8. The chef offers up to five courses for dinner, and special dietary needs can be met with a little notice. The bar, where an open fire keeps things cosy on chilly evenings, is a good place to relax and plan the next day's activities - the area has a great deal to interest walkers and sightseers. Smoking is not allowed at the hotel except in the conservatory or rear garden. Dogs are welcome as long as they are kept on a lead.

HENSLEIGH HOTEL

Lower Sea Lane, Charmouth, Dorset DT6 6LW
Tel: 01297 560830 Fax: 01297 560207

John and Caroline Davis run the **Hensleigh Hotel**, a truly delightful establishment in a seaside village at the heart of the Dorset Heritage Coast. Jane Austen described the village as 'sweet and retired', and it remains a place of great charm, with a bypass adding to the tranquillity. The hotel, which has a large private car park, offers ten comfortably furnished en suite bedrooms, some of them on the ground floor, all with central heating, tv and

hospitality tray. English or Continental breakfast starts the day, and an evening meal is served in the dining room or conservatory. Local fish is a speciality. The other day rooms comprise a snug bar and relaxing lounge, where, as in the rest of the hotel, a non-smoking policy operates. The hotel is handily

placed for all the amenities of the village and is just a short stroll from the cliffs and the beach, which stretches on either side of the River Char as it enters the sea. The area is rich in fossils, and informative talks on how and where to search for them are given in the Charmouth Heritage Coast Centre, established in 1985 to tell visitors about the beauty and scientific interest of the area, and also of the potential hazards of the cliffs. The coastal path leads westward to Lyme Regis, two miles away, and in the other direction to Seatown and Golden Cap, the highest point on the South Coast.

CHARLESTON HOLIDAY COTTAGES

Grosvenor Cottage, The Street, Charmouth,
Dorset DT6 6NX
Tel: 01297 560053

Charleston House and Charleston Cottage, which lie together in a walled garden, are an ideal base for families exploring the scenic delights of the Dorset countryside and coast. Converted from an early 19th century public house, Charleston Holiday Cottages have their own car parking spaces, garden and patio, and the owners, Kim and Kevin Wood, have provided everything needed for a comfortable self-catering holiday. Charleston House comprises a ground-floor lounge-diner with tv, fully equipped kitchen, three well-furnished upstairs bedrooms (one with bunk beds and toys), a bathroom with WC and a separate WC. Charleston Cottage is similarly kitted out, but with two upstairs bedrooms. Both the properties are centrally heated. Children

are very welcome, but pets cannot be accommodated. The village shops are within a five-minute walk, with supermarkets an easy drive away in Bridport and Axminster. In Charmouth itself there's a bakery and café, fish and chip shop and pubs, and a market on Mondays in summer. The main attraction is naturally the coast, with safe bathing for children, golden sands and a pebble beach that is recognised as one of the finest fossil beaches in Europe. The beach has been designated a Site of Special Scientific Interest (SSSI), and the Heritage Coast Centre, almost at the water's edge, tells visitors all about finding and identifying fossils.

of the mouth of the Char, was established in 1985 as an education/information centre to help the public understand and appreciate the area's scientific wealth, its natural beauty and the potential dangers posed by the unstable cliffs. Visitors (50,000 a year) can see the Jurassic Theatre Audio-Visual Show, where and how to find fossils and how to identify them, the Aquarium and the Weather Station.

MONKTON WYLD
4 miles N of Lyme Regis off the A358

The 1848 Church of St Andrew is well worth a visit.

WHITCHURCH CANONICORUM
5 miles NE of Lyme Regis off the A35

Clinging to the steep hillside above the valley of the River Char, on the edge of the Marshwood Vale, Whitchurch Canonicorum is notable for its enchanting setting and for its **Church of**

St Candida and Holy Cross, often known as the Cathedral of the Vale. This noble building with its Norman arches and an imposing tower built around 1400 is remarkable for being one of only two churches in England still possessing a shrine to a saint (the other is that of Edward the Confessor in Westminster Abbey). St Candida was a Saxon woman named Wite, which the Normans took to be the Saxon for white and Latinised it to Candida, the Latin for white. She lives as a hermit but was murdered by a Viking raiding party in 831AD. During the Middle Ages a cult grew up around her memory and it was thought that she could effect miracle cures; a large shrine was built of golden Purbeck stone, its lower level pierced by three large ovals ('limb holes') into which the sick and the maimed would thrust their limbs, their head or even their whole body, in the hope of being cured. The cult of St Wite

HIGHER POUND FARM

Monkton Wyld, Nr Lyme Regis,
Dorset DT6 6DD
Tel: 01297 678345 Fax: 01297 678730

Visitors to this lovely part of the country will find abundant peace and serenity at Jill and Jeremy White's **Higher Pound Farm**. Set in rolling Dorset countryside three miles north of Charmouth, the farm's 65 acres of pasture, paddocks and woodland incorporate a Grade ll listed 18th century farmhouse, an equestrian centre and holiday letting cottages.

Old stone barns have been skilfully and sympathetically converted into six really delightful cottages, very attractively furnished and equipped with all the modern conveniences to provide a comfortable base for a getting-away-from-it-all self-catering holiday at any time of year. The cottages can accommodate up to 4 or 6 guests each, and all offer parking (for two cars per property); electricity and gas are included in the letting tariff, and standard equipment includes gas cooker, microwave oven, patio with furniture and shared payphone and laundry room. Dogs are welcome in two of the cottages but must be kept on a lead at all times. The cottages are not suitable for guests with mobility difficulties. A shared large garden has picnic and barbecue facilities; children are very well catered for with a Wendy house and plenty of space to romp or play games.

Guests can say hello to the owners' horses and goats, and the riding school on the premises is for all ages, shapes and sizes - book in advance. Nature-lovers can spot rare birds, deer and badgers, and there is direct access to adjoining Forestry Commission land with its many walks and trails. The farm itself affords superb views down the Char valley to the sea at Lyme Bay, just four miles away. The medieval port of Lyme Regis is well worth a few hours' exploration, so, too, the pleasant market town of Axminster, just two miles away in Devon, and the whole stretch of coast offers many attractions, including sandy beaches, spectacular cliffs, boating, fishing, windsurfing and fossil hunting.

The farm, which is signposted from the B3165, lies near the borders of three counties and, with the main A35 only a mile distant, is an excellent base for forays around Dorset and into Somerset and Devon. Among the places within easy reach is the Golden Cap, at over 600 feet the highest cliff on the entire Channel coast.

thrived until the Reformation, when all such 'monuments of feigned miracles' were swept away. That might have been the end of the story of St Wite, but during the winter of 1899-1900 the foundations of the church settled and cracked open a 13th century tomb chest. Inside was a lead casket with a Latin inscription stating that 'Here rest the relics of St Wite' and inside, the bones of a small woman about 40 years of age. The shrine still attracts pilgrims today and the donations which they leave in the openings beneath the tomb are devoted to causes which aid health and healing. (Canonicorum was added to the name of the village after 1242 when the Canons of Wells and Salisbury took the majority of the tithes.)

South of Whitchurch is the village of **Morcombelake**, home of the famous Dorset knobs and other old-fashioned biscuits made in Moore's Biscuit Bakery.

So ends a brief visit to the county of Dorset, which offers the visitor an irresistible mix of glorious countryside and equally glorious coast, of thousands of years of history and a wide range of up-to-date amenities - but not a single racecourse!

Above all this is **Thomas Hardy's** county, and Dorset's Tourist Information Centres and the **Thomas Hardy Society** produce a wealth of leaflets concerning the great man. They have also devised inner and outer tours, the former with a natural starting point of Dorchester.

Many of the towns and villages in this Guide were well known to Hardy, and today's visitors will recognise many of the buildings and geographical features that appear in the novels. The major points on the tours, with the equivalent names used by Hardy and the stories in which they appear, include the following:

Dorchester:
  Casterbridge; The Mayor of Casterbridge

Stinsford:
  Mellstock; Under the Greenwood Tree
Higher Bockhampton:
  Upper Mellstock; Under the Greenwood Tree
Bere Regis:
  Kingsbere; Tess of the d'Urbervilles
Athelhampton:
  Athelhall
Puddletown:
  Weatherbury; Far From the Madding Crowd
Cerne Abbas:
  Abbot's Cerne; Tess, The Woodlanders, The Dynasts
Weymouth:
  Budmouth Regis; Under the Greenwood Tree, The Trumpet-Major, Far From the Madding Crowd
Swanage:
  Knollsea; The Hand of Ethelberta
Bournemouth:
  Sandbourne; The Hand of Ethelberta
Poole:
  Havenpool; The Mayor of Casterbridge
Shaftesbury:
  Shaston; Jude the Obscure
Sturminster Newton:
  Stourcastle
Sherborne:
  Sherton Abbas; The Woodlanders
Melbury Osmond:
  Great Hintock; The Woodlanders
Beaminster:
  Emminster; Tess of the d'Urbervilles
Bridport:
  Port Bredy; Fellow-Townsmen
Portland:
  Isle of Slingers; The Trumpet-Major, the Well-Beloved

Happy touring. Happy reading.

List of Tourist Information Centres

DORSET

BLANDFORD FORUM

Marsh & Ham Car Park, West Street,
Blandford Forum, Dorset DT11 7AW
Tel/Fax: 01258 454770

BOURNEMOUTH

Westover Road, Bournemouth,
Dorset BH1 2BU
Tel: 0906 8020234

BRIDPORT

32 South Street, Bridport,
Dorset DT6 3NQ
Tel: 01308 424901 Fax: 01308 421060

CHRISTCHURCH

23 High Street, Christchurch,
Dorset BH23 1AB
Tel: 01202 471780

DORCHESTER

Unit 11, Antelope Walk, Dorchester,
Dorset DT11 1BE
Tel: 01305 267992 Fax: 01305 266079

LYME REGIS

Guildhal Cottage, Church Street, Lyme Regis,
Dorset DT7 3BS
Tel: 01297 442138 Fax: 01297 444668

LYMINGTON

St Barbe Museum, New Street, Lymington,
Dorset SO41 9BH
Tel: 01590 672422
Summer months only

POOLE

Waterfront Museum, 4 High Street, Poole,
Dorset BH15 1BW
Tel: 01202 253253 Fax: 01202 262684

SHAFTESBURY

8 Bell Street, Shaftesbury,
Dorset SP7 8AE
Tel: 01747 853514

SHERBORNE

3 Tilton Court, Digby Street, Sherborne,
Dorset DT9 3NL
Tel: 01935 815341 Fax: 01935 817210

SWANAGE

The White House, Shore Road, Swanage,
Dorset BH19 1LB
Tel: 01929 422885 Fax: 01929 423423

WAREHAM

Trinity Church, South Street, Wareham,
Dorset BH20 4LU
Tel: 01929 552740 Fax: 01929 554491

WEYMOUTH

The King's Statue, The Esplanade,
Weymouth, Dorset DT4 7AN
Tel: 01305 785747 Fax: 01305 788092

WIMBORNE MINSTER

29 High Street, Wimborne Minster,
Dorset BH21 1H R
Tel: 01202 886116

HAMPSHIRE

ALDERSHOT

Military Museum, Queens Avenue,
Aldershot, Hampshire GU11 2LG
Tel/Fax: 01252 320968

ALTON

7 Cross and Pillory, Alton,
Hampshire GU34 1HL
Tel: 01420 88448 Fax: 01420 543916

ANDOVER

Town Mill House, Bridge Street, Andover,
Hampshire SP10 1BL
Tel: 01264 324320

BASINGSTOKE

Willis Museum, Old Town Hall,
Market Place, Basingstoke,
Hampshire RG21 7QD
Tel: 01256 817618 Fax: 01256 356231

EASTLEIGH

The Point, Leigh Road, Eastleigh,
Hampshire SO50 9DE
Tel: 02380 641261 Fax: 02380 641261

FAREHAM

Westbury Manor, West Street, Fareham,
Hampshire PO16 0JJ
Tel: 01329 221342 Fax: 01329 282959

FLEET

Harlington Centre, Harlington Way, Fleet,
Hampshire GU13 8BY
Tel: 01252 811151

FORDINGBRIDGE

Roman Quay, High Street, Fordingbridge,
Hampshire SP6 1RL
Tel: 01425 654560
Summer months only

GOSPORT

1 High Street, Gosport,
Hampshire PO12 1BX
Tel: 02392 522944 Fax: 02392 511687

HAVANT

1 Park Road South, Havant,
Hampshire PO9 1HA
Tel: 02392 480024

HAYLING ISLAND

Beachlands Seafront, Hayling Island,
Hampshire PO11 0AG
Tel: 02392 467111 Fax: 02392 463297

LYNDHURST

New Forest Museum & Visitor Centre,
Main Car Park, Lyndhurst,
Hampshire SO43 7NY
Tel: 02380 282269

PETERSFIELD

County Library, 27 The Square, Petersfield,
Hampshire GU32 3HH
Tel: 01730 268829 Fax: 01730 266679

PORTSMOUTH

The Hard, Portsmouth,
Hampshire PO1 3QJ
Tel: 02392 826722

PORTSMOUTH

102 Commercial Road, Portsmouth,
Hampshire PO1 1EJ
Tel: 02392 838382

PORTSMOUTH

Clarence Esplanade, Southsea,
Hampshire PO5 3ST
Tel: 02392 832464

RINGWOOD

The Furlong, Ringwwod,
Hampshire BH24 1AZ
Tel: 01425 470896
Summer months only

ROMSEY

1 Latimer Street, Romsey,
Hampshire SO51 8DF
Tel: 02392 512987

ROWNHAMS

M27 Services (Westbound),
Hampshire SO16 8AW
Tel: 02380 730345

SOUTHAMPTON

9 Civic Centre Road, Southampton,
Hampshire SO14 7LP
Tel: 02380 221106 Fax: 02380 832082

SOUTHAMPTON INTERNATIONAL AIRPORT

Wilde Lane, Eastleigh,
Hampshire SO18 2HC
Tel: 02380 627235

WINCHESTER

Guildhall, The Broadway, Winchester,
Hampshire SO23 9LJ
Tel: 01962 840500 Fax: 10962 850348

ISLE OF WIGHT

COWES

The Arcade, Fountain Quay West, Cowes,
Isle of Wight PO31 3AR
Tel: 01983 291914

NEWPORT

Car Park, Bus Station, Newport,
Isle of Wight PO30 1JU
Tel: 01983 525450

RYDE

Western Esplanade, Ryde,
Isle of Wight PO33 2LW
Tel: 01983 562905

SANDOWN

8 High Street, Sandown,
Isle of Wight PO36 0DG
Tel: 01983 403886

SHANKLIN

67 High Street, Shanklin,
Isle of Wight PO37 6JJ
Tel: 01983 862942

VENTNOR

34 High Street, Ventnor,
Isle of Wight PO38 1RZ
Tel: 01983 853625
Summer months only

YARMOUTH

The Quay, Yarmouth,
Isle of Wight PO41 4PQ
Tel: 01983 760015

Index of Towns, Villages and Places of Interest

List of Advertisers

A

B

C

Hidden Places Order Form

To order any of our publications just fill in the payment details below and complete the order form *overleaf*. For orders of less than 4 copies please add £1 per book for postage and packing. Orders over 4 copies are P & P free.

Please Complete Either:

I enclose a cheque for £ [＿＿＿＿＿] made payable to Travel Publishing Ltd

Or:

Card No: [＿＿＿＿＿＿＿＿]

Expiry Date: [＿＿＿]

Signature: [＿＿＿＿＿＿＿]

NAME: [＿＿＿＿＿＿＿]

ADDRESS: [＿＿＿＿＿＿＿]

POSTCODE: [＿＿＿＿＿＿＿]

TEL NO: [＿＿＿＿＿＿＿]

Please either send or telephone your order to:

Travel Publishing Ltd
7a Apollo House
Calleva Park
Aldermaston
Berks, RG7 8TN

Tel : 0118 981 7777
Fax: 0118 982 0077

	PRICE	QUANTITY	VALUE

Hidden Places Regional Titles

	PRICE	QUANTITY	VALUE
Cambs & Lincolnshire	£7.99	....	....
Chilterns	£8.99	....	....
Cornwall	£8.99	....	....
Derbyshire	£7.99	....	....
Devon	£8.99	....	....
Dorset, Hants & Isle of Wight	£8.99	....	....
East Anglia	£8.99	....	....
Gloucestershire & Wiltshire	£7.99	....	....
Heart of England	£7.99	....	....
Hereford, Worcs & Shropshire	£7.99	....	....
Highlands & Islands	£7.99	....	....
Kent	£8.99	....	....
Lake District & Cumbria	£8.99	....	....
Lancashire & Cheshire	£8.99	....	....
Lincolnshire	£8.99	....	....
Northumberland & Durham	£8.99	....	....
Somerset	£7.99	....	....
Sussex	£7.99	....	....
Thames Valley	£7.99	....	....
Yorkshire	£7.99	....	....

Hidden Places National Titles

	PRICE	QUANTITY	VALUE
England	£9.99	....	....
Ireland	£9.99	....	....
Scotland	£9.99	....	....
Wales	£9.99	....	....

Hidden Inns Titles

	PRICE	QUANTITY	VALUE
South	£5.99	....	....
South East	£5.99	....	....
South and Central Scotland	£5.99	....	....
Wales	£5.99	....	....
Welsh Borders	£5.99	....	....
West Country	£5.99	....	....

*For orders of less than 4 copies please add £1 per book for
postage & packing. Orders over 4 copies P & P free.*

Hidden Places Reader Reaction

The *Hidden Places* research team would like to receive reader's comments on any visitor attractions or places reviewed in the book and also recommendations for suitable entries to be included in the next edition. This will help ensure that the *Hidden Places* series continues to provide its readers with useful information on the more interesting, unusual or unique features of each attraction or place ensuring that their stay in the local area is an enjoyable and stimulating experience. To provide your comments or recommendations would you please complete the forms below and overleaf as indicated and send to:

The Research Department, Travel Publishing Ltd,
7a Apollo House, Calleva Park, Aldermaston, Reading, RG7 8TN.

Your Name:

Your Address:

Your Telephone Number:

Please tick as appropriate: Comments ☐   Recommendation ☐

Name of *"Hidden Place"*:

Address:

Telephone Number:

Name of Contact:

Hidden Places Reader Reaction

Comment or Reason for Recommendation:

....

....

....

....

....

....

....

....

....

....

....

....

....